The Task

of

Post-Contemporary Education

ESSAYS IN BEHALF OF A HUMAN FUTURE

The Task
of
Post-Contemporary Education

ESSAYS IN BEHALF OF A HUMAN FUTURE

Kenneth D. Benne

Teachers College, Columbia University
New York • London

Essay 1 was originally published as "The Diagnosis of Our Time," in *Studies in Philosophy and Education*, 1976, Vol. 9, no. 3, pp. 211–29 and is reprinted here by permission of Kluwer Academic Publishers. Essay 2, "The Meanings of Democracy in a Collective World," is reprinted with permission from *Society as Educator in an Age of Transition*, Kenneth D. Benne and Steven Tozer, editors, Eighty-Sixth Yearbook of the National Society for the Study of Education, Part II (Chicago: University of Chicago Press, 1987). "The Learning Community," Essay 3, is reprinted with permission of the Philosophy of Education Society, from *Philosophy of Education*, 1984, pp. 27–52. Essay 4, "Technology and Community: Conflicting Bases of Educational Authority," first appeared in *Work, Technology, and Education*, edited by Walter Feinberg and Harry Rosemont, pp. 142–165, © 1975 by the Board of Trustees of the University of Illinois. Reprinted by permission of the University of Illinois Press. Essay 5 is based on "The Idea of a University in 1965," published in *The University in the American Future*, edited by Thomas Stroup, pp. 1–51, © 1966 by the University of Kentucky Press. Reprinted by permission of the publishers. The material in Essay 7, "The Theory and Practice of Reeducation: Kurt Lewin's Contributions," is taken from an essay first published in *The Planning of Change*, Third Edition, by Warren Bennis, Kenneth Benne, and Robert Chin, © 1976 by Holt, Rinehart and Winston, Inc. Reprinted by permission of the publisher. Essay 8, "On Learning to Believe in Persons," appeared in *Mid-Twentieth Century American Philosophy*, edited by Peter A. Bertocci, pp. 1–19, © 1974, Humanities Press. Reprinted by permission. "Toward a Morality of Hope for the Future," Essay 9, was published in *Educational Reconstruction*, edited by Nobuo Shimahara, pp. 392–426, © 1973 by Charles Merrill. Reprinted by permission of Nobuo Shimahara.

Published by Teachers College Press, 1234 Amsterdam Avenue, New York, NY 10027

Copyright © 1990 by Teachers College, Columbia University

Library of Congress Cataloging-in-Publication Data

Benne, Kenneth Dean, 1908–
    The task of post-contemporary education : essays in behalf of a human future / Kenneth D. Benne.
    p. cm.
    Collection of essays published over the past twenty-five years.
    Includes bibliographical references.
    ISBN 0-8077-3013-0.   ISBN 0-8077-3012-2 (pbk.)
    1. Benne, Kenneth Dean, 1908– . 2. Education—Philosophy.
I. Title.
LB885.B38 1990
370'.1—dc20   89–48912
                                                                    CIP

Manufactured in the United States of America. Printed on acid-free paper.

97 96 95 94 93 92 91 90   8 7 6 5 4 3 2 1

To
Paul E. Blackwood

Contents

Preface

THESE ESSAYS ON POST-CONTEMPORARY EDUCATION might properly be named "prophetic," if prophecy is clearly distinguished from prediction and foretelling. All are oriented toward the future. But there the similarity between prophecy and the other two ends.

Foretelling purports to describe what the established goals, ways and manners of institutions, programs and practices—in this case, those which are named "educational"—will be, a generation or more from now. Foretelling is dubious on both cognitive and moral grounds. Foretellers must assume that knowledge of the determinants operating in or upon educational institutions, which will give shape to these institutions in the future, are now available to them along with knowledge of the strengths of those determinants. Such knowledge may come from secular or sacred sources. I pretend to no such knowledge. And I doubt that it is available to anyone, for new determinants will emerge, and present determinants will interact and lose or gain in power, whether due to changes in technologies, to shifts in the hierarchy of values, or to the effects of the meeting and confrontation between newly desegregated cultures and subcultures.

Moreover, I doubt the morality of attempts to foretell the future in any detail. The effect of this is to discourage the acceptance of responsibility by those now in charge of educational planning for making the many decisions concerning educational policy and practice that press upon them today. For, if influential planners were to believe that the future shape of education is predictable, historically predetermined, and independent of the actual choices they are making today and tomorrow, they might understandably hesitate to take their decision making seriously. Such planners might lean toward the foretold future in selecting one among several alternatives, thus attempting to hasten the "inevitable." They might not probe the alternative values at stake in their present choices, nor agonize, individually and dialogically, concerning the alternatives competing in the arena of choice. Nor might they work to create and negotiate optimal resolutions in mediating currently conflicting value orientations.

In brief, they might well underestimate the potential power of human volition, manifested in responsible human choices, to give meaningful and consensual shape to the forms and functions of emerging educational programs and institutions.

I have considerably more respect for probings of the future when these take the form of "prophecy" rather than "foretelling." The prophet summons his or her audience to quickened and deepened moral concern with the choices that confront us here and now. The prophet may speak for viable and valid traditional values now threatened by current historical trends and fashions in life and in education. He or she may call for a reinterpretation of traditional values to make them more applicable to changed and changing conditions of life and learning. Or the prophet may speak for new values, ones that are potential, yet inadequately actualized in the contemporary, balanced imbalance of established powers and policies. Prophets may seek to persuade their audiences to integrate valid and viable—but now segregated and competing—values, both traditional and novel. They may urge others to support the integration of outlooks in making decisions about what should be done, not in a fantasized future but in the actuality of today, in behalf of a better tomorrow. In short, prophecy seeks to focus, clarify, and strengthen, rather than to discount and diminish, human volition as a determinant in the process of history. It is as a prophet, I hope, not a foreteller, that I wish to speak to contemporary educators of post-contemporary education.

Ours is a time in dire need of prophecy. We are living in a deepening and continuing crisis of culture. Crisis, as I am using the term, does not denote an unfortunate emergency, a temporary upset of established practices and aspirations to which life will return after the emergency has been handled and managed. Crisis rather denotes to me a turning point in human history, an *axial* period as Karl Jaspers (1961) once named our contemporary historical situation. It is marked by a crumbling of traditional assumptions, a dissolution of outmoded orthodoxies. Important traditional value orientations, largely functioning below the level of collective consciousness, lead to radically unexpected outcomes, often contrary to the consequences sought, when these orientations shape collective decisions. Multiplication of contradictions between professed intentions and actual consequences in their actions leads men and women to despair of the relevance of rationality in the conduct of private or public affairs.

Karl Mannheim (1943), who, so far as I know, was the first social theorist to describe the current human condition of Western societies as a "crisis of valuation," identified some of the conflicts in beliefs that attend the current crisis. The similarity between the conflicts named by Mannheim in 1943 and those persisting today underlines the fact that crisis in culture is no overnight emergency.

> In the very same social environment we now have the most contradictory philosophies of life. First, there is the religion of love and universal brotherhood, mainly inspired by Christian tradition, as a measuring-rod for our situation. Then there is the philosophy of Enlightenment and Liberalism, with its emphasis on freedom and personality, and its appreciation of wealth, security, happiness, tolerance and philanthropy as the means of achieving them. Then we have the challenge of Socialists, who rate equality, social justice, basic security and a planned social order as the chief desiderata of the age. But beyond all this we have . . . the most recent philosophy, with the demoniac image of man emphasizing fertility, race, power, and the tribal and military virtues of conquest, discipline and blind obedience [fascism]. . . . we have no agreed-upon educational policy for our normal citizens, since the further we progress the less we know what we are educating for. On the primary levels of education we are undecided whether to aim at creating millions of rationalists who discard custom and tradition and judge each case on its own merits, or whether the chief aim of education should be the handing on of that social and national inheritance which is focused in religion. On the higher levels of education we do not know whether to educate for specialization, which is urgently needed in an industrialized society with a strict division of labor, or whether we should cater for all-round personalities with a philosophical background. (pp. 15–16)

Choices by educators in a culture in crisis, as in contemporary America, are far from easy. But the life of an educator may nevertheless be an exciting lot if prophecy is not only tolerated but welcomed. Prophecy today must, of course, look beyond the crisis in our nation and take a transnational, global view of the contemporary human condition.

On the world scene, contradictory forms of life, espoused by people in cultures once segregated but now forced into uneasy confrontation, impel leaders and members of these national or tribal cultures into unmediated struggle. The struggle is initially billed by each as a defense of a traditional way of life, a way of life already weakened by internal contradictions, as already noted. It is difficult and sometimes impossible to prevent the struggle from degenerating into efforts by each to impose its way of life, oversimplified and sloganized into a battle cry, upon the other. Peoples now live precariously, protected by a dubious balance of terror. The instruments of mutual decimation now available for use threaten the very continuance of human life on earth. We are indeed headed toward (perhaps we are already in) a new era in human history. The extinction of our own and of other species can, of course, put an end to history and historical eras on earth.

The end of the modern era has for some years been proclaimed, especially by continental European Jeremiahs, often under the banner of one post-modernism or another. I have preferred the title of post-contemporary instead of post-modern for my essays. My hope is that I can maintain a future-oriented perspective toward our current historical situation and avoid being embroiled in backward-looking polemics concerning the date and occasion of modernity's demise.

I would continually remind myself and others that, in some sense, we are already living in a post-modern era, but one still able to be shaped by devoted human efforts. We are tempted to forget the fact that our future is dubious, that familiar ways of living our lives, private and public, are outmoded. We need somehow to rise above our compelling present and acknowledge the enormity of our life-world which Walker Percy (1975) has wittily described:

> There is a lag between the end of an age and the discovery of the end. The denizens of such a time are like the cartoon cat that runs off a cliff and for a while is suspended, still running, in midair but sooner or later looks down and sees there is nothing under him. (p. 19)

Nuclear weapons are, of course, only the most drastic example of developing and developed technologies which, without moral and political controls over their use, now militate against human survival. Can prophetic reeducation stimulate contemporary persons and cultures toward the control of technology and toward the creative mediation of conflicts in the interest of species survival? Can educational policies and programs be created and employed to make a post-contemporary life for humankind more probable than it now appears to be?

The essays in this volume attempt to prophesy about various aspects of these basic educative and reeducative questions. Contemporary educators are certain to confront these questions, if and when they think seriously and responsibly about priorities in their current choices and activities. The essays are tuned to an American audience but the issues they discuss are of world wide importance.

My effort to illuminate some educational aspects of our contemporary crisis is mainly interpretive, critical and diagnostic. Whatever "answers" to the basic questions may be suggested in my essays are provisional and in need of refutation, replacement or further development. "Answers" that are both wise and viable for humankind will emerge only out of far-flung communal dialogues and collaborative projects. The dialogues and collaborations required must be sustained international, interreligious, interracial, interclass, intergender, and intergenerational conversations and cooperations, if their outcomes are to be both wise and effective. My highest hope is that these essays might give some small impetus to the joining of such pluralistic conversations.

Acknowledgments

EACH ESSAY IN THIS BOOK is based on a previously published journal article or lecture. All have been revised, some rather drastically, for this volume. I appreciate the permission to reprint that has been granted by the various holders of copyright.

Essay 1, "Diagnosis of Our Time," was first published in 1976 in *Studies in Philosophy and Education, 9*(3), 211–29.

Essay 2, "The Meanings of Democracy in a Collective World," was printed in one of the two 1987 Yearbooks of the National Society for the Study of Education (pp. 1–23). This yearbook, which Steven Tozer and I edited, was entitled *Society as Educator in an Age of Transition.*

Essay 3, "The Learning Community," first appeared in the 1984 proceedings of *The Philosophy of Education Society,* pp. 27–52.

Essay 4, "Technology and Community: Conflicting Bases of Educational Authority," was written for a 1975 symposium volume, *Work, Technology, and Education,* edited by Walter Feinberg and Harry Rosemont and published by the University of Illinois Press.

Essay 5, "The Idea of a University in 2000 C.E.," was first printed in *The University in the American Future,* edited by Thomas Stroup and published by the University of Kentucky Press in 1966. My essay was based on a public lecture I delivered in 1965 as a visiting professor at the University of Kentucky during its centennial year. This lecture was thoroughly revised and delivered again at the University of Kentucky in 1981. Since then I have continued to study and brood over the failure of American "multiversities" to redefine their form and mission as "universities" and seek to fulfill their reconstructed form and mission. This study and brooding have led to the present version of my re-revised essay.

Essay 6, "From Pedagogy to Anthropogogy," was originally delivered as the sixth Charles DeGarmo Lecture and published by the Society of Professors of Education in 1981.

Essay 7, "The Theory and Practice of Reeducation: Kurt Lewin's Contributions," was first published in 1976 as "The Process of Reeducation: An Assessment of Kurt Lewin's Views" in the third edition of *The Planning of Change* (pp. 315–326), edited by Warren Bennis, myself, and Robert Chin and published by Holt, Rinehart and Winston. The essay was also included in the fourth edition of that work, published in 1986.

Essay 8, "On Learning to Believe in Persons," was originally included in a volume called *Mid-Twentieth Century American Philosophy* (pp. 1–19), published by the Humanities Press in 1974. The editor, Peter Bertocci, put together personal statements of belief by 15 American philosophers.

Essay 9, "Toward a Morality of Hope for the Future," was the concluding chapter of *Educational Reconstruction*, edited by Nobuo Shimahara and published by Charles Merrill in 1973.

I thank Jeanne Connell and Steven Tozer for helping to get my references into their final shape. I gratefully acknowledge the help of Teachers College Press editors Sarah Biondello, Susan Liddicoat, and Nina George in guiding this book through the process of publication.

The Task
of
Post-Contemporary Education
ESSAYS IN BEHALF OF A HUMAN FUTURE

1 · Diagnosis of Our Time

"Each of us, in his own life," concludes Jacques Ellul [1964], "must seek ways of resisting and transcending technological determinants. . . . Our own desires and aspirations can change nothing." Technology is not yet wholly autonomous, nor do we have to accept the "Fatality of its rules", which at that are diverse, shifting, and sometimes inconsistent. It is not too clear on his grounds how we can still have "our own desires and aspirations", but . . . we have managed to retain some, and I assume they can change something. . . . I think we still have some measure of choice in futures. What with all our knowledge and our awareness . . . we at least have less excuse for failing than did all the civilizations of the past.

Herbert J. Muller
The Children of Frankenstein

1

IN 1943, KARL MANNHEIM PUBLISHED AN ESSAY with the same title I am using here. In adopting his title, I am not indicating total acceptance of his analysis of the human condition in 1941–1943 as apt to our "earthling" situation today, though indeed there are elements of his diagnosis that have never received the attention, thought, or testing in action that they deserve. In fact, for the most part, post-World War II educators eschewed attempts, like Mannheim's, to seek direction for educational efforts in a continuing diagnosis of human societies and cultures in their contemporary travail. In various ways, they avoided facing and acknowledging the pervasive "crisis of valuation," with which Mannheim's diagnosis began, in formulating educational "problems" and projecting policy and programmatic "solutions" to these "problems" and testing these formulations experimentally. For, to face the "crisis in valuation" and take it seriously is to recognize the need for structural, systemic changes in our basic institutions—familial, economic, political, and educational. Further, it is to recognize the need for focusing efforts, especially educational efforts, on developing a commitment to a common basis of valuation, in order to guide the comprehensive planning that our interdependent condition of life now inescapably requires. Most educators have chosen to work on the counterassumption that our contemporary institutions are systemically, structurally sound. Where they have been most influential, they have, therefore, served to aggravate, rather than meliorate, the crisis in which we live and move and have our being.

It is the spirit of Mannheim that I would wish to bring to my diagnosis, along with his title, rather than the letter of his analysis. He did not hesitate to formulate "outrageous hypotheses," to use Robert Lynd's (1935, see Ch. 6) phrase, where "outrageous situations" require such hypotheses. And he held these hypotheses with commitment, yet nondogmatically. He was an "intellectual," in Talcott Parsons' (1969) definition of that term, in that he put "cultural considerations above social in defining his commitments."

> Social systems are organized about the exigencies of interaction among acting units, both individual persons and collective units. Cultural systems, on the other hand, are organized about the patterning of meaning in symbolic systems. Relative to action . . . meaning systems are always in some respects normative in their significance; they specify what in some sense *should* be done and evaluate the actual performance accordingly, rather than either describing what in fact is done or predicting what will be. (p. 3)

Yet Mannheim was a "responsible" intellectual in the sense that he was always attentive to the social system patternings that underlie

2

conflicts in ideas and values and to the importance of working out a compatible and supporting social organization to implement novel idea and value systems as they are applied in practice. Democratic ideas and values, for example, cannot be learned well in a school system or classroom organized in an authoritarian pattern. "Cultural" transformation requires "social" change. And Mannheim was responsibly attentive to the social changes required in the implementation of the value and ideal commitments to which his intellectual analyses led him. I would be a responsible intellectual in my diagnosis, as Mannheim tried to be in his.

THE OUTLINES OF MANNHEIM'S DIAGNOSIS

The broad outlines of Mannheim's (1943) analysis of our contemporary plight can be stated briefly.

> We are living in an age of transition from laissez faire to a planned society. The planned society that will come may take one of two shapes: it will be ruled either by a minority in terms of a dictatorship or by a new form of government which, in spite of its increased power, will still be democratically controlled. (p. 1)

Mannheim saw the novel element in modern society as the emergence of knowledge-based techniques for deliberately producing various intended effects, though often inattentive to various unintended consequences. Among the various developed and developing technologies for extending human control over the environment, he was especially impressed with the significance of what he called "social techniques." These included powerful techniques for forming and manipulating public opinion—telecommunications, the press (print and electronic), and systematic schooling. He recognized that scientific studies of human behavior were spawning techniques that made possible the invasion, by those in public control, of areas once demarcated as personal and private; they also made possible the manipulation of emotional dynamics and subjugation of psychological processes by those who monopolistically possessed and wielded them. He saw the application of these techniques in therapy, social work, advertising, and "scientific" corporate management, as well as in thought control as exercised by Nazi, fascist, and Soviet dictatorships.

> The reason why I lay such emphasis on these social techniques is that they limit the direction in which modern society can develop at

all. The nature of these social techniques is even more fundamental to society than the economic structure or the social stratification of a given order. By their aid one can hamper or remould the working of the economic system, destroy social classes and set others in their place. (p. 3)

Modern technologies—social, physiochemical, electronic, and military—tend to foster centralization of decision making and so the possibility and efficacy of dictatorial control in and over a society. Effective decisions about the deployment and utilization of human and nonhuman resources can be and are increasingly made from a limited number of key positions in a society. Planning has become not only possible but virtually inevitable.

A refugee from Nazi-controlled central Europe, Mannheim made his diagnosis in the presence of emergent totalitarian states and dictatorships and in the midst of their struggle with "democratic" capitalist societies. His effort was to find an effective and militant democratic alternative both to unplanned capitalism and totalitarianisms of left and right. He found "the democracies" divided within themselves by fundamentally conflicting philosophies of life—suffering, in his term, from a "crisis of valuation." The problem of democratic societies, as he saw it, was to find or construct and develop a sufficient community of direction and commitment to sustain an effective system of economic and social planning, while maintaining the democratic freedoms of expression, voluntary grouping, opinion formation, and participation in public decisions. His diagnostic and prescriptive effort was to conceive and promulgate effective processes of planning through and for personal and group freedom and participation. He saw consonant processes of guided learning as centrally important in the tasks of reeducating people for life and participation in a planning society. When he came to England, he insisted on being named a professor of both sociology and the philosophy of education. This underlines the importance Mannheim attached to education and reeducation in cultural renovation. (Mannheim often identifies "education" with "schooling," an identification I will argue in later essays is today mischievous and misleading.)

WHAT OF MANNHEIM'S DIAGNOSIS TODAY?

It is important to criticize the adequacy of Mannheim's diagnosis for the human condition today. I am sure he would criticize, revise, and reconstruct it, were he alive today. The grounds of the criticism would be mainly historical experiences and developments during the past half century, along with developments in knowledge and technology, including social technology, not available to the past generation.

Evaluation of Mannheim's diagnosis must take account of the "neo-conservative" movement in the United States (and, perhaps, to a lesser degree in Western Europe and in Japan and other Asiatic countries), which crested during the 1980s. Leaders in this movement advocated a return to sound bourgeois capitalist principles. This required a radical reduction of governmental interventions in the regulation and direction of the economy. Interventions by the federal government were seen as especially detrimental. Ideologically, neo-conservative leaders touted unregulated market operations as the only modes of economic control compatible with a "free" society. This view is, of course, antithetical to Mannheim's belief in the necessity of overall planning, with government an active partner in the control of a technologically driven and increasingly interdependent economy. What has the neo-conservative adventure revealed about the relevance and adequacy of Mannheim's view?

In its results in America, neo-conservatism has actually underlined the soundness of Mannheim's general diagnosis. The neo-conservatives sought to restore "traditionally sound" principles to preeminence in the management of our political and economic life. F. S. C. Northrop, in his *The Meeting of East and West* (1946), made a striking observation concerning attempts by any nation or other group to enthrone "sound" principles from the past as necessarily good in our radically changed national and world environment, and to oversimplify various patterns of international and intergroup relations in terms of "good" and "bad."

> Neither war nor the peace-time problems of our world can be diagnosed as a simple issue between the good and the bad. . . . The very number and diversity of what the good and the divine is give the lie to any such diagnosis, and to the ever-present proposal that a return to the traditional morality and religion is a cure for all our ills. All that such proposals accomplish is the return of each person, and religious denomination, each political group or nation to its own pet traditional doctrine. And since this doctrine (or the sentiments it has conditioned) varies from person to person, group to group, nation to nation, and East to West, this emphasis upon traditional morality generates conflicts and thus intensifies rather than solves our problems. This in fact is the basic paradox of our time: our religion, our morality and our "sound" economic and political

theory tend to destroy the state of affairs they aim to achieve. (pp. 4, 5–6)

Is Northrop's basic paradox evident in the results of the attempt to implement neo-conservative policies in the United States? I believe that it is. I offer here only a few of the evidences that bolster my belief.

Ronald Reagan's neo-conservative administration sought to reduce the power of the federal government over American industry and commerce by deregulation and by lowering taxes, especially taxes upon the wealthy and upon private corporations. These moves were based on traditional capitalist "sound" principles: "That government is best which governs least" and "free competitive market control of the economy leads to greater and more efficient production of goods and services" and is "the only type of control consistent with a free society." The aim was to stimulate investment in new and more effective means and methods of production and trade. The results, paradoxically, were quite different. Many of the funds made available to putative investors through lowered taxes did not flow into the creation of more productive and efficient plants but into stock market speculations and augmented consumption of foreign goods. Competition was not increased in our economy through deregulation but rather was reduced through rampant mergers and take-overs, hostile and friendly. Multinational corporations thrived at the expense of domestic employment. Economic arrangements are now more collectivistic than they were before, in the sense of larger and fewer aggregations of productive capital and fewer and more massive centers of private economic decision making and control. And our international trade deficit has continued to grow.

The Reagan administration dedicated itself to less government control over economic activity, but, in attempts to enforce "sound" sexual morality and reduce women's control over the management of their pregnancies, it also projected and advocated augmented governmental interventions into the private lives of women and families. A general doctrine of freedom may thus lead to less freedom of choice when "sound" moral principles, espoused by neo-conservatives, are widely threatened and contravened.

Further, neo-conservatives have tended to commit our country to increasing "national strength" primarily through a radical buildup of destructive military power. The avowed purposes are greater security within the nation and augmented respect from other nations. One result, when combined with reduced revenues, is a staggering increase in national indebtedness, much of it to foreign creditors. It has also augmented Americans' feelings of insecurity in the ominously deepening shadow of enlarged nuclear capabilities in our country and our world. It has sapped, not strengthened, the moral leadership of our nation in the world of nations.

Northrop's paradox is evident in these and other results of neo-conservative policies. And Mannheim's case for planning is obscured by widespread propagandistic identification of public "planning" as, of necessity, a feature only of totalitarian regimes and as somehow antithetical to "democracy." This mistaken view has been abetted by use of the very social technology whose misuses Mannheim feared. Such false neo-conservative assumptions require a giant task of un-learning and relearning for Americans before Mannheim's arguments can be sanely evaluated by the American public, and his general rec-ommendations seriously considered as necessary means for human survival.

But there are other cultural developments, since 1943, that re-quire reevaluation of Mannheim's diagnosis. Mannheim focused on European aspects of cultural and social crises in industrialized na-tions and, by extension, the crises in the United States, Canada, and Australia. He did not bring Asia, Africa, and Latin America into the range of his diagnosis. As a result, "Third World" phenomena, as we have come to name them—the disparities in power and accumulated and accumulating capital between "have" and "have not" nations, the new "colonialisms," and the ethnic and racial dimensions of social and political conflicts—did not enter into his analysis, as they must into ours today.

Moreover, Mannheim did not know two of the most powerful social techniques that can be used to facilitate or to bypass and vitiate democratic planning—television and computer technology. We, as a people, are still fumbling with the social meanings of these powerful instruments of the "information revolution." Many now available electronic aids to the invasion of privacy were unknown to Mann-heim.

The controlled release of atomic energy had not, in Mannheim's time as it has in ours, dramatized mankind's power to destroy and pollute the biosupport systems necessary for the maintenance of hu-man and other forms of life on earth. Our consciousness of less dra-matic and more insidious ways in which urbanized and industrialized men and women are polluting their nest has grown in the train of our awareness of the totally destructive potentialities of radioactive pol-lution.

The pressure of uncontrolled population growth, in collusion with medical techniques for prolonging human life, upon resources of food, fuel, and fiber was not in the forefront of Mannheim's conscious planning for humankind's future as it should be in ours.

Mannheim had not reckoned with the wave of liberation movements in America and elsewhere, which stem from persons and groups of persons who feel alienated from the mainstream of life, alienated from themselves and their "real" natures and potentialities, and oppressed by the forms and conventions of established society. Protests against oppressive conditions of life and against those who were seen as oppressors began with racial groups, particularly blacks in America, and have spread to women, students and young people, oppressed poor people, homosexuals, peaceniks, and environmentalists. The incidence of protests in the United States abated during the Reagan years, but fresh protests have arisen since Reagan left the presidency. Sometimes the rhetoric of protest is borrowed from Marxism. More often the rhetoric of protest is populist and anarchist. Almost invariably, the language of protest is a language of "power"; the goal of protest, in addition to local and occasional goals, is a redistribution of maldistributed power. Protests have been "mass" movements, but most often the professed aim has been to encourage persons to lift themselves out of the mass, to accept and affirm themselves as persons, and to reject prevailing attributions of inferiority, powerlessness, and helplessness that those in established society have placed upon them. The "new" consciousness has led toward the politicizing of traditional relationships, emphasizing their "power" dimension. But the consciousness raising and affirming actions advocated are "therapeutic" in intention as they seek self-acceptance and self-assertion by those whom the "establishment" has put down. The protest movements have often embodied qualities of religious commitment, putting faith above conventional and "worldly" knowledge and wisdom. At times, the religious dimensions of protest are explicit, as in liberation theologies. Institutionalized compartmentalizations of "politics," "therapy," and "religion" are breaking down. Are new mergers of purpose and method and alternative institutions implicit in the razing of old boundaries and old walls?

Some of the protest movements, especially those defined along generational lines—young versus old—cut across national boundaries and have emerged in capitalist, communist, and socialist countries, and in both developed and developing countries. Are there intimations of a nascent world culture in these youth movements, a nascent consciousness and culture, pressing against the confines of repressive and outmoded social organization and controls, as Margaret Mead (1970) has suggested? Mannheim's diagnosis was couched in essentially sociological and anthropological terms. A contemporary diagnosis, if liberation and protest movements are granted evidential status, must involve psychobiological and spiritual concepts and dimensions as well.

In a review of Mannheim's early work in *Daedalus*, Shils (1974) has raised critical questions of a different order. While Shils focused his criticism on *Ideology and Utopia* and not on Mannheim's later work, including *Diagnosis of Our Time*, the criticisms are apt, in some measure, to his later more applied work as well. In brief, Shils notes that Mannheim never overcame his early prejudice against individualism nor the historicism that he learned from Hegel and the historical materialism that he took over in a nondogmatic way from Marx. As a result, he did not find in knowledge an independent element in the determination of action and cultural change. He tended to discount "the autonomy of the observing, imagining and reasoning (individual) mind." "He had little sense of the social institutional processes which are directly involved in the transmission, establishment and acceptance of knowledge." "He found no place for the investigation of the cognitive element in action or of the influence of natural or social science in society" (pp. 83 ff.).

Shils emphasizes the cognitive relativism in which Mannheim's sociology of knowledge involved him. From an applied point of view this led Mannheim to discount the role that disinterested knowledge can play in processes of planning that involve conflicting group interests in the outcomes of action. The place of "facts" in planning can be and frequently is overstated. But without "facts" and some shared cognitive agreements on what the "facts" are, the prospects for effective planning in areas of intergroup conflict are dim indeed.

I would generalize Shils' criticism beyond the area of knowledge production and utilization. Mannheim tended to share the view of the self as environmentally determined, not only cognitively but morally and aesthetically as well, that has characterized mainline human studies in both "liberal" and "socialist" circles in the modern period of Western thought and practice. The self has not been viewed as potentially a free, creative, proactive center in the generation and testing of meanings (within the limitations of environmental constraints, of course). Recently, existential modes of thinking about persons have challenged familiar and unexamined assumptions about environmentally determined selves in the social and human sciences and in their application. It is liberation movements, with their affinity for existential viewpoints and approaches, that have transformed views of the potent and influential self into practical processes of social change and planning. Certainly, assumptions about self make a difference in one's views about the ways in which institutions can be (and should be) changed and in the processes through which planning for the human future can be (and should be) institutionalized.

What remains valid in Mannheim's diagnosis for our own time? The need for social planning is even more evident in our time than in 1941–1943. The ever-present threat of the use of modern technologies to instate and maintain dictatorial regimes in and among nations has been underlined both by historic events and by refinements and extensions of social techniques since Mannheim's day. It can happen here—the Watergate scandal and, even more vividly, the Iran-Contra affair, remind us that it is *covertly* happening here. The development of militant democratic planning as an alternative to totalitarian planning is still an unfinished task. Some historic events and some knowledge and technical developments in the last generation have dimmed Mannheim's hope as a feasible alternative to totalitarian planning and social control, but others have brightened the hope. The educational project of developing persons capable of and committed to participation in democratic planning is largely a neglected task, though no less important now than in Mannheim's day.

I wish now to explore a few aspects of a diagnosis of our time that the already outlined developments in history, knowledge, and technology since World War II have put on the agenda of planners for the melioration of the human condition. I will raise more questions than I will answer. But this is no condemnation of the effort when the task is diagnosis.

THE MALDISTRIBUTION OF POWER
AND THE DECLINE OF AUTHORITY

It is impossible to ignore or deny differentials in power between persons and among groups in our power-conscious age. (For a well-documented analysis of the maldistribution of power in contemporary America, see Tozer, 1987.) One effect of the liberation movements already discussed has been to stimulate widespread reexamination of various traditional relationships, which have been taken for granted, in terms of the power differentials involved in them. Relations between racial majorities and minorities, between the young and the old, between women and men, and between people at different levels within hierarchical organizations are only a few of the relationships that have been exposed and reexamined in the past generation. In my opinion, this "new" extended consciousness of the operation of power within the maintenance and alteration of relationships and institutions is salutary and required. But I do not endorse all of the conceptions of power that direct this process of exposure or the recommendations about changes in relationships that revelation of power differentials leads many liberationists to make. Awareness of power as an ingredient factor in social stability and change is certainly a necessity for those who would plan directions and methods for social, economic, and educational change.

For power is to social dynamics what energy is to physiochemical dynamics. One cannot understand or change a human system without taking the uses and distribution of power into account. We desperately need to understand the operation of power if we are to plan democratically.

Let me state tersely, if not dogmatically, some of the erroneous assumptions that characterize much current thinking about power. The correction of these errors in thought and practice will have an important bearing upon the resolution and management of many aspects of the crisis in which we live today. First, there is no fixed sum of power in human situations, as many assume. Our familiar win–lose strategies for managing conflict are based on and perpetuate the fallacy of thinking of power as existing in fixed amounts and incapable of enlargement or diminution. In this view, the less powerful in a situation must acquire some of the power of the more powerful, leaving "one side" weaker if "the other" is to become more powerful. In a family, for example, must a husband give up power if a less powerful wife is to become more potent? A similar question can be asked about conflicts between parents and children. I think we have all experienced relationships in which the achievement of augmented power by less potent members of a group has generated more power for the entire group and all its members. The group is able to enjoy and achieve more as the potency of all members is increased. But this has occurred only when openness and trust among members have increased, when common goals seen as good by all have been envisaged and accepted at least provisionally, when useful information is shared among members, rather than hoarded and withheld—in brief, when win–win, cooperative strategies for managing differences and conflicts, rather than win–lose strategies of competition, have been employed.

In the international situation, would "have" nations be strengthened economically if "have not" nations were strengthened economically? Many students of international economics answer yes. How can the conditions that support win–win strategies of managing differences and conflicts be built between people in "have" and "have not" nations?

I suggest that false and limited notions of "power" and its inherent scarcity block the human search for ways of equalizing power differentials through generating new power rather than through struggling over the reallocation of existing power, assumed to be somehow limited and scarce.

Second, power is frequently seen as independent of shared goals and values. Actually, power is a function of shared goals and values. Those who believe in a cause will generate and focus power in its behalf. Those who disbelieve in a cause must be bribed or compelled to serve it. Napoleon was once reminded that a general could do everything with bayonets but sit on them. Without belief in the purposes toward which their leaders are leading them, soldiers can turn their weapons on their officers rather than "the enemy" as defined by the officers and by others who seek to direct their efforts. The widespread incidence of "fragging" in the American army in Vietnam attests to the actuality of this. Clarification of joint commitment to goals is one way, perhaps the only human way, of generating power in a human system where morale is low, where "power" is at low ebb, and where existing power is wasted in defensive and "rewarding" operations. Participation in setting goals as well as in implementing goals set by others is not an idealistic frill in generating power. It is a necessity in democratic planning.

Third, knowledge and information, along with clarified and accepted goals, are important ingredients of power. This is emphatically true in a society that bases its plans and decisions on knowledge of situations and of act–consequence relations within situations rather than on traditions and customary ways of producing and distributing goods. The shift in modern decision making and policy setting from tradition direction to dependence on amassed and evaluated knowledge and information in relation to consciously formulated goals and outcomes has moved a long way in industrialized societies. This is, of course, another way of underlining the necessity of planning in industrialized societies. Those with access to relevant information have power to make realistic decisions about plans and policies. Those without access to relevant information are deprived of power to make or share in making realistic and workable decisions. Computer technology has vastly increased human power to store, process, and retrieve information relevant to decisions. I will comment later on the crucial problem of access to information in democratic planning today.

Finally, there is widespread confusion between authority and other forms of power both in the human sciences and in action planning today. (See Benne, 1943/1971, 1970, and 1986.) In brief, authority operates where its bearer exercises power in the service of a need of subjects who are unable to meet this need through their own unaided powers. Moreover, the relation holds for some delimited field of transactions between bearer and subjects, not in all areas of life. "Authority" relations are thus relations of interdependence, not of dependence on the part of subjects and independence on the part of bearers.

Many traditional authority relations have ceased to be authority relations today. For example, students often see the power of school systems over them as naked, illegitimate power, not authority, when they perceive the resources of the schools oriented not to meeting their needs for free and responsible learning and growth as they envision these, but rather to meeting the teachers' needs to propagate their specialist "disciplines" or to meeting the manpower needs of one or another established bureaucracy—school, industry, or government department, including the military.

When I wrote *A Conception of Authority* nearly 50 years ago, I noted that, with all the rejection of the authority of traditional rules, roles, and statuses in industrialized societies, there was an almost unquestioned acceptance of the authority of specialized expertise. I saw then that much of this acceptance rested on the prestige of empirical science, from the findings of which modern specialized expertise draws its power to predict and control phenomena. (I say "prestige" rather than "authority" of science, because most of us in many areas of our lives have too little understanding of the world view or spirit of science to grant it genuine authority in the management of our lives.) I see more clearly now that the willing obedience of many to the dictates of experts rested also in a generalized deification of technology. The unplanned uses of technology may have precipitated the crisis of humankind, but we have tended to believe that further technology and technological solutions would in the long run save us from the bad effects of its misuse.

Our technological god has now failed us. Uncontrolled by common, human values, the development and use of technology, which once promised to liberate and fulfill us, now threatens literally to destroy us. The conversion of matter into energy gave us our first chilling intimation of the lethal powers of previously trusted technological expertise. The further work of environmentalists has shown the more insidious but nevertheless lethal ways in which many of our uses of technology are destroying the support systems on which the continuity of human and other forms of life depends.

The failure of our technological god has lent a distinctive quality to the desperation and loss of hope among men and women in the United States and other industrialized cultures. Our continued dependence on technology in a thousand ways is extreme. The ramifying effects of the petroleum shortage in the 1970s, however engineered, in undercutting our habitual style of life as persons and consumers and in grinding interrelated processes of transport, manufacture, and distribution to a halt are evidence of this dependence.

Reactions to this loss of authority in our lives are various. Among the "foolish" reactions are efforts to "return to nature," opposing the artificiality of our "ersatz" environment and way of life to the "naturalness" of a romanticized version of preindustrial life and society. Another "foolish" response is to embrace unscientific or antiscientific guides to living—whether astrology, numerology, fundamentalist religion, parapsychology, or I Ching.

It was out of a similar desperation that "advanced" industrial societies accepted totalitarian planning by self-appointed elites as a way to bring order, at large cost, into their fundamentally disordered lives. Mannheim understood and feared this reaction. We should understand it better today and fear it more. But do we? Do we see how close the Vietnam War and the Cold War with the USSR once brought us to a police state?

Mannheim sought an alternative in democratic planning. This is, in my judgment, still our best alternative. But we must see today that the restoration of community within industrialized societies where it has been destroyed and the building of community among peoples of various nations where it has not existed before are necessary to provide commonly acceptable authority for effectively planning and enforcing humane uses of technology and for the education and reeducation of people in planning. Mannheim saw and emphasized that democratic planning must include planning for freedom. This is still essential. But democratic planning must include planning for freedom in and through community as well as for the uses of technologies according to priorities set in and through processes of participative planning. Reeducation must be part of the task of planning—reeducation of people from laissez faire modes of living where these have been the rule and reeducation from dependence on autocratic control by others where this has been the rule.

CAPITALISM AND SOCIALISM

Contemporary liberation movements, with their vivified conscious-ness of oppression, their commitment to finding relief from oppres-sion, and their recognition of the necessity for transferring power from oppressor groups and classes to the oppressed, have led to a renewed interest in Marxism in America and elsewhere in the capital-ist world. Finding the locus of oppression within the established sys-tem and its normative structures, coalescing with our new awareness of "social system" as a powerful cross-disciplinary tool of analysis in human affairs, has led to an identification of the "capitalist system" as the "cause" of dehumanization and alienation in the minds of many liberationists in capitalist countries. It may be apropos to note that liberationists in the USSR attribute to the "socialist system" com-parable ills of dehumanization and alienation there.

I tend to agree with Mannheim that questions of the uses to which technology, including social techniques, are put and of who makes the decisions about these uses are more fundamental than the issue between a capitalist or socialist organization of the economy. I say this without discounting the importance of economic policies and operations within a society and without apologizing for the patholo-gies and injustices inherent in our American capitalist economy.

Ownership of the means of production is not the crucial control element in developed economies, as it seemed to Marx in the nine-teenth century. Ownership has to some large degree been separated from managerial control of economic policies and decisions, as Berle, Means, Galbraith, and others have emphasized. Control of economic policies is now in the hands of a "techno-structure," as Galbraith (1967) has observed. This techno-structure represents a coalition be-tween managerial interests within the private and the public (govern-mental) structure of our political economy. There are contradictions between current controls of our economy and the possibilities and desirabilities of using our productive powers fully and humanely. The system cannot generate the purchasing power required to keep itself profitably employed. Profit motivation works against maintaining and restoring the biosupport systems that human and other forms of life require. Our profit system cannot channel capital investment into economically unprofitable or less profitable but humanly necessary areas of adequate housing and health care for all people. The adver-tising system devised to get people to buy what manufacturers plan to produce diverts people from assessing their own basic needs and directing productivity toward meeting these needs. And so on and on.

Our economic system does need changing. But social ownership is hardly an adequate answer to all the changes now required. Public ownership is probably long overdue in some areas of our economy—the mines and the railroads, for example. But the more fundamental need is to set and enforce priorities for use and development of our productive capacities. Informed and effective participation in policy determination by persons, groups, and interests now outside the controlling techno-structure is more crucial than the transfer of "ownership" of productive capacity. This redistribution and transfer of power in planning will take many forms, as it now presents both opportunities and barriers to democratization. (For nonidolatrous treatments of contemporary technology and its effects on work, see Waks and Roy, 1987, and Wirth, 1987.) I will try to locate some of these more specific lines of change in the sections that follow.

I do not mean, in what I have just written, to dismiss the relevance or value of a Marxist orientation to humankind and society. I realize that the Marxist literature is being reworked along humanist lines, partly as a result of the dialectic between existentialist and Marxist modes of thought. If the main import of Marx' labor theory of value is an emphasis on people as the creators of value—indeed the only creators of value—and if Marx' theory of alienation is focused on ways of restoring people to "ownership" of the processes and products of their creation of value, as some Marxist scholars seem to say, I am happy to be to that extent a Marxist. (Treatments of current Marxist thought that I have found useful are Harrington, 1972; Ollman, 1971; and Schaff, 1963.)

ETHNICITY, NATIONALITY, AND PERSONAL IDENTITY

The Marxist conception of class consciousness and solidarity is based on a "rationalistic" conception of humankind and human motivation and action. That conscious recognition of contradictory economic self-interests among social classes will provide a ground for class solidarity across national and ethnic lines is at the heart of Marxist thought. Yet it was nationalist identifications that destroyed international working class solidarity during World War I and in other crucial events as well. Men and women seek identity through other and deeper identifications than those of economic self-interest.

The reemergence of ethnicity as a basis of personal identification and political action is widely apparent in contemporary societies. The Black Power movement and the growth of ethnic backlash movements in the United States, and the upsurge of ethnic identification as a counterpower to colonialism and imperialism throughout the Third World, illustrate such reemergence. At the risk of undue simplification, I see two quite different bases of group formation and identification within the need systems of men and women. One is based on what Giddings (1908) once called "consciousness of kind." Ethnic and national identifications are of this sort: I am a black; a Puerto Rican; a Jew; a Ghanian; an Italo-American. Others of this kind are "like" me—I belong with them and they with me. The basis of such familial identification does not admit of fully rational analysis or definition. It just is, in some factual and undefinable sense. The other basis of group formation and identification is grounded in a division of labor among members, as emphasized by students of social behavior like Durkheim and Lewin. It is based not on ascribed similarity of members but on a differentiation of function, and presumably of character and abilities, among members. Any group formed to achieve a complex goal or set of goals is of this sort—a work group, a team, a problem-solving or planning task force. This basis of group formation is capable of rationalization in terms of effectiveness and efficiency in the performance of some commonly accepted and valued task.

In a society, these two kinds of groupings may be opposed or mutually reenforcing. A society, wise about the bases of its cohesion, continuity, and perpetuity, must take account of both bases of grouping and seek to reconcile the two bases of group loyalty and personal identification and identity. In a pluralistic "community," the two bases of personal identity are, if not reconciled and mutually reenforcing, both honored; and commonly acceptable processes of reconciliation are available and institutionalized for use when and where the two fall apart and into conflict.

The eclipse of community in industrial societies and in their fundamental institutions—family, school, and work organization—has helped to release and lend reactive and defensive power to various kinds of "ethnic," "racial," and "religious" groupings. Where loyalty has been transferred from tribes and local communities to nations, heightened nonrational feelings of nationality take precedence over other identifications.

I think we must learn to respect the reality of ethnic and national identifications even as we learn to organize *working* systems of membership across ethnic lines in setting and serving larger common goals. Babad, Birnbaum, and Benne (1983) provide a description of the education required. Practical rationality and judgment in reorganizing societies to meet novel demands with both high morale and effectiveness require such learnings and their application. "Change agents," trained to unusual sensitivity and understanding of group and intergroup phenomena and dynamics, and skilled in applying knowledge in conflict situations, must be made available to all parts of our increasingly interdependent but dangerously noncommunal societies.

BEYOND BUREAUCRACY

I owe the name of this section to the title of a book written by my friend and colleague, Warren Bennis (1973). Bennis documents the inability of bureaucratic organizations to respond flexibly and mindedly to internal and external demands for changes in goals and methods of achieving them. Yet change is the predominant quality of life in contemporary societies and an expectation for the future. The inabilities of bureaucracies—and Bennis includes among bureaucracies private organizations in industry, health care, welfare, and religion along with public and governmental organizations—to assess needs for change and to plan and effect changes in roles, rules, internal and external relations, and methods of operation are due to several features of bureaucratic organization. It is not alone their large size. Their pyramidal structure, with decisions concentrated at the top of the pyramid; their mechanical assignment of partial tasks to segregated departments, which operate without awareness of or responsibility for the whole mission of the organization; their dependence for the motivation of persons on external rewards rather than on commitment to the purposes of the organization—all of these and other characteristics make for inflexible, mindless, and dehumanized operations.

Organizations are being forced to depend on temporary systems to plan for meeting novel demands. These temporary, project-type organizations cross departmental and disciplinary lines to bring together resources needed for dealing with particular situations, stress equal participation by members in decisions, and are more organic and less mechanically formal in relations among members. In brief, they have more of the characteristics of democratic communities than of bureaucratic organizations. Bennis argues that we must become more inventive in creating forms of social organization tailored to facilitate planning for management of social and technical change. The temporary systems he describes have come out of the necessity for adaptive responses to changing conditions of life. Planning for change requires not only new and valid goals and priorities. It requires deliberate formation and reformation of organizational forms consonant with new and changing goals and priorities. Bennis, Benne, and Chin (1986) discuss various approaches to the changing of organizations.

All of us in education know how a rigid, bureaucratic organization has subverted new ideas and practices in schooling. Protesting students in the 1960s were typically more radical in projecting ideal democratic goals than in inventing democratic forms of organization to support and advance these goals. Adult radicals have often fallen into the same contradictory practices. Michael Harrington (1972), in emphasizing how Soviet communism subverted its professed socialist goals by its dependence on bureaucratic forms controlled by an elite, names its form of economic organization "bureaucratic socialism."

Alternatives to bureaucratic organization are emerging. But the creation of alternative forms of social organization consistent with changing goals and personnel, and a turbulent social environment must become an integral part of social planning. Again, training persons to participate in forming new groups and organizations must become an integral part of general, democratic education.

ACCESS TO INFORMATION

I mentioned earlier how computer technology and instantaneous means of transmitting information are involving us in an "information revolution." We now have ways of storing vast quantities of information, processing it, selectively retrieving it relevant to decisions to be made, and transmitting it instantaneously to any part of the earth and beyond. This is familiar to all of us and is commonly regarded as a wonder of modern technology.

The bearing of this new powerful technology upon future forms of social and political control is perhaps less often probed and assessed. It seems true that control of access to information makes possible a form of tyranny more concentrated and complete than any we have known in the past. In a planning society, policy decisions and tactical decisions as well are based on information and knowledge rather than on customary and traditional principles and usages. Those who have access to information are able to make realistic and workable decisions. Those without access are dependent on others for making the decisions that control their lives.

There is no necessity that access to information be limited to a few people. (I realize that claims of alleged national security and competitive advantage are used frequently to make a virtue of limited access.) In some measure, limited access is a correlate of hierarchical social organization and control by those at the top. There is no impossibility in making computers available to all members of a society, along with skills in storing and retrieving information. Democratic planning must make equal access to information as fundamental a right as equality of income and equal participation in processes of planning, important as these latter are.

I realize also that new ways of storing, retrieving, and transmitting information, along with refined techniques of electronic surveillance, constitute grave threats to personal privacy. Although traditionally private rights, such as rights of private productive property, are being redefined, and must be, in an age of public planning, new areas of privacy must be defined and protected in democratic planning, if healthy, creative personalities are to be developed and protected.

One way of helping this along may be to make a minimum family income the right of every family. There is a protection of private patterns and styles of life in guaranteeing to each individual a command of private uncontrolled economic means. Private ownership of homes for those who want and need them should be assisted. And the protection of individuals in their homes and private areas of consumption and sexual activity should be a part of what is to be planned for in a good society.

ALTERATIONS IN SEXUAL AND GENDER RELATIONSHIPS

Sexual mores have undergone marked changes in the last generation in all industrialized societies and perhaps in developing countries as well. Sexual practices have tended to pass out of the realm of more or less rigid social control into the realm of control by personal taste and preference. While modern productive and distributive technology, in increasing economic interdependence, has tended to take productive property out of the realm of private into the realm of public control, techniques of contraception have made it possible to leave sexual practices more to private control. It has already been noted that resurgent conservatism in "religious" politics is seeking to delay this process through governmental coercion.

Regarded rationally, population control has now become imbued with the public interest. Problems of poverty and of pressure of growing populations against limited resources make "family planning" an important aspect of social planning. Whatever resistances to the use of contraceptives and abortion traditional moralists may exert, people's access to information about contraception and abortion has led and will continue to lead to their more extensive use. Social planning, with due respect for private judgment and moral scruples, should hasten processes of family planning in all parts of the world.

With widespread use of contraceptives, variations in sexual taste and preference are almost certain to manifest themselves. Acceptance of these variations by society at large is likely to follow. Redefinition of family patterns and childrearing practices will follow in their train. The eventual effects upon children's mental and moral development of the increasing incidence of growing up in one-parent families and of spending considerable time in day-care centers cannot now be confidently assessed. But these effects are bound to be of great significance to post-contemporary educators.

The increasingly successful efforts by women to attain vocational and civic opportunities equal to those now enjoyed by men (at least by white men) and to receive equal rewards for equal work will alter the gender stereotypes in our and other nations. Educators must be prepared to help boys and girls, men and women, to achieve self-images consonant with these crumbling stereotypic roles. The effort should be to prevent the freezing of new gender stereotypes and to help both men and women develop affirmative individualized views *of* themselves that are liberating *for* themselves. Elise Boulding (1987) has assessed authoritatively the present trends and tensions in changing gender roles in familial, occupational, and civic settings. Only such a rounded view of alterations in sex and gender developments will serve educators well.

One important aspect of the effects of changes in patterns of sexual activity and of inter-gender relationships has not been explored as fully as it deserves. This is the relationship between changes in interpersonal relationships and changes in larger economic and political institutional patterns. How, if at all, will sexual "liberation" affect the personal commitments of those "liberated" to the achievement of wider social change?

I have found Reimut Reiche's (1971) treatment of sexuality and the class struggle of interest in this connection. Like many Marxists, Reiche is suspicious of any social movement that diverts persons from commitment toward efforts to create a classless society. But he is by no means dogmatic in his tentative "answers" concerning the relationship. His investigation raises questions about a wider range of social movements and their interrelations. What is the relationship between various liberation movements that focus on changes in personal expression and taste, and movements that press toward changed economic-political patterns and practices? We can be quite sure that Charles Reich (1970) in his book, *The Greening of America*, overstated the "causal" relationship between his Consciousness III, manifesting itself in novel patterns of personal and interpersonal functioning (as in the communes of the 1960s), and an emerging new cultural and social order. But it would be foolish to deny some interactive relationship between the two. Educators, who typically seek to affect the consciousness of the individuals whose learning they attempt to influence, should always be alive to the interrelations between learning at the personal level and social change.

THE BANKRUPTCY OF THE NATIONAL STATE

I have left this element in the diagnosis of our time of troubles to the last, not because of its lesser importance, but partly because it is difficult to see beyond the international anarchy in which we live our lives today. It is clear that there is no effective political control of the economic and social interdependence that is today worldwide. We have no effective world institutions to support effective planning with respect to worldwide problems. And democracy, partial as it is in our country, is notably missing on the world scene.

Our efforts to build a basis for participatory planning with respect to world problems must be piecemeal and fragmentary at the present time. We can support moves to limit armaments, to outlaw nuclear weapons, to find effective processes of negotiation as a substitute for war in settling international disputes. We can work for world citizenship as an alternative or adjunct to national citizenship, become world citizens ourselves, and encourage others to become world citizens also. We can support various forms of people-to-people interaction and exchange across national lines. We can encourage transnational planning to solve genuine world problems in which all peoples of the world have a stake in solving—the maintenance of biosupport systems through antipollution measures (to stop the dwindling of the ozone layer and thwart the greenhouse effect, for example), effective implementation of the declaration of human rights, strengthening programs of international aid to developing countries, nuclear disarmament, and the control of international terrorist activities.

We can encourage futurist thinking about problems, believing with Margaret Mead (1965) that the future is the only viable basis for developing a shared culture—a future culture to which various traditional cultures can contribute. And we can look for breaks in the system of inadequate national controls and try to introduce transnational controls at these breaking points.

In conclusion, I will quote once again the heart of Mannheim's (1943) diagnosis of our time, which, however much in need of qualification and elaboration, still seems generally valid to me.

> We are living in an age of transition from laissez faire to a planned society. The planned society that will come may take one of two shapes: it will be ruled either by a minority in terms of a dictatorship or by a new form of government which, in spite of its increased power, will still be democratically controlled. (p. 1)

2 · The Meanings of Democracy in a Collective World

Though often repudiated in practice by both the individual and the mass and though but vaguely defined and understood by the average citizen, democracy remains today a vital and powerful force in American life—one of the major necessities to be reckoned with in every venture in statecraft or education. Here is the basic ethical reality in the history of the nation.

George S. Counts
The Social Foundations of Education

I submit that an overwhelming majority of Americans believe that it is only fair that those who have a stake in the collective action should have a voice in shaping it. This belief colors our consciousness from the first game of hide-and-seek or scrub baseball. The consensus for this principle is based not only on rational grounds; it is part of the common moral intuition. It may be called our fundamental moral reflex.

Harry S. Broudy
"Education in a Pluralistic Society"

WHY ASSESS THE MEANINGS OF DEMOCRACY
IN A WORK ON EDUCATION?

That the United States of America as a nation is the exemplar and principal defender of democracy in today's world is the professed belief of a vast majority of Americans. That educational opportunity for all people, at public expense if necessary, is a manifestation and a bulwark of democracy is still believed by a majority of Americans, although the belief may be less firmly entrenched than it was a generation ago. The early American democratic idea of developing an enlightened citizenry and, later, the idea of equality of educational opportunity for each person to develop his or her capacities, were two democratic ideals that contributed to the extension of schooling throughout the nineteenth and early twentieth centuries in America.

It can be argued that, in a society that professes allegiance to democratic processes, the very idea of education cannot be understood adequately without attention to the meaning of democracy. This is to say more than to agree with Thomas Jefferson that political democracy depends on an educated populace for its effective operation. The point is rather that, in a society like that of the United States, the idea of public education depends for its normative meaning on the meaning attributed to democracy. If this is true, better and richer understandings of democracy contribute to better and richer understandings of education. To understand barriers to the actualization of democracy is to understand barriers to the actualization of an adequate education for ourselves and our fellow citizens.

In what sense is this linkage true? It has become a commonplace to recognize that education always takes place in relation to a particular social context. What it means "to be educated" in any particular culture depends on the demands and expectations which that culture places upon its members. The meaning of "being educated" as a Plains Indian in the eighteenth century was distinctively different from the meaning of "being educated" as a citizen in twentieth-century America. This is because the social institutions, norms, and ideals of the two cultures are distinctly different. "Literacy" in the two cultures has different meanings. Shooting accurately with bow and arrows, dancing, tracking animals, and fighting human enemies were probably elements in the "literacy" of a developing Plains Indian, or at least a brave. Reading, writing, and computing are elements of "literacy" for a twentieth-century American.

In addition to instrumental "literacy," developing young people are shaped to understand and internalize values, ideals, and beliefs considered important in the culture in which they are gaining membership. For the Plains Indian, tribal loyalty, respect for animals, and a feeling of oneness with "nature" may have been such values. In twentieth-century America, acceptance of many values and beliefs is expected of *bona fide* members of American society, though these expectations vary from group to group in our heterogeneous society. Few if any of these are so fundamental to the characterization and justification of our social order as a belief in "democracy." We are brought up to believe in it, however imperfectly it may be understood by most members of society.

Ours is a society, as Abraham Lincoln said at Gettysburg, "conceived in liberty and dedicated to the proposition that all men are created equal." In 1934, George Counts declared that democracy is our "basic ethical reality" (p. 11). In 1980, Harry Broudy argued that the democratic process is our "fundamental moral reflex" (p. 20). If these observers are correct, then democracy has such a central place in our culture that the culture cannot be adequately understood without an understanding of the meaning(s) of democracy itself. If educational practice is meaningful only in relation to its cultural context, then understanding the meaning(s) of democracy in our culture is necessary to an adequate understanding and evaluation of educational practice in that culture. We learn to read and write, and we learn to make judgments in accord with certain ideals, democracy among them. We know fairly clearly what we mean by reading and writing, but we know less clearly what we mean by "democracy."

None of these observers of American society would have claimed that our social institutions and practices adequately embody democratic ideals. Nor, indeed, would they probably have agreed completely on what these ideals are or ought to be. Yet all, like many other students of American society, have evoked democratic values as normative criteria by which social, economic, and educational arrangements should be evaluated.

There is still an even more fundamental linkage between democracy and education, which students and practitioners of education in America should keep in mind. This has to do with the educational benefits to individual persons who participate in the process of democracy. It is common to argue for education as instrumental to effective democratic participation. Carole Pateman (1970), however, has argued for the converse of this proposition: We should value democracy because we value education. Citing John Stuart Mill, Jean Jacques Rousseau, and others, Pateman points to the proposition that, in principle, a democratic system of community life, more than any alternative, provides opportunities for individual persons to take responsibility for their own relations with others and thus to develop the capacities necessary to conduct those relations effectively and freely. Pateman argues, in effect, that a fundamental aim of democracy is to educate its members through their participation in self-management of their chosen enterprises. Looked at in this way, the relationship between democracy and education is ideally of mutual benefit, one to the other.

THE MINIMAL MEANINGS OF DEMOCRACY

We have noted Counts' (1934) observation that for average Americans the meaning of democracy is "but vaguely defined and understood" (p. 11). Such vague understanding probably becomes evident when questions are raised that take the answers beyond the minimal meanings of democracy that "everyone" is willing to grant. Most often these minimal meanings hold that democracy is a form of rule (by the people, by representation) and that it is an embodiment of freedoms (religious or political, for example).

Democracy as a Form of Rule

Traditionally, "democracy" has referred to a form of government. The etymology of the word (Greek, *demos:* people, + *kratein:* to rule) underlines this meaning. That democracy is "rule by the people" is one of the first definitions schoolchildren typically learn. The people rule themselves by debating and voting on controverted questions and, in most forms of democracy, the majority determines the policy that is taken as established. (In Quaker circles, as well as for other devotees of democracy, a consensus is required for legitimation of a decision.)

Participation by all in forming, discussing, and deciding upon policies becomes difficult, if not impossible, where large masses of people are involved, as in our modern nation-states as opposed to the small city-states in classical Greece. In such cases, direct democracy yields to representative democracy. People elect their representatives after campaigns in which various views of current issues are aired and discussed. People can attempt to influence these representatives in office, fail to reelect them if dissatisfied with their records, or, in extreme cases, recall them before their terms of office have expired.

Rule by the people, majority rule, and rule by representation are three variations on the democratic theme of government by the consent of the governed, which attends to rulership in democratic society. All represent a view of democracy that is serviceable at the level of a thumbnail sketch or a slogan, but that fails to reveal deeper meanings of the democratic ideal.

Democracy as the Embodiment of Freedoms

For many Americans, the claim that "we are a democratic society" is synonymous with "we are a free society." A democracy embodies and protects for citizens a variety of freedoms, such as political, religious, or intellectual freedom, and democratic forms of governance should seek to protect citizens in the exercise of those freedoms. Majority rule, for example, is not adequately democratic if it does not effectively protect the freedoms of minorities; hence John Stuart Mill's fear of "the tyranny of majorities." Democracy understood as a form of rule, then, is part of a larger, commonly held view that attends to the freedoms democracy ideally seeks to embody. These dimensions of freedom commonly associated with democratic life are civil, political, and economic.

The distinction between civil liberty and political liberty was made by Aristotle in his *Politics* (1946) and it is reflected in American thinking about democracy. For Aristotle, civil liberty was the freedom to live as one chooses to—to pursue the good life as one understands it. Aristotle explained political freedom as the freedom to participate in making the laws—"ruling and being ruled"—that protect the interests of individuals. Since individuals are the best judges of their own interests, he reasoned, they must have the opportunity to structure the social order to protect those interests. The importance of the action of political freedom, which we might think of as political participation, is illustrated in Mill's criticism of the "benevolent despot." Such a despot, who could perhaps effectively protect civil liberties, would be antidemocratic in that the despot alone, rather than the people themselves, would be free to determine the laws that governed people's lives.

The popular equation of democracy with "free enterprise" and "the free market system" is evidence of the "economic freedom" dimension of democratic ideals. Democratic life, it is believed, embodies the freedom to become as rich or as poor as one's talents and efforts allow, without the regulating influence of government. This notion of economic freedom as a democratic ideal is a product of the Enlightenment effort to free individuals from oppressive feudal or mercantilist political economies, and it has become a central dimension of what most Americans consider the democratic ideal to represent.

These three dimensions of freedom, then, are as much a part of the minimal meanings of democracy as are rule by the people, majority rule, and rule by representation. They operate together to form popular conceptions of democracy that attend both to forms of rule and dimensions of freedom.

Majority rule, it is believed, must not be allowed to interfere with continuing attempts by dissident persons, groups, and minorities to defend their interests and to work for changes in governing policies. So the civil liberties of persons are guaranteed, as in the Bill of Rights of our federal Constitution—freedom of speech, assembly, petition, and so on, and the disestablishment of any and all religious denominations. One function of government is to guarantee the civil liberties of all citizens, especially minority persons and groups. The Bill of Rights also prohibits the establishment of any one religion and offers protection to persons in worshiping or not worshiping in the manner of their choice.

Another function of government is to maintain a fair and orderly mechanism for balancing conflicting interests against one another. The U.S. Constitution is a classic effort to structure that balance via political participation in a representative democracy—one that embodies, to one degree or another, Aristotle's ideal of political freedom.

Finally, government is popularly thought to protect economic freedom. Regardless of how elaborately government agencies seek to regulate economic life today, the American public clings to its high regard for the "free enterprise system," and too rigorous efforts to regulate that system in the interests of economic equality and consumer protection are publicly denounced as "socialistic." Of course, socialism may be understood and practiced as democratic in some societies. But the popular allegiance to economic freedom in the United States continues to serve as an obstacle to overtly socialist policies in, for example, health care or job security.

Our representation of the "minimal meanings" of democracy in contemporary U.S. society, then, focuses on both personal and civic aspects of democracy. The personal aspects are dimensions of freedom. The civic aspects sketch a form of governance. Probably few "average Americans" would grow restless or incoherent if those who raise questions concerning the meaning of democracy stayed within the boundaries of such minimal meanings. But the course of history has seen, in America and elsewhere too, a widening and deepening of the meanings of democracy. And, in this widening and deepening, controversies have appeared within the public, and established practices and customs have been challenged and changed in the name of democracy. Conflicts have appeared among those who profess "democracy" as well as between proponents of democracy and proponents of other forms of rule and other conceptions of legitimate freedom.

BROADENING AND DEEPENING OF THE MEANING OF DEMOCRACY

There are numerous areas in which the meaning of "democracy" has been broadened and deepened since the time of Thomas Jefferson. Six of them have been chosen for treatment here. Some of these have resulted from applying the concepts of democracy to areas of human living where other forms of control have operated traditionally. Others have been articulated in response to changing conditions of life or to the challenge of nondemocratic modes, traditional or novel, of organizing and controlling human enterprises. Most of them evoke controversy, even among proponents of democracy.

Democracy as a Form of Rule versus Democracy as a Way of Life

In modern societies, politics has been isolated from other aspects of life, unlike the integration of politics with other phases of life which prevailed in the Greek *polis*. "Government" has been separated from "industry," "business," "family," "religion," "entertainment," "the arts," and many forms of "mass communication."[1]

Some of these aspects of life have traditionally operated or have come to operate under a form of control and management that is undemocratic or antidemocratic in character. Industry may be taken as an example. Under the assumed "inalienable" rights of private property, owners of industry, especially as units of industry have grown in size, have instated authoritarian forms of rule and management. Workers who had once partially controlled the conditions of their labor came to have little or no voice in making or enforcing the policies and practices that prevailed in their workplaces. Families, schools, hospitals, and other institutions have often operated and still operate with similar authoritarian forms of rule.

Proponents of democracy have long criticized the inconsistency of these arrangements with the freedom to live or work as one chooses and to participate in the decisions that affect one's interests. They have further noted the contradictions of our society and have sought to extend the notions of democratic life, first in idea and then in practice, beyond the area of "politics" to other aspects of our common life—industrial democracy, democracy in schools and classrooms, democracy in family relations, and so on. In industries, for example, unions of workers developed power through organization to gain a collaborative voice in decisions affecting their lives, most often in such limited areas of policy making as wages and working conditions. Like some turn-of-the-century workers who resisted collective bargaining with respect to wages because it condoned an autocratic workplace in favor of limited concessions by owners, theorists of industrial democracy envisioned a wider range of collaborative (democratic) policy making and participative management in all areas of industrial life.

In actual practice, the extension of democracy into the areas of power traditionally exercised by ownership and management has been resisted, and conflict rather than collaboration has tended to result. Of late, collaboration among management, labor, and public representatives in operating and managing industrial and business enterprises has made greater headway in theory and to a lesser extent in practice. Such management goals as enhanced productivity and more effective learning about and readier acceptance of changed technology and changed ways of working have probably been more powerful than devotion to democratic values in motivating such extended democratic collaboration. But the effect is to bring democracy into operation, however inchoately, in an area of social control where it was until recently resisted and denied.

The most succinct way of describing the extension of democracy from politics to other aspects of society is to contrast democracy as a "political form" with democracy as an "ethical way of life," applicable to all interpersonal, intergroup, and organizational relationships. John Dewey (1916) made a strong case for democracy as a way of life in its educational bearings. If persons in our society are to learn that a regard for democratic life is more than a regard for rules of voting and representative government, democracy must come to be seen as an ethos, applicable to political relationships between leaders and other citizens, but equally applicable to workers and managers in industry, to school boards, administration, teachers, and students in formal education, and so on. Dewey (1948) argued that democracy is not limited in its meaning to forms and procedures in government, but has a moral significance rooted in what we value in human social life.

> Government, business, art, religion, all social institutions have a meaning, a purpose. That purpose is to set free and to develop the capacities of human individuals without respect to race, sex, class or economic status. And this is all one with saying that the test of their value is the extent to which they educate every individual into the full stature of his possibility. Democracy has many meanings, but if it has a moral meaning, it is found in resolving that the supreme test of all political institutions and industrial arrangements shall be the contribution they make to the all-around growth of every member of society. (p. 186)

Civil Rights as Well as Civil Liberties

Civil liberties have been recognized and, in most part, accepted in principle as essential aspects of political democracy in the United States since the addition of the Bill of Rights to the federal Constitution in 1791. These generally take the form of limitations upon government (and other agencies) against depriving persons of guaranteed freedoms of speech and assembly, and freedom from unreasonable searches of one's residence and person, imprisonment without trial, and so on. But civil liberties throughout history have been unevenly distributed among our people. They were denied to black slaves until emancipation in 1863, and to most black citizens afterward by various devices until the civil rights protests of the 1950s and 1960s led to the outlawing of the Jim Crow laws of Southern states. Women were denied their rights as property holders, public speakers, voters, and independent citizens with recourse to due process until well into the twentieth century. Both blacks and women are still victims of discrimination, though less flagrantly than before.

After World War II, liberation movements powered by organized minorities flourished and sought the extension of legal guarantees of various civil rights as well as the traditional civil liberties. Instead of civil liberties conceived as freedom from any interference by government, government was appealed to for the establishment and protection of civil rights. Civil rights, as opposed to civil liberties, tended to take the form of entitlements and negation of discriminatory practices rather than exemption from limitations upon specified personal and small-group freedoms. Blacks, Hispanics, Asians, women, homosexuals, and handicapped persons are among the minorities who have mounted liberation movements directed toward abolition of discrimination against them in employment and in access to public accommodations, housing, and education. In general, the target of liberation movements has been the abolition of second-class citizenship for all persons, whether because of race, ethnicity, sexual preference, gender, or disability. Their goal was to extend democratic rights and equal protection under the law to groups and persons who within our socially heterogeneous society had been denied these rights, whether because of unexamined traditional practices and attitudes or because of conscious prejudices and prejudicial actions.

The struggle for extension of rights has by no means been fully won for and by these groups. For example, differential rewards for men and women doing the same work still prevail. The right to a job for those who wish to work and the right to merited promotions are still aspirations for those devoted to the addition of civil rights to our traditional civil liberties.

But the liberation movements of the 1950s and 1960s have had a tremendous educational effect within our citizenry. Many more people are now conscious of unfinished tasks of achieving democracy than before minorities organized to publicize their democratic demands. Increased consciousness has led to more open conflict among those who view differently the desirability of complete equality of various minorities before the law. One example of this is found in the ongoing struggle to establish an Equal Rights Amendment to the Constitution, which would confirm women's equal status with men in our most fundamental law. This and other efforts to legislate equality where it does not exist have caused many to argue that equality as a value should not be pressed to the point of jeopardizing traditional commitments to liberty.

Proponents of democracy who are individualistic in their view of persons and societies tend to stress liberty as the heart of democracy. They often find an impassable gulf between liberty and equality. This alleged incompatibility arises in part from a confusion of equality with identity and sameness. People, it is argued, are not the same; they are naturally uniquely different. Only an "unnatural" regime can impose equality upon the members of a society, and such imposition is an affront to their freedoms. As John Randolph is alleged to have said before the Virginia legislature in the eighteenth century: "I am a democrat. I hate equality; I love liberty."

On the other hand, equality is perhaps best seen not as identity among persons, but as equal access to the resources required by each person for his or her unique development. In this view, the inconsistency between equality and liberty is relieved. If freedom is conceived as including opportunity and power to actualize one's choices, along with the absence of legal barriers to choosing and acting as one wills, equality in this sense of ready and equitable access to resources becomes a necessary condition of freedom, rather than an opponent to it.

In a money economy, access to resources is, of course, related to command of wealth in the case of many resources. So equality is jeopardized by large discrepancies in wealth between members of the same society. The widening gap in incomes among groups of citizens of the United States is one of the principal barriers to democracy. Measures undertaken by government to narrow the gaps in income are necessary, it appears, to preserve and advance democracy in our society. The Lockean conception that the government is best that governs least is a remnant of the individualistic tradition that has become a foe both of democracy and of individuality in our collective society.

Finally, in our heterogeneous society, though gains have been made in reducing discrimination against nonwhites, women, and homosexuals in employment, vocational advancement, and distribution of economic rewards, prejudice is still rampant, even though it is widely denied. Sexism and racism remain deep within our culture and stand athwart the development of the fraternity that is necessary to sustain fully the liberty and equality that democracy requires.

Political Representation, Participatory Democracy

It is not often remarked that the Constitution of the United States originally provided that only one-half of one of the three main branches of the federal government would be elected by popular ballot. The others were to be elected by designated electors or appointed. Since that time, the role of the federal government in the lives of citizens has grown, and the president, vice president, and senators are, essentially, popularly elected. At the same time, appointive regulatory commissions and governing agencies have continuously multiplied since the eighteenth century.

While leaving national governance in the hands of a relatively elite selection of citizens, the authors of the Constitution envisioned a society in which citizens governed their local affairs democratically, both by popular assembly and by local representative government. If casting a vote for a representative or a local official is taken as evidence of democracy, then the United States can offer such evidence, for local and national officeholders are elected by the people, although often by a minority of eligible voters. Yet voting for representatives is at best a minimal requirement for democracy, and such voting takes place in totalitarian societies as well. In those cases, Americans are likely to deny the democracy of voting procedures on the grounds that no real choice is offered, that only one party is represented, and so on. For Aristotle, democracies allowed citizens to govern and be governed in turn, an arrangement that representative government allows. The aim of representative government, it may be argued, is for citizens to participate effectively in their own governance. It is relatively clear that, in the United States today, most citizens do not effectively participate in their own governance, either in national affairs or in local institutions such as the workplace and the schools.

In part, these conditions arise from the overwhelming influence of the "scientific management" movements in industry and in regulation by professionals in national and local governments and in the schools, which took root in the urbanizing, industrializing society of the early twentieth century. The belief that management of institutions by experts would be most efficient and beneficial to all seemed to justify the decreased participation by common citizens in the decisions that affected their lives. A burgeoning management profession appropriated planning and decision making from workers (often in spite of bitter struggles), from local ward representatives, and from neighborhood school boards. This is part of the allegedly more "efficient" but less democratic legacy of the movement toward professionalization and the power of specialized expertise. Decision making and planning became ever more centralized in the hands of experts whose professional training appeared to qualify them to make policy decisions on behalf of all. Today, broad foreign and domestic policy planning at the national level falls to appointed officials who are expertly trained in those areas; city planners and city managers make plans for local communities; and school policy is planned by curriculum specialists in a central office.

It is somewhat ironic, then, that many people fear collective social planning as a way of meeting the future, because they connect it with totalitarian regimes and imposed plans that are centrally formed and enforced. In Dewey's words, planning by "a class of experts" has been upon us for some time, however unrecognized this may be. Indeed, in recent years planning has been advocated and practiced more assiduously by totalitarian regimes than by political democracies. But there is no necessary linkage between dictatorships and planning as a substitute for improvisation and historical drift in finding direction toward our ambiguous and conflicted future. Democracy, in its fuller meaning as an ethos, should save planning from dictatorial imposition or domination by experts, if we can find ways of infusing its spirit and practice into our processes of planning from locality to nation and world.

Plans should be subject to ready alteration in light of evaluation of developing experiences with them, including surprises and unforeseen consequences. And all affected by them should be involved in evaluating and criticizing plans and policies in need of attention.

Planning should be from the bottom up, not from the top down. In order to save its economy from the imposition of centrally contrived plans, as in the Soviet Union, Yugoslavia provided for planning to begin in each local factory and business; workers decide on their next year's plan based on joint planning with experts. Local plans are combined and reconciled centrally and differences negotiated. Such an arrangement provides for participation in planning by each person affected by the plan. There is no impassable barrier to decentralization of planning in the development of national or even transnational plans.

Economic Freedom versus Economic Planning

The extension of participation by workers in making decisions on problems arising within a factory or other place of business has already been briefly discussed. But the nonideological factors that have reinforced this extension of democracy have only been mentioned. Problems encountered in all industrialized nations that have introduced mass production methods have been the building and maintenance among workers of a will to work, a commitment to high quality of product or service, and a high morale.

In general, it has been found that these motivations cannot be bought from workers either by increased pay or attractive working conditions. Workers must come to feel a sense of psychological ownership toward their work and workplace before they will work to their fullest capacity, strive to maintain high quality in their product, or accept willingly the changes in jobs and relationships that a changing technology thrusts upon all industries and businesses today. Carole Pateman (1970) identified this sense of ownership as one of the fundamental aims and benefits of participatory democracy, as found, for example, in the writings of Mill and Rousseau. A feeling of psychological ownership can best be generated by participation of workers in making decisions about production goals and about the quality of their work and working conditions. "Democracy" is thus not an obstacle, but a means to greater productivity, as it enhances morale and promotes more adequate quality control.

Two able students of organizational behavior, Slater and Bennis (1964), were so convinced of the necessity of workplace democracy for optimal productivity and product quality as to argue that "democracy is inevitable." No doubt they were much too sanguine in asserting this inevitability. The question whether a feeling of psychological ownership in their work can be attained or maintained by workers without the establishment of common legal ownership remains unanswered.

Cooperative decision making is in some ways not compatible with the tradition of competition that still pervades the American economy. Merle Curti once called John Locke the philosopher of America. Certainly, Locke's conception of the human being as an atomic individual motivated primarily (if not exclusively) by self-interest, normally related to others competitively, and joining with others only to serve his or her self-interest or protect his or her security, is still strong in American thinking about human affairs. Competition is seen as the prime motivator of individuals toward achievement. (This view has been strong traditionally in the life of schools, where cooperation among students in schoolwork is frequently seen as cheating, and ranking students is seen as a desirable prod toward good work. How those who fail in the ranking race are motivated by competition is typically left unexplained. In contrast, teamwork is encouraged in play and games, and is typically instrumental to success in competition with other teams.)

Such a view of persons was not a serious distortion of economic reality in a time of many small enterprises in fabrication, business, and commerce. Competition may well have served as a way of sorting out individuals on a scale of productivity and efficiency and in eliminating the inefficient. The free competitive market may well have served to regulate the distribution of effort and investment and the effective allocation of rewards.

But conditions have changed radically since the time of Adam Smith. Large corporations dominate the economic landscape. The small entrepreneur succeeds only against great odds. Corporations grow ever larger in size and fewer in number. Most people live and work within the framework of a collective world in work as well as in the provision of health, welfare, and educational services. In reality, cooperation has become a virtue in a collective world. Yet our individualistic mentality still attributes virtue to competition in the rhetoric and practice of resistance to public control of enterprises by government.

Ideally, democracy makes a virtue of cooperation. This, of course, does not mean that conflict, as opposed to deliberately engendered competition, has no place within a democratic system. It is precisely because of conflicts of interests among persons and groups that a way of settling the conflicts in a manner satisfactory to all parties is required. Democracy provides for the participation of all parties, along with those who represent the public not directly involved in the conflict, in a process of what Max Otto once called "creative bargaining," to attain a novel resolution of the conflict more satisfactory to all parties than the resolutions initially favored by the conflicting parties.

To understand democracy, the process of creation that comes out of the confrontation of conflicting viewpoints and out of the dialogic search for a common view needs to be emphasized. To the individualist, compromise is the best that can be hoped for from the settlement between conflicting parties. To the democrat, learning by persons, one from the other, makes dialogue and discussion a creative process, engendering new and better social arrangements.

This involves a view of the human person different from that of the atomic individual. The view is of human persons as inherently social, with internalized social relations as well as the conventional external relations that Locke posited as the only relations between atomic persons. This is not to deny that each person is unique as well as socialized. It is this uniqueness that lends support to the idea of participation by all persons affected by a decision in forming that decision, in the interest of a maximum induction from various experiences in the solution. Persons have the capacity to take the role of other persons, however different in outlook, and to communicate differences in the interest of creating new solutions to perplexing difficulties. But this capacity needs to be learned through use.

We live in a collective world. It is also a conflicted world. Creative cooperation is needed as never before in the history of humankind. The excitement of competition should be available to people in games and other experiences governed by rules cooperatively made and agreed upon. But the capacity for democratic cooperation must be a prime goal for education in a collective and conflicted world, if humankind is to survive. The minimalist notion of economic freedom that values competition and disparages cooperative control results in contemporary economic arrangements that serve the interest of some at great expense to others. The "economic freedom" of the poor is not experienced as freedom but instead as an oppressive burden, one that requires bringing collective efforts to bear.

Intellectual Freedom versus Democratic Education

One dimension of freedom embedded in the classical liberal conception of civil liberty is intellectual freedom. This was expressed in the First Amendment to the Constitution in terms of freedom of speech and assembly, and it was fundamental to the colonial and early national regard for freedom of worship—particularly as expressed, for example, in Jefferson's Bill for Religious Freedom in Virginia. In his *Notes on Virginia*, Jefferson argued for a free marketplace of ideas in which the truth of beliefs, religious and scientific, could be allowed to stand by itself without the support of government.

> The Newtonian principle of gravitation is now more firmly established, on the basis of reason, than it would be were the government to step in and to make it an article of necessary faith. Reason and experiment have been indulged, and error has fled before them. It is error alone which needs the support of government. Truth can stand by itself. . . . Reason and persuasion are the only practiceable instruments. To make way for these, free inquiry must be indulged. (quoted in Lee, 1964, p. 64).

This faith in the free marketplace of ideas, and in the ability of an informed citizenry to judge wisely, supported Jefferson's famous dictum: "Were it left to me to decide whether we should have a government without newspapers, or newspapers without a government, I should not hesitate a moment to prefer the latter" (p. 65).

This Jeffersonian optimism in the ability of an informed public to identify and protect its interests stems in part from a classical liberal faith in the inevitability of progress—a faith represented in Adam Smith's invisible hand and earlier in Bacon's *New Atlantis*. By the late nineteenth century, however, that faith had been shaken in the United States by a devastating civil war, depressions, and pervasive labor troubles. In Edward Bellamy's influential and enormously popular *Looking Backward* (1960), the twentieth-century citizen proclaims to his nineteenth-century audience that "the idea of indefinite progress in a right line was a chimera of the imagination, with no analogue in nature" (p. 31). Intellectual freedom was not enough, warned Bellamy. The free marketplace of ideas was as likely to produce chaos as truth, and only a society based on planning, cooperation, and expert intelligence could meet the demands of the future.

In practice, such thinking emphasized expertise rather than democratic processes, and the rule by experts that Bellamy envisioned has become one obstacle to democracy in twentieth-century American society, as already noted. We are reminded of the Athenian mistrust of specialized expertise as constituting uneven power among citizens, and of Harold's Laski's (1931) oft-repeated warning concerning the limitations of the narrow expert. In modern life, the concentration of specialized power in the hands of experts who form social policy, as well as write specialized textbooks, serves effectively to exclude most citizens from policy debate and influence. While we have "intellectual freedom" to an important degree, that freedom bears only a weak connection to the generic problems of democratic governance in contemporary society.

Other limitations on the value of "intellectual freedom" as a measure of democratic life are the control of mass media by a relatively few figures who must rely in turn on the government for the great bulk of their information about domestic and international affairs, and the role of profit-motivated advertising in shaping the tastes and values of citizens. The point to be made here is that in the "free marketplace of ideas" a few powerful groups do most of the selling, and significantly divergent points of view are not readily available to the public. Jefferson had assumed that dissenting voices would be heard if censorship by government were prevented, but he did not envision a narrowing of public debate by more subtle and yet more powerful means.

Jefferson, however, recognized that free debate through the newspapers was no guarantee of an informed citizenry. He qualified his rhetorical preference for government by newspapers by adding: "But I should mean that every man should receive those papers and be capable of reading them" (quoted in Lee, 1964, p. 65). He was prepared, as many of his colleagues in the Virginia legislature were not, to establish a school system to provide the literacy necessary to democratic life. Today we are beset with rampant illiteracy not just of the traditional kind, but of another kind as well: that which some scholars have called "critical illiteracy." If the "intellectual freedom" we now have does not provide an effective critical perspective to the citizenry, then that intellectual freedom falls short of the democratic ideal.

John Dewey (1916) argued for something akin to critical intelligence by proposing education in a humanized scientific method for all schoolchildren, so that common people would be able rationally to judge for themselves the worth of social and industrial arrangements. Boyd Bode (1957) later argued that "the school is, par excellence, the institution to which a democratic society is entitled to look for a clarification of the meaning of democracy" (p. 95). Both Dewey and Bode recognized that one looks in vain to capitalist institutions for a sustained democratic critique of contemporary society. Only the schools, they believed, were potentially equipped to develop such critical understandings among the populace. But neither Bode nor Dewey adequately foresaw the pervasive ideological grip that antidemocratic commitments would come to have, not only on industry and advertising, for example, but on the powerful medium of television, on government, and even on schools themselves. An effective education appropriate to today's conditions cannot settle for "intellectual freedom" conceived only as prohibitions against government censorship. It must seek out some means of equipping people of all ages to see critically and to resist the hegemony of expertise, the power of advertising, the profit-bound commitments of the government, and other antidemocratic forces in American life.

Another foe to the intellectual freedom that democracy requires is dogmatic belief in ideas and principles, which those who espouse them hold as absolutes. To regard ideas and principles in this way is to exempt them from criticism and from confrontation with ideas and evidence that challenge their adequacy. Such devotion to formal ideas and beliefs is found often among devotees of a religious creed that is allegedly based on supernatural revelation. Absolutists in religion regard those who question their dogmas as enemies and, in extreme cases, as evil enemies. They are often tempted to impose their moral absolutes through the power of government, or public opinion, on others who do not share those absolutist beliefs. They also resent educational efforts to expose their absolutes to critical examination, when necessary, along with the cherished beliefs of others. This undercuts the critical dialogue on which democratic policy making depends, whether the issue is the legalization of abortion, the elimination of discrimination against homosexuals in employment, or any other controversial issue.

Absolutism in beliefs is, of course, not limited to religious believers. Extreme nationalists hold their patriotic slogans with a fervor akin to that of religionists who find all truth in the Bible or some interpretation of it. Such absolutism makes it very difficult to achieve free and critical dialogue concerning such questions as the strengthening of international rule and the consequent weakening of national sovereignty, or the compromising of our national interests with those of another nation in the interest of peace, even where a vast majority of people will such dialogue.

The Future of Individuality in Democracy

We live in a collective world. We live also in a continually changing world. Through research and the application of its results in a radically changing technology, we have created a world in which traditional ways of managing and directing human affairs can no longer attain or maintain a livable order. We must, as responsible human beings, use our communal intelligence to guide our way into the future. We have used a part of our ingenuity and intelligence in creating a high technology world. It is necessary to use all of our social intelligence to maintain and improve a human way of life in a world possessed of the power for good or ill inherent in that technology.

We can no longer depend on finding direction by following uncritically our own familiar traditions. Finding direction for the future by projecting the forms and values of our traditional culture upon the future has been further undermined by the ever-present fact of intercultural contact and confrontation within and between nations. The development of vast networks of interdependence, the spread of mass media, and reduced security in spatial and political boundaries between cultures, due to space-destroying means of transportation, have brought about uneasy contact and confrontation between traditionally segregated nations, classes, races, and subcultures. As we seek new bases for an interdependent future across these cleavages in culture by projecting the traditions of any one culture upon the future, the futility of this way of defining the future for purposes of policy making becomes more and more apparent. If there is to be a common future, it must be constructed by men and women from aspects of various cultures in a way that leads beyond the present maze of conflicting traditions. Men and women must design and create the framework for cooperative planning by their own continuing dialogue on a hundred fronts.

Does this undercutting of direction by tradition mean an end to the cultivation and honoring of individuality in persons, which have been part of our democratic tradition at its best? The answer is no! We must invent a future that inescapably will be novel in many respects. We will need original, inventive, and creative ideas as never before. The source of creative novelty will, as in the past, be the minds of individual persons who, out of their uniqueness, see the world differently from the prevailing common-sense view. Actually, the liberation of thought and action from direction by a dominant tradition should free persons to trust their powers of creative imagination more than before and to give a hearing to heterodox opinions and ideas as providing possible mindholds on a desirable future. The ideas of atomic individualism that were once joined with the democratic view of humankind and society are no longer viable. The alternative idea of persons emerging out of dialogue between human beings, and of considering and testing the novel ideas that continuing dialogue between persons who differ always engenders, gives individuality a valued basis in the minds of all persons, especially perhaps of those concerned with education. Traditional individualism is no longer the friend of individuality. But individuality is, of necessity, to be valued as never before.

Does the weakening of tradition-dependence undercut reliance on the democratic tradition in guiding men and women in planning their desirable direction into the future and inventing ways of moving toward it? It does mean that democratic traditions must be criticized, like all other traditions, and not followed blindly. And it does mean that forms and institutions of democracy, as they have developed in America and acquired a distinctively American shape and flavor, cannot be successfully imposed on other cultures.

But the central meanings of democracy still seem to offer the best chance of incorporating the most desirable values from different cultures into an emerging outlook toward a human future. That objective requires the critical and responsible participation of persons from all cultures in the formation and continuing revision of such a future. The recent reemergence of political democracy to supplant dictatorial regimes in country after country—Argentina, Brazil, Uruguay, the Philippines—may indicate agreement with this view on the part of widely divergent peoples.

THE ARTS OF DEMOCRACY

I once attempted to formulate the basic arts of democratic citizenship, shorn of their distinctive American accretions (Benne, 1967). These arts promise effectiveness when learned and used by persons and groups engaged in planning for the human future.

1. The art of effective criticism as well as veneration of our traditions.
2. The art of listening to opinions and expressed attitudes and practices different from our own and answering these in light of the full human meaning of what we hear.
3. The art of dealing with conflicts creatively and integratively.

4. The art of evaluating the virtues and limitations of experts and of expert opinion and knowledge, and of using expertise not subserviently but wisely.
5. The art of evaluating openly and intersubjectively the results in practice of decisions formed in the passionate heat of controversy and conflict.

These arts of democratic citizenship portray democracy as a way of living rather than merely as a mechanism of voting or as freedom from governmental interference. These arts require of citizens that they be educated to understand the deeper meanings of democracy and that they care enough about those deeper meanings to measure against them the quality of their participation in such institutions as government at all levels; the workplace; the churches, temples, and mosques; and the schools. Further, these democratic arts engage people in processes that are educational in themselves. The art of evaluating the virtues and limitations of experts, or the art of intersubjectively evaluating social decisions and practices, requires that one continually learn new information and understand conflicting points of view in order to participate effectively. These arts demonstrate the point made earlier that, in its deepest meanings, democracy not only requires an educated populace, but serves to educate that populace. Dewey's (1948) moral meaning of democracy, that "the supreme test of all political institutions . . . (is) the contribution they make to the all-around growth of every member of society" (p. 186), becomes a standard much more useful for measuring the practices of contemporary life than such a minimal meaning of democracy as, for example, "representative government."

The above arts of democracy suggest criteria for measuring our schools and other educative agencies as well. Do they equip our citizens to exercise those arts? Or do they rather equip our citizens, by and large, to accept without critical examination self-congratulatory rhetoric about contemporary America as the world's exemplar of the free enterprise system and as the last, best hope of democracy on earth?

3 · The Learning Community

Wherever there is conjoint activity whose consequences are appreciated as good by all singular persons who take part in it, and where the realization of the good is such as to effect an energetic desire and effort to sustain it in being just because it is a good shared by all, there is in so far a community. The clear consciousness of a communal life, in all its implications, constitutes the idea of democracy.

John Dewey
The Public and Its Problems

But the essence of man is no abstraction inhering in each single individual. In its actuality it is the ensemble of social relationships.

Karl Marx
"Theses on Feuerbach," #6

47

PERHAPS ALBERT EINSTEIN (1960) HAS SUGGESTED as succinctly as anyone the vast reeducative task that recent developments in human mastery of our nonhuman environment have placed upon our generation. "The unleashed power of the atom has changed everything save our modes of thinking, and we thus drift toward unparalleled catastrophes" (p. 376). In the sound, time-tested modes of thinking that Einstein saw as now tending toward catastrophe, he very likely included normative assumptions about self and others; about dealing with differences; about war; about national sovereignty; about human beings, collectively and individually, in their world; about a viable environment, physical and biological, and human responsibility for its maintenance or destruction. Such assumptions, along with the rationale they provide for living—these to one national, ethnic, or religious group; those to another—are acquired by persons in the processes of their enculturation, for the most part provincially and preconsciously. Educators have never before assumed responsibility for the deliberate reenculturation of persons of all ages at the level of normative assumptions about self, society, and world.

Lest we think that unleashing of atomic power is the only development in our generation that drives us toward recognizing the fatal alternative to the fundamental reorientation of the thinking of humankind, we might well consider a wise person among geneticists saying quite as truly as Einstein spoke as a physicist: "The unleashing of human power in recombinant genetic engineering to create new living species, perhaps basically and irreversibly inimical to the human species, has changed everything save our modes of thinking, and we thus drift toward unparalleled catastrophes." And so the litany might run through fields of robotization of work, toxic wastes, lasers, and other areas of technology and applied sciences.

The need for human reenculturation is dramatically evident in the contemporary human inability to control morally and politically the use of powers with which recent developments in science and technology have endowed those in charge of "developed" societies. The barrier lies in unchanged traditional modes of thinking and valuing. My purpose in this essay is not to propose a substantive curriculum appropriate to the compelling task of reeducation implied. I do believe philosophers of education should be stimulating and leading dialogues across lines of cultural cleavage concerning the issues involved in the needed changes and the problems involved in their educational treatment, as Northrop (1946) began to do in the 1940s, unfortunately with few successors. I along with some colleagues have been nibbling at the task for some years, though I will not attempt to share the results of my nibbling with you in this essay (see Benne and Birnbaum, 1978; Babad, Birnbaum, and Benne, 1983).

Rather, what I aim to do is to explore some of the complexities of the processes and structures of reenculturation and resocialization that educators must create and learn to use if human modes of thinking are to be modified in a way to mitigate the "unparalleled catastrophes" against which Einstein warned. This involves for me an understanding of the integral place that learning in and through community occupies in achieving changes in basic modes of thinking.

The process for effecting changes in basic modes of thinking in persons is as integrally a social process as their original acquisition was. It involves experience in dialogic community with others who think and act on the basis of various basic assumptions and outlooks. In our individualistically oriented society and our over-psychologized, professional treatment of formal learning, the integrally social character of personal reeducation must, I fear, today be argued. Such a proposition would not have needed argument in fifth- or fourth-century Athens with Plato or Aristotle, or indeed with Aeschylus or Sophocles. Nor would it have needed argument in the classical period of American philosophy, as Max Fisch (1950) named the era of Peirce, Royce, James, Dewey, Santayana, and Mead—and, by mutual adoption, A. N. Whitehead. If Fisch is right, and I think that he is, all these philosophers found in the concept of "community" a significant key to the understanding of human personality, society, and history, whatever their differences in ontology and epistemology. But a generation of American philosophers has alienated itself from classical American philosophy by self-elected recolonization, mainly to the latest version of a long succession of British nominalisms and, in lesser degree, to continental European phenomenology or Hindu-Buddhist metaphysics.

So I feel that the necessity of learning communities for the task of reoriented thinking that Einstein saw as the alternative to catastrophe must now be argued. And this is what I propose to do. (It need hardly be said that I am not predicting that learning communities will be understood or built sufficiently or strategically enough to avert "unparalleled catastrophes." But I am recommending that the effort be made.)

THE BEGINNING OF WISDOM IN DISCUSSIONS OF LEARNING AND SOCIETY

I once argued (Benne, 1943/1971) that the beginning of pedagogical wisdom requires keeping three mighty commonplaces steadily and faithfully in mind.

1. Every human being is a community animal. From the social act in which a person is conceived to the conjoint rites over his or her bier, a healthy and sane human life is in large measure supported and sustained by a group way of life. At each turning point of a life career, as well as during the "routine" intervals between, each person—even the most original and creative of persons—plays out with relatively minor variations the role defined for human beings and for members of their community, whether by custom, by formal rule or law, or by the inclusive and uncongealed "atmosphere," the spirit, the symbolic life of shared meanings and purposes, in and through which the person and his or her fellows live and move.

2. Human beings are born excommunicated. Human infants are born without the habits, commitments, and attitudes; the equipment of language and symbolization; the mind and personality that are the necessary equipment for mature members of any community. Nor is the threat of excommunication ever entirely removed from any human person, throughout his or her lifetime. Each person, even the doughtiest parent, is always somebody's child. The alien and the immature present a continuous and central problem in the life of any and every social group.

3. Despite all falterings, failures, and evasions; despite all persistent infancy in people, all the persistent alienations of deviate persons from the community process, all the arbitrary barriers to communication that develop and operate in the life of human groups; and despite the prevalence of widespread brute coercions within human relationships, in some measure the contradiction between the conditions described in (1) and (2) is met in every community. The alien and immature are brought to find their way in the group way of life. The once alien and immature become the carriers and in turn transmitters of the common way of life to still other partially alien and immature human beings. The pedagogical process that oper-

ates to solve this contradiction is inherent in the going processes of community life, however much its management and extension may be "delegated" to special groups (or institutions) within the society.

I am quite aware that "pedagogy," both etymologically and in its common usage, refers to the stimulation, support, guidance, and evaluation of processes of learning in, with, and by children. As such, it fails to encompass the stimulation, support, guidance, and evaluation of learning processes in, with, and by persons who are no longer children chronologically. I have suggested "anthropogogy" as a more adequate term than pedagogy for today's education (Benne, 1970; see also Essay 6 in this book).

As already noted, my original purpose in enunciating the three mighty commonplaces was to establish the inherently and inescapably sociocultural and interpersonal context, or, more abstractly, the relational and dialogic form, of basic anthropogogical processes. There are some who might question the validity of my semantic shift from "anthropogogical" to "learning" processes. "Anthropogogy," they might willingly grant, is inherently sociocultural. But "learning," they might go on to claim, is individual in nature. And, in the spirit of Rousseau (the Rousseau of *Emile,* not the author of *The Social Contract*) and of Ivan Illich, they might go on to claim that "learning" is a "natural" and "individual" process. Institutionalized schooling and pedagogy have thwarted, suppressed, and distorted this natural individual process of learning and must be diminished or abolished in order that natural human learning may flourish. This seems nonsense to me. To abolish schools is not to abolish anthropogogy. It is rather to change the venue of anthropogogy to some other institution or institutional complex.

But, it may be argued, to insist on social and cultural "reality" as a necessary term of reference, indeed as an indispensable source of criteria, in evaluating visions of more or less desirable processes of learning may be to discourage the very creative processes in individuals on which hope for a more viable and desirable future for humankind depends. I will argue later that there is a creative and transcendent dimension to all desirable human learning. But no process of human creation is creation *ex nihilo.* The materials that are reshaped and re-formed in a creative vision are materials drawn selectively and recombinatively from the society and culture of the creative person. Herman Melville, had he been born into a land-locked, sub-Saharan culture, might have sought to project a dramatic vision of the human struggle with cosmic good and evil. But it would not have been *Moby Dick*, a vision compounded of clipper ships, whales, and diabolically perfectionist sea captains. Nor is it likely that his vision would have found expression in the form of a novel.

One thing I do mean by my counsel is a caution against well-intentioned overemphasis on "individualizing learning." Properly limited, "individualized learning" is a useful slogan against attempts to enforce upon all persons in a learning situation uniform and inflexible standards with respect to style, rate, or content of learning. There are good grounds for opposing the imposition of nonadaptive, uniform, socially prescribed standards upon all in a group of learners. But to take "individualized learning" as the only alternative to prescribed uniform expectations about desirable processes and products of learning may be equally inimical to the assumption of an intrinsic motivation to learn by individual persons. A sometimes touted example of "individualized instruction" may help to make this point clear.

Accessibility by individuals to instructional programs stored in computers is frequently "sold" as an aid to "individualized learning." The individual learner takes his or her questions to a well-stocked computer, which, impersonally and with a minimum of human static, gives correct answers. Or if the learner's "answers" to some question require a process of calculation or other thinking on his or her part, the learner can compare his or her "answer" to the correct answer stored in the computer and may receive impersonal corrections to the process of calculation or thinking where these are faulty.

It should be noted first of all that individualized learning in this version has not eliminated the "social-transactional" element from the process of learning. If I am right, the social-transactional element can never be eliminated from learning processes. Rather, what individualized learning has done is to abstract the individual learner from the interactional matrix of flesh-and-blood peers, teachers, parents, siblings, and neighbors in which his or her personal and interpersonal life is lived and to focus learning on a transaction with remote, impersonalized, perhaps depersonalized, authoritative beings who respond to the learner's questions through the computer medium. People have stocked the computer. People operate and maintain the computer. People coach the learner to couch questions in appropriate computer language. But the learner's relations with these remote and minimally accessible persons or roles have been shaped functionally to his or her ready acquisition of questions that somebody else thinks it is important for the learner to ask and to answer. There is dialogue involved, but it is a dialogue "unhampered" by the feelings and fears, the confused identities and conflicting interests and aspirations, that characterize the reality of the society in which presumably the student is learning to live and that characterize his or her present identity as a member of that society as well. By dramatic definitions of dialogue, it is a truncated and attenuated dialogue, ill-designed to lead to deeper understanding of self or of others as persons.[1]

In our "individualistic" society and culture, the "individual" and the "personal" are often identified and so confused. A limerick that went the rounds a few years ago makes just such a point about the depersonalized quality of much individualized instruction.

> The news is now out, clear and clean,
> That, by aid of a teaching machine,
> King Oedipus Rex
> Has learned all about sex
> Without ever touching the queen.

SOCIALIZATION, ENCULTURATION, AND LEARNING

It follows from my emphasis on the three mighty commonplaces that I would search for exemplars and prototypes of desirable learning within processes of growing up, processes that in learned circles we have come to call socialization and/or enculturation. Though there is much in contemporary socialization and enculturation to criticize and discard, as I have already suggested, I would seek for models of the learning process there rather than in the learning that goes on in schools, colleges, scholars' studies, or scientific laboratories.

One reason is that the latter type of learning process is focused on the actualization of a limited range of human capacities and potentialities. The focus is on the stimulation and support—the cultivation—of cognitive powers and on the development and refinement of skills, particularly skills functionally necessary in the effective pursuit and acquisition of knowledge. It is, of course, true that effectiveness in the development and use of cognitive capacities and ancillary skills also requires consonant, noncognitive value orientations, attributes of self and character, and interpersonal competences. But scholarly and scientific enterprisers are, for the most part, parasitic upon processes of socialization and enculturation in nonacademic settings for developing such essential, noncognitive capacities in those they recruit into their specialized, learned associations. They select products of nonacademic enculturation, who more or less adventitiously have developed in a way to meet their requirements. And not seldom, scientists and scholars, even social scientists, attribute efficacy or nonefficacy in these noncognitive requisites for productive cognitive work to favorable or unfavorable "genetic" factors, not to excellences or deficiencies in learning experiences. In this respect, scientists and scholars are little different from most rank-and-file members of modern societies who tend to code processes and products of noncognitive socialization as "natural," not as learned and so improvable through appropriate human interventions. It is partly in this obsessive coding that the drift toward unparalleled catastrophes lies.

Some years ago, a few of us proposed that each person is possessed of two kinds of interlinked characters—a substantive and a methodological character (Raup, Axtelle, Benne, & Smith, 1962). The substantive character refers to our habitually patterned ways of handling choices and actions within familiar and routine aspects of our lives. The methodological character refers to our accustomed ways of coping with discrepancies, conflicts, strangenesses, and strangers encountered within our existential worlds. It is not at all surprising that the substantive character of each of us is, with individual variations in emphasis and organization, our internalized version of the meanings, roles, values, and life orientations prevalent in the culture and its subcultures as we have been induced to participate in them. But persons with similar substantive characters may have quite different methodological characters. My methodological character will have much to do with how assiduously I will seek to learn my way through conflicts and doubts; how able I will be to see and turn to others different from myself as resources in learning a "new" substantive character, if necessary; and how committed I am to sustained dialogue. Alternatively, my methodological character will influence how readily and ardently I will adopt other ways of coping with doubts and discrepancies in my lived world—defensiveness, dependence on authority, aggression, denial, or evasion, among others. Those who wish better to understand the learning now required of all of us should be focally concerned with the ways in which persons build and rebuild, learn and relearn their methodological characters. My proposal is that a pluralistic society requires persons with similar methodological characters, however varied their substantive characters may be or become. This is why I seek community rather than unity through learning.

It has long puzzled me why a society and culture of immigrants like America did not become more fully aware of the learning processes in resocialization and reenculturation of thousands of adults, which were occurring throughout our society during the nineteenth and early twentieth centuries. The programs of adult education that arose to help immigrants comply with the legal requirements of naturalization tended to be cognitively oriented, even in materials designed to instill American patriotism, and to employ traditional scholastic methods of instruction. The "melting pot" goal, however mistaken or unsuccessful, blinded people to the persistent heterogeneity of basic modes of thinking. Perhaps that was why practitioners in these Americanization programs developed such limited insight into the deeper processes of human adaptation that their students were undergoing or failing to undergo.

Margaret Mead, an anthropologist who, more than many of her colleagues, saw enculturation in terms of interpersonal and social learning and relearning, did seek to draw wisdom from the experiences of immigrants in America and to apply this wisdom to the dramatic need for apt and effective models of relearning—a need now experienced by persons in both technologically developed and developing cultures. Mead (1970) came to believe that the accentuated gap between generations, dramatically evident in youthful protests in the 1960s and driven underground into more passive forms of resistance in the 1970s and 1980s, occurring as it does in capitalist, socialist, and communist nations is signaling the emergence of a world culture still largely to be built. It is a culture in which traditional forms of human enculturation have become outmoded and altered forms required.

All of us, Mead argued, are living today as if we were immigrants in a new and strange society and culture. We can derive help in our plight from insight into how immigrants, young and old, handled problems of reenculturation in a strange land, that is, from our historic American experience. Adult immigrants to America could not teach, coach, and guide younger members of their families in learning ways to cope with a culture that was perforce alien to them. They were forced to depend on their children, who were learning the ways of the new culture through participative experiences in and hard-won initiations into cross-cultural groupings, both inside and outside schools. The younger members of families assumed leadership in participative processes with their parents and other elders, who were forced unaccustomedly to follow the lead of the youngsters in learning a new way of life.

In what Mead called post-figurational cultures, where slowly evolving traditions guide processes of enculturation, children learned the traditional way of life through participation in and initiation into group membership, processes controlled and led by the elders. But the balance shifted, of necessity, in immigrant families and generations in a strange land. Their lives were lived in what Mead called a co-figurational culture, in which processes of peer learning of a new way of life found uneasy equilibrium with quasi-clandestine, tradition-directed patterns of enculturation into the ways of the "old" country.

In Mead's terminology, all of us—younger and older—are now living in a pre-figurational culture. In this culture, the traditions of neither "old" nor "host" countries can furnish confident guidance into a clouded future. We are all immigrants in an alien land. We must seek and develop patterns of learning in which young and old will collaborate in the invention of a future way of life, if there is to be a future way of life. A rigid hierarchy of old over young or of young over old (or indeed of indigenous over alien or of alien over indigenous) in planning, conducting, and evaluating processes of learning and relearning will not work. At times, the younger, the alienated, and the deviate will be closer to the pulsebeat of the future as it reveals itself in the present than the older and the oversocialized "squares" among us are or can be.

Yet future-oriented life and learning, if they are to be sane, must maintain a living continuity with their multi-cultural past. A viable future needs a past. So at times the older will rightly take the lead in initiating and directing learning processes. The main lesson to be learned is perhaps that the rightful locus of authority in learning processes must be negotiated and renegotiated continually. Fixed authority of status, whether based on age, expertise, or prior residence, has little or no rightful place in future-oriented reeducation in a pre-figurational culture.

The occasion and indeed the basic motivation for learning is a person's desire to extend and deepen his or her membership in or identification with some human association significant to him or her. The desire is not, in the first instance, a wish passively to conform to othermade patterns of performance, valuation, or thought. It is rather a proactive wish to become more potent in shaping and managing the environment in which the learning person lives or aspires to live.

The established way of life in a culture provides both resources and barriers to the aspirant to growth and learning, once the aspiration moves from the status of passing fancy into a state of provisional psychological reality. Its resources may include positive and negative role-and-person models, knowledges, skills, and competences required for functioning confidently in the human estate to which the learner aspires, and norms for guiding, directing, and evaluating progress and performance. It is characteristic of our culture that such resources are better articulated and more readily available to aspirants to a paid vocational career than to aspirants to competence as citizen or lover or to other unpaid estates of sainthood and/or sinnerhood. Only spottily available in our society are groups of caring persons to provide the open challenge and support that adequate maturing of an aspiration requires, that is, "communities." It should be underlined that an adequate validating community for learning is not a circle of uncritical and doting yea-sayers. It is adequate only if its members are capable of providing negative and positive "feedback" to each other in a context of caring and acceptance.

The basic method of learning in socialization and enculturation is participative, experiential, and dialogic. It is through experience of participation that relevant resources of the culture are internalized, and that reality-based barriers to fuller and freer functioning are overcome or accepted. (Irrational barriers, of which exclusionary prejudices are an example, may have various effects on proactive aspirants to learning—they may cease to be proactive and develop habits of hopelessness, self-alienation, passivity, and conformity in future learning; they may maintain unhealthy compartmentalizations between their personal worlds of fantasy and their lives in an alien world of public "reality"; they may develop resentful commitments to social rebellion.) The effects of participative and experiential learning on persons are simultaneously cognitive, motoric, moral, and esthetic. These various dimensions of learning may be internalized with varying degrees of consciousness on the part of learners. William Kilpatrick pointed out long ago the reality and inevitability of concomitant, along with focally intended, learnings. In a pre-figurational culture, it is important that significant concomitant learnings be raised to the level of consciousness. This is accomplished through personal reflection on chosen action carried through in relation to its intended and unintended consequences with the assistance of "feedback" from a validating community of peers. Consciousness raising lifts concomitant learnings from mute conditionings to conceptualized act–consequence relationships. It makes for more intelligent transfer of learnings to situations other than the situation of origin. It increases the probability of later revision and relearning that new aspirations and new life conditions may require. Such consciousness raising requires open dialogue with other persons in and near the learning situation—an interrelating of actor and observer stances toward the process of learning. Adequate learning, since it requires participation, is always a personal-social transaction. Fully adequate basic learning requires an appropriate dialogic, community context.

INDIVIDUALS, SELVES, AND PERSONS

One reason many Americans find it easy to believe that learning is basically an individual affair is the prevalence and persistence of an individualistic ideology in American society. Its advocates, Reaganites and others, have become more strident in its defense as its orientations fail more and more to provide adequate normative guidance to life choices in the increasingly collective conditions in which American lives are lived.

A conception of learning adequate to the demands of a prefigurational and interdependent culture on human inventiveness and creativity requires exorcism from our thinking of misconceptions of the individual embedded in our traditional individualistic ideology. Individualism has become the foe not the friend of individuality in contemporary culture. More adequate conceptions of self and person have emerged from a variety of sources—sociologists like Charles H. Cooley, social philosophers like George Mead, philosopher-theologians like Martin Buber, psychotherapists like Erich Fromm and Harry Stack Sullivan, and educational philosophers like W. H. Kilpatrick. I can only sample this large body of work with my main purpose in mind of understanding better the emergence, maintenance, and rebuilding of selves and persons in the processes of a learning community. Unfortunately, with the exception of Kilpatrick, none of the classic theorists of the self as emergent in processes of social interaction elaborated the meanings of self–other processes for human learning. So I am forced to depend for these elaborations more on my own experiences and speculations than I might otherwise wish to do.

These theorists sought the locus and origin of the human self not in neurology or genetics, nor analogically in the operation of human artifacts like computers, nor in extrapolations to human societies of the structures and processes of more instinctually determined insect societies.[2] Rather, they sought and found the origin of the human self in interpersonal relations and interactions and in personal-social transactions.

Martin Buber (1970) showed that the I and the Thou, the self and the other, emerge in the same process of interpersonal confrontation and dialogue. There can be no experience of I without experience of an Other. Nor is it enough for self-emergence to experience others as objects, as instruments, as extensions of my will, as Its. Full realization of selfhood comes only in the awe-ful experience of others as Thous, as subjective, proactive centers of valuation and choice. Only in such experiences with others do I come to realize and accept myself as proactive agent and responsible center of valuation and choice. In Buber's language, the actualization of self occurs only in dialogue, in the experience of I–Thou relations. (These concepts will be useful later in distinguishing between collectivity and community.)

In the experience of self is the additional capacity to objectify myself as the agent of my own actions. This capacity underlies the power to assume responsibility for my own actions and, in this sense, is the root of ethical conduct. It also underlies the capacity of persons to build into their methodological characters commitment to learning as a way through the stress of doubt, discrepancy, and strangeness as these intrude into the boundaries of their personal worlds. This makes possible the sharing with others of the responsibility for creating the conflicts encountered and for creating a mutually viable resolution or compromise of these conflicts. George Mead (1931) found the genesis of this ability in the capacity to be at once, or at least alternately, an actor, observer, and critic of one's own actions in processes of interpersonal communication. Through the agency of symbols, I can take the role of the other; I can enter symbolically into the viewpoint of the other and from this vantage point objectify my own actions and their consequences to myself and to others. The other person can similarly come to see his or her actions and their meanings from my perspective. Selfhood makes possible the "objectification" of both our social and our physical worlds and the accumulation of shared and intersubjectively tested meanings transmissible from generation to generation and from group to group. Persons in the same circle of communication develop a perspective of perspectives, a Generalized Other, as Mead named it, which, while varying in specific meaning, from person to person and from group to group, provides an "intersubjective" framework in which to define social reality for members of a society. It is in this sense that Kilpatrick (1947) argued for intimate interrelations between "selfhood and civilization" in his unfortunately neglected book, which bears that name, and for the necessity of rounded processes of personal and communal learning in the creation and maintenance of both.

While the self–other process emerges in the early years of socialization, in which a system of language and symbolization is internalized and developed, it continues throughout the lifetime of persons. While reality-oriented selves develop and function within limits set by biological potentiality, it is an error to identify self and person with the biologic individual, the choices and actions of which it influences intimately and, in some measure, comes to direct. Selves are personal-social constructs whose maintenance and continuity depend not alone on the maintenance of life in the organism to which they are "attached" but on an appropriately supportive and challenging interpersonal and social environment as well. Harry Stack Sullivan (1953) was one of the first students of personality derangements to emphasize the place of consensual validation in the construction, maintenance, and growth of selves. Persons maintain their sanity through continual validation of themselves and their perceptions of reality against the perceptions of others with whom they are in contact and communication. Isolation experiments with human subjects have revealed that the boundaries of self disappear, that the boundary between fantasy and reality vanishes, when persons are deprived of self-validating feedback from their environment, particularly their social environment.

That persons continually fantasize and dream, clothing their worlds with meaning, is to me irrefutable evidence of their basic proactivity and creativity. Persons do create the worlds in which they choose and act and have their being. But it is through the self–other process, where this has been learned well, that shared reality is constructed and maintained. As Santayana (1939b) once remarked, "Truth is a tragic segment through the realm of essence." Or, as Dewey once put a similar point, the world of meaning is infinitely wider than the world of fact.

Persons construct selves through choice and enactment of life-projects, including, but by no means limited to, vocations and careers. In his classic discussion of the self, William James (1950, Ch. 10) emphasized that every major choice is not alone an actualization of a potential self but a denial, if not annihilation, of other potential selves. If I am to fulfill, through appropriate learnings and disciplines, my aspiration to be a celibate monk, I must deny or inhibit my potentialities to become a great lover of women. I do choose and learn, with some degree of uniqueness, my selves, but, quite unavoidably, within a context of communication and participation with others. In Buber's language (1970), human life and learning are lived and learned in a process of dialogue.

It is commonplace to think of a society as a complex linkage, through formal and informal organizations, through networks and affiliations, members, roles, and groups. It is less commonplace, but useful to me at least, to think of each human person as an internalized society of selves, conjoined functionally with a living biological organism. Like external societies, a person maintains or seeks to maintain a viable order, a workable organization, between and among his or her not always harmonious or tractable constituent selves. This organization may be, in whole or in part, rigid or fluid, hierarchical or flat, compartmentalized or dialogically interactive, conflicting or harmonious, democratic or authoritarian. Plato once defined thought or reasoning as a debate within the assembly of the human breast. To me, this is more than an analogy. There are internal processes of dialogue, confrontation, debate and reality testing between and among the interdependent parts of persons. Persons do important parts of their thinking and learning in, for, and by themselves. But these inner processes maintain their sanity, their reality orientation, their relevance and effectiveness in the public world of praxis and action only through continually renewed dialogue with other persons, dialogue like that out of which selves and persons emerged in the first place.

COLLECTIVITY AND COMMUNITY

Thus far in my arguments for an integral interrelation between learning and society, I have not noted or analyzed different forms of human organization in terms of their hospitality toward and support of learning and growth by members through their participation in interactions and transactions that the organization legitimizes and sanctions. Organizations quite different in this respect operate side by side in our society and in other societies as well. Persons must learn to accommodate contrasting forms and norms of human organization in living various aspects of their lives. Tensions within the inner societies of persons result. The achievement of personal wholeness and integrity, however ardently and cogently its virtues may be extolled by spokespersons for religion and for mental health, receives minimal support and facilitation for most persons in contemporary American society.

I will concentrate here on a distinction between two forms of social organization in my attempt to clarify the idea of a learning community. This is an oversimplification, as all two-term typologies are. But the oversimplification may nevertheless be useful to my purpose of clarification. The distinction is between "collectivity" and "community."

Buber (1935) has expressed the distinction in his characteristic gnomic style.

Collectivity is not a binding but a bundling together; individuals packed together, armed and equipped in common, with only as much life from man to man as will inflame the marching step. But community . . . is the being no longer side by side but with one another of a multitude of persons. And this multitude, though it also moves toward one goal, yet experiences everywhere a turning to, a dynamic facing of, the other, a flowering from I to Thou. . . . Collectivity is based on an organized atrophy of personal existence, community on its increase and confirmation in life lived toward another. (p. 31)

It is not entirely easy to locate concrete referents for Buber's "collectivity" and "community." Perhaps the organization of a traditional army best typifies collectivity. It is an organization in which member persons become "objects." It is shaped, trained, and ordered to achieve the goal of an efficient killing mechanism. Members are trained to exclude personal feelings, aspirations, fears, hopes, and despairs from their relations with one another. The legitimate relations are task-determined role relations, not voluntary interpersonal relations. Task-related communications must move up and down the hierarchical chain of command through prescribed channels. Intelligence relevant to operations is accumulated in centralized places of command. Decisions and commands issue from these centers, and the prescribed virtue down the line is prompt and unquestioning obedience to legitimate commands. (It need hardly be stated that such ideal mechanization of relationships and interactions was never fully achieved in any army. In Santayana's phrase (1939a), "The sweet herbs" of friendship and enmity, resentment and loyalty, love and hate "flourished on their little earth." But it would be foolish to deny that such mechanization of member-to-member relations was sought and trained for.)

Perhaps Buber's prototype of community was one of Israel's *kibbutzim*, of which he was an ardent advocate. In a *kibbutz*, members care for each other as persons. There is work to be done, but assignments to tasks are made through participative dialogue in which not only the task requirements but also the powers, capacities, and limitations—the learning aspirations and interests—of the kibbutz members concerned are taken into account and, insofar as possible, reconciled. The members concerned speak their interests, aspirations, and preferences openly in the decision-making councils. The *kibbutz* aspires to be an organization committed at once to work and task achievement and to the support and nurturance of personal growth and development. (As in the case of the army, this description is an idealization.)

The examples of army and *kibbutz* may be useful in concretizing the contrasting meanings implicit in Buber's distinction. But we must generalize from these examples in applying the distinctions more widely. Perhaps an historical detour may aid this process of generalization. The distinction between *Gemeinschaft* and *Gesellschaft*, which preoccupied Tönnies and other classic German sociologists, overlaps Buber's distinction. *Gemeinschaft* referred to the way of ordering societal life in medieval Europe. *Gemeinschaft* "communities" incorporated traditionally defined and socially inherited statuses for the various grades of people within them. Obligations, services, and loyalties between persons at different levels are mutual and reciprocal, though unequal. The lord, for example, took care of the workers on his land when they were too old to work, as they in turn paid him a share of the product of their labors on the land and furnished footsoldiers for his armies in defense of the realm. The order of "community" life was tradition-directed and usually religiously sanctioned.

Gesellschaft reflected the modern shift, in the language of Sir Henry Maine, from status to contract in the ordering of human relations. Workers contracted with employers for their services, and mutual obligations beyond the terms of the time-limited contract were minimal or nonexistent. The form of social organization of work that emerged eventually, along with *Gesellschaft*, was bureaucracy, a form that owed much in its inception to the organization of the armies of the time. It was a hierarchical organization of roles and role relationships rather than of persons and personal relationships. Channels of communication and authority were carefully defined by the book and not by tradition. Intelligence collection and decision making were concentrated at the top of the hierarchy.

Max Weber and other macro-sociologists of his time saw a widening victory of *Gesellschaft* and bureaucracy over *Gemeinschaft* communalism as the earmark and the "price" of modernization in the organization of work and of social relations more generally. They were partly right in their prediction. Increasing dependence on scientifically based technology led to greater and greater dependence on technically specialized roles and an ever more intricate division of labor to be bureaucratically managed in the production of goods and services. Bureaucratization spread beyond the organization of persons into worker roles to encompass other of their roles—as citizen, as student and teacher, as consumer, and as client in quest of health, recreational, and welfare services as well.

The growth of worldwide social interdependence, which Woodrow Wilson once called the emergence of the Great Society in the West, has been accompanied by the bureaucratization of life and work, as the increasing prevalence and power of multinational corporations attest. In the building of a vast society in the West, we have shattered traditional communities—economically self-sufficient local, agrarian, or village communities—and have failed to build new bases for and forms of community within or between the imposing social structures on which we have come uneasily to depend for our biologic survival (see, for example, Stein, 1960).

I said before that classic nineteenth-century sociologists were correct in one part of their predictions. Where they were wrong was in their belief that the human need for "community," once satisfied in *Gemeinschaft* villages and neighborhoods, would disappear, or perhaps that the person-sustaining loyalties, once generated and renewed through life in these associations, could be transferred to other social aggregates—to professional and vocational associations, to nations, or even to "leagues of nations."

The human need for communities, associations in which members are accepted as persons, valued and cared for as persons, not valued primarily as specialized role occupants capable of providing some useful expertise in a collective endeavor, has not disappeared in the Great Society. If I have been right in my claim that consensual validation is necessary to the maintenance of a sane and viable personal identity, it is not surprising that people have sought and found substitutes for traditional local communities as these have been eroded and destroyed. Some have come to attach their personal allegiance to the particular racial or ethnic segment of society into which they were born (this is especially characteristic of members of minority groups); some to a vocational or professional association; some to an ideological cause; some to a charismatic religious cult, whether novel or traditional; some to an age group. The validation of one's self and person against a social circle of acceptant and meaningful response tends to be limited to one segment of society, not to a social unit that is capable of sustaining its members, at least potentially, in all their life functions—in that sense, a community. The identification of the person is to an association that, because it is special in its interests, tends in the stress of political competition and conflict to become a closed rather than an open "society." Processes of public policy making become win–lose competitions. In these struggles, members of other groups are ascriptively dehumanized, even demonized. The Great Society tends to become like Hobbes' pre-contractual Leviathan, a war of all against all, although indeed the warring units are groups rather than individuals—a struggle of particulars masquerading as universals, as Harold Laski once described the class struggle.

While all of us are appalled by the results of misplaced questings for community, we, or at least I, can also be encouraged by the unwillingness of people to live their lives as Its in the impersonalized and depersonalized structures of collectivity, however "scientifically" and beneficently managed these may be. The tragedy is that in unintelligent and nonlearningful struggles to escape the confines of one collectivity, people fall into or create another collectivity, perhaps less beneficent than the former. We cannot sanely ignore the social and political effects of misplaced questings for community. But it is the effects on the kind and quality of human learning with which we are primarily concerned in this essay. Of course, the two sets of effects are interrelated, because learning and society are organically linked, as I have set out to argue.

Persons who seek the resource of community as a support to their functioning as whole, though unique, beings through more or less total commitment to some partial association—some segmental slice through societal complexity and interdependence—are doomed to disappointment. The greatest price persons pay lies perhaps in the suppression and denial of opportunities to develop themselves in directions that do not fit the specialized purposes of the association to which they have committed themselves. Because the association is "at war" with competing associations within the larger society, it must maintain a more or less rigid internal discipline among its members. This means a narrowing of the range of permitted and supported member learnings and deviations from the associational norm. Opportunities for developing self–other relationships between members of competing associations do not occur "naturally" and may be actively discouraged. It is the development of self–other relationships between competing associations that might objectify their situation to themselves and support the development of mutually acceptable win–win resolutions to their conflicts. More typically, limited resources are committed to defensive operations, both external and internal, reducing further the resources available for support and fostering of freely chosen directions of actualization by persons who are committed members of the association.

Blind devotion to our variegated pasts necessarily divides us. Our present is dominated by collectivity and social fragmentation, both inhospitable to the nurture of the persons and the invention of the forms of human organization that our pre-figurational culture requires. The only place for us to turn, in order to build viable community and shared culture, is the future. Margaret Mead (1965) has reminded us that variegated cultures and traditions, personal and group differences, can come to be seen and accepted as welcome resources, but this is likely to happen only if persons from across various current lines of social cleavage can come to see the future as an open project for joint construction, through their own participative and learningful choices and actions. But such a turning around will occur only as they together build learning communities to furnish themselves an alternative basis of support and security—alternative to the segmental associations to which they now desperately cling.

The most hopeful way through and beyond the desert of collectivity, social fragmentation, and impending self-inflicted doom in which we now wander is for persons thirsting for a fuller life to unite in building community within contemporary collectivities and between and among contemporary fragmentations. It is in the processes of such building that they may learn both more person-and-community centered forms of human organization and more viable models of personhood for life in a pluralistic and pre-figurational culture.

BUILDING LEARNING COMMUNITIES
AND LEARNING THROUGH THEM

My suggested model of learning and of learning communities has so far been general and visionary. But can it be made to work? Can its ideas, however plausible they may sound in theory, be operationalized in practical projects and programs of learning? Practical readers, and the author too, who likes to think of himself as a practitioner as well as a theorist, may feel that something needs to be added. They, like Ko Ko in Gilbert and Sullivan's *Mikado*, may feel that what is needed is "corroborative detail to give versimilitude to an otherwise bald and unconvincing narrative." Fortunately, the author, unlike Ko Ko who had to draw upon his imagination for corroborative details, can draw upon a considerable body of action research and evaluated experience.

Since 1947, I, along with an increasing number of colleagues, have been experimenting with and elaborating and refining ways of building learning communities in collectivized and fragmented societies, both inside and outside America and sometimes across national boundaries (see Essay 7 for a discussion of the origin of these reeducative efforts). I refer to the development of what are commonly called laboratory methods of learning, associated with such organizations as the National Training Laboratories. I am quite aware that other approaches to the building of learning communities have developed during the same period, in America and elsewhere. I hope I will be pardoned for concentrating here upon the methodologies with which I am most familiar.

The developers of laboratory methods have brought together and integrated processes of personal and social changing that in our highly departmentalized universities and society are often researched and practiced under the auspices of different, often noncommunicating, disciplines and professions. Perhaps the clearest way of presenting a rounded view of laboratory methods is, therefore, to discuss it from six different viewpoints, keeping in mind that what is intended is a multi-perspectival account of a more or less unified body of methods for building learning communities and for stimulating and supporting personal and communal learning within them. A fuller account of laboratory methods is available in Benne, Bradford, Gibb and Lippitt (1975).

A Process of Participative and Experiential Learning

Perhaps most fundamentally, the methods are ways by which persons learn how to learn for themselves. (From previous discussions of self and person, it should be clear that this does not typically mean learning by themselves, in solitude, though voluntary personal withdrawal and meditation are not foreign to the method.) This learning goal may be phrased in another way: to support persons in building into their methodological characters a commitment to participative and experiential learning as a way of coping with doubt, discrepancy, and conflict.

The notion of learning through participation and experience is not new in the history of educational thought. But it has often been constricted and distorted in its application in formal education by other dominant ideas and unexamined assumptions. The first of these is that education is primarily a process of transmitting a cultural heritage to the immature and, by extension, to alienated and deviate members of a society. A second assumption is that those who are knowledgeable about a culture, as it has come to be out of its past, and who occupy established positions of authority in its structures, know better what learners need to learn than the learners themselves. A third, closely related assumption is that learning experiences should be planned, managed, and evaluated by those who know best what learners need to achieve.

Responsible participation of learners is reduced by these assumptions in highly significant ways: in determining what they need to learn; in inventing and testing ways to pursue their chosen learning goals effectively; in managing the behavioral conditions of learning—motivational, affective, and emotional states, and power and authority relations—as these contribute to or thwart learning; and in developing and using criteria to evaluate learning outcomes and processes. Learners are, by these assumptions, maintained (or oppressed, as Paolo Freire would have it) in a dependent position within the learning situation. They do learn prescribed content, but they do not learn autonomy in initiating, conducting, and evaluating their own learning projects and enterprises. The full potential in participative and experiential learning, especially the value of learning how to learn, is not actualized.

Practitioners of laboratory methods of learning work on quite different assumptions. They view learning and relearning not primarily as cultural transmission, but as a future-oriented process of personal and cultural renewal. This view calls for a different relationship between "teachers" and "learners," and "outside" resources needed to achieve the learnings sought. Learning experiences are seen as "experiments" designed to link creatively needs and resources. As "experiments," learning experiences are problematic; the outcomes cannot be fully known in advance. In evaluating learning outcomes, processes of planning, conducting, and managing learning are lifted up into consciousness. The behaviors of all persons in the learning situation are evaluated (not judged) in terms of their effects on learning processes and outcomes. Power and authority relations are observed, analyzed, and renegotiated as needs for change are determined. A major learning outcome sought is self-knowledge and communal knowledge about processes of participative and experiential learning and about ways of transferring such knowledge to other social situations in which members are now involved or will be involved in the foreseeable future.

I said earlier that I saw important uses for computer assistance in personal and communal learning. Computers with information stored so that it may be retrieved relevantly to the policy-and-practice-oriented questings by most members of a learning community, not only relevantly to the concerns of specialized researchers or bureaucratic managers, can help significantly to meet the information needs of communities of learners. Barriers to accessibility by learners to relevant stored information must be reduced, so long as the right of persons to privacy is not infringed. Conflicts between these two sets of rights must be resolved collaboratively by the learning community.

A Way of Understanding and Managing Interpersonal, Group, and Social Dynamics

Developers of laboratory methods have emphasized the importance of experiential content, often neglected in traditional education, in building and utilizing learning communities. This content is the process side of learning, its interactional context, in which the operation of interpersonal, group, intergroup, and organizational dynamics becomes apparent to those attuned to the observation and analysis of social processes. In traditional learning situations, the attention of learners is directed away from this "interpersonal underworld." Attention is directed toward "objective" learning goals and cognitive content considered relevant to these goals. Yet questions about control and domination, about dependence and counter-dependence, about intimacy and distance, and about inclusion and exclusion are present in the minds of some persons, though unexpressed, in every learning situation. But traditionally these have not been regarded as questions appropriate or fruitful for open inquiry and learning.

Practitioners of laboratory methods encourage responsible inquiry into such questions as they arise. This requires the public expression of feelings and immediate perceptions about self and others. The purpose is that member feelings and perceptions of self and others be surfaced, shared, reflected upon, interpreted, and corrected and altered in the process. Wise decisions about improvement of the social medium and climate of participative learning will come only out of diagnosis of such data and their responsible analysis and interpretation.

The reason for such raising and focusing of consciousness upon processes and interactions in learning situations seems to me easy to justify. As already emphasized, traditional bases of community have been eroded and often replaced by forms of social organization inhospitable or inimical to continuing participative and experiential learning by members. We can no longer depend on mute and nonconscious historical evolution to develop the communities required by sane personal and social development. Community building and development must become deliberate and conscious. Such development requires persons able to observe, interpret, and change, where needed, human relationships and social dynamics in the image of community.

A Way of Planned Change

The innovators of laboratory methods were as much concerned with helping persons learn skills and understandings relevant to planning and achieving change in their social environment as they were in personal development and renewal. The transfer of skills, values, and insights achieved by persons in specially contrived learning laboratories to social situations outside the laboratories required persons to make these outside situations more hospitable to and supportive of their newly internalized capacities and commitments. This required them to learn methods of social change along with methods of participative personal learning.

It was thus a "natural" extension of laboratory methods to move them outside the residential laboratories where they were first elaborated and tested, into projects and programs for developing ongoing organizations and larger social systems in the image of community. Laboratory methods have been extended to the invention, testing, and improvement of methods of organizational and social planning, action, and changing, as well as to the invention and testing of methods for stimulating and supporting personal and interpersonal learning and growth. Their practitioners typically seek to link and integrate these two levels of behavioral changing. Learning and re-learning by persons need to be important ingredients of social action and changing. Programs of social action should assume responsibility for the effects of the action on the learning and growth of all persons involved in and affected by it.

A Process of Cooperative Action Research

Wide communication gaps now exist within our departmentalized society between practitioners of basic social research, practitioners in the helping professions, and the laypersons and groups who are suffering the effects of debilitating and dehumanizing social conditions and who, where they have not surrendered to despair, are struggling, often ineffectively, to meliorate these conditions. (I do not mean to imply that researchers and professionals are not also victims of our crisis culture.) How can these gaps be bridged? Part of the problem is to invent ways of improving the tempo and quality of utilization of research-tested social knowledge and professional know-how in forming and improving the life practices of persons and groups in various associational and institutional settings. This objective of laboratory methods will be discussed in the next section.

But more fundamental is the problem of infusing the value orientations, the commitment to cooperative inquiry, now characteristic of basic researchers in dealing with problems set by their specialized disciplines, into the practical efforts by human beings better to diagnose their social and cultural life-environments and to modify these in the light of their diagnoses. These orientations and commitments are also part of the methodological characters of scientifically oriented practice professionals as well. Can persons who are not social scientists or highly trained professionals learn to use a research approach in clarifying researchable questions in the problematic situations that confront them, in collecting and interpreting relevant data, and in building a valid information base for projecting and testing solutions?

Kurt Lewin was one of the first social scientists to answer these questions affirmatively. As explained in Essay 7, Lewin's cooperative action research became a model of learning and relearning for the social scientists and helping professionals and assorted laypersons who set out to build and test laboratories for reeducative learning in the late 1940s. Some such mix of human resources and competences seems necessary for effective action research. The model conjoins research, self-directed learning, and cooperative action. Here, as elsewhere, the effective use of laboratory methods requires attention to the "subjective" problems rising out of unaccustomed peer relations and concern for relevant, valid, factual, and sometimes technical information about situations being studied, with the purpose of improving them as sites for human living and learning.

A Process of Knowledge Utilization

I have suggested before that part of the motivation of developers of laboratory methods of learning was to find and test ways of facilitating the utilization and application of research-tested social and behavioral knowledge by men and women of practice and action. This was particularly true of knowledge of behavioral dynamics at various levels of human organization. Such knowledge, it was believed, if it can be internalized by men and women of practice and action, can assist them in making more dependable diagnoses of the personal and social difficulties in which they are involved and in mobilizing more effectively their own and others' resources in meliorating these difficulties.

New knowledge of person, group, organization, society, or culture can be internalized and utilized by men and women now unacquainted with it only as the new knowledge is chosen as promising to meet better their requirements for maintenance, continuity, and growth than do the knowledge components of their present belief and value systems. People must see a need for change in their present belief systems before they can seriously entertain knowledge of person, group, or society alternative to the modes of explanation and interpretation they are currently employing to make sense of their lived worlds. Persons must acknowledge to themselves inconsistencies, discrepancies, and inadequacies in their present ways of seeing, classifying, and interpreting their phenomenal experiences. New sources of knowledge must become more credible and trustworthy than the other persons against whom they now consensually validate their perceptions of and beliefs about "reality." Persons, as Kurt Lewin has argued, find and accept new beliefs and value orientations as they find and accept membership in a new community with value and cognitive orientations different from those of other significant associations to which they now belong. There is an inescapable connection between believing and belonging. Persons must participate in building new validating communities for themselves.

In general, practitioners of laboratory methods maintain that problems of better utilization of tested social and psychological knowledge can be solved only as men and women of knowledge and men and women of action, both with self-acknowledged needs for better understanding of themselves and of their life-situations than they now possess, can meet together in processes of collaborative inquiry. Ordinarily, the building of the required community will call for the good offices of third-party helpers—persons skilled in bridging and linking hitherto segregated human systems—a role sometimes called that of "change agent."

A Way of Resocialization and Reenculturation

Human organisms, as already emphasized and reemphasized, become persons and selves as they enter into membership in various human associations and, in this process, internalize the language, the moral and esthetic standards, the ways of thinking and behaving that prevail as a way of life in these associations. Much of the learning of ways of valuing, thinking, and behaving occurs through nonconscious accommodation of member responses toward the modal ways of the association into which persons are born or to which they aspire and seek to belong. If and as persons develop self–other capacities to think and choose for themselves, they incorporate cultural content more critically and selectively, and they create their own distinctive life-orientations and value systems. These enable persons to exercise a larger measure of free and responsible control over the processes of their own continuing socialization and enculturation.

In a rapidly changing society like our own—in which unexamined traditions furnish no dependable basis for choice, and in which creative responses to novel conditions of life must be invented and learned, both individually and communally, as a condition of human survival—people, young and older, must learn to assume greater responsibility for consciously directing the processes of their own continuing enculturation and reenculturation. It is a corollary of this proposition that continuing socialization and resocialization occur throughout the lifetimes of persons and that societies can no longer rely upon a fixed shaping of character in early socialization. But this means that persons must be enabled in correcting and modifying the persisting effects of early socialization where these have become dysfunctional in coping with changed and changing life conditions and challenges. Such reeducation is often interpreted as a "therapeutic" process focused on the curing of "pathologies" engendered in some large part by faulty processes of early socialization.

While not denying the existence of pathologies in the lives of some persons or the needs of these persons for therapy, practitioners of laboratory methods assume a preventive, a learning and growth, posture toward the needs for resocialization that are now prevalent throughout our culture. Their orientation is toward strengthening the coping powers of persons, toward supporting persons in developing more learning-prone and adaptive methodological characters, not toward the curing of hang-ups engendered in past experiences. Socializing processes occur for persons as members of all groups and organizations in the life and work in which they become involved. The learning task is to support persons in becoming more aware of the socialization demands placed upon them by the human systems to which they belong, to develop support from others in becoming more aware of these demands and more critical of them, and to seek to shape the decision-making processes of these systems toward more participative and communal forms—in brief, to work to make at least some of their associations more mentally healthy places in which to live, in terms of their regard for the maintenance and growth needs of all persons affected by the operations and demands of the systems. The aim is to stimulate and support persons in learning the arts of joining with others in managing their own continuing socialization and enculturation, not alone in specially constructed and assembled learning communities, but ideally in more and more of the associations in which learning processes are occurring.

4 · Technology and Community

Conflicting Bases of Educational Authority

To set free the technical forces of production, including the construction of cybernetic and learning machines which can simulate the complete sphere of the functions of rational goal-directed action far beyond the capacity of natural consciousness, and thus substitute for human effort, is not identical with the development of norms which could fulfill the dialectic of moral relationships in an interaction free of domination, on the basis of a reciprocity allowed to have its full and non-coercive scope. Liberation from hunger and misery *does not necessarily converge with* liberation from servitude and degradation *for there is no automatic developmental relation between labor and interaction.*

Jürgen Habermas
Theory and Practice

If the technical expert, as such, is assigned the task of perfecting new powers of chemical, bacteriological, or atomic destruction, his morality as technical expert requires only that he apply himself to his task as effectively as possible. The question of what the new force might mean, as released into a social texture emotionally and intellectually unfit to control it, or as surrendered to men whose speciality is professional killing—well, that is simply "none of our business," as specialists, however great may be his misgivings as father of a family, or as citizen of his nation and of the world.

Kenneth Burke
A Rhetoric of Motives

WESTERN CIVILIZATION IN ITS MODERN PHASE has frequently been described as Faustian civilization. To recall the legend of Dr. Faustus is an appropriate beginning for this discussion. It was for the augmentation of his personal power, through knowledge and mastery of technology, that Faustus bargained with Mephistopheles. The price that he paid for the mastery of technics was his soul. Without a soul to guide the powers with which his technology endowed him, he became a threat to his human community and ceased to be a person. Unable to love or to trust others, he was equally unable to accept love and trust from them.

The salvation of Faustus, in Goethe's version of the legend, came through his restoration to humanity, to membership in the human community. It came also in the utilization of his unusual technical powers for humanly constructive purposes—the draining of the swamps. The angels chanted, as they carried the restored soul of Faustus to his eternal reward, "Whose restless striving never ceases, him we have power to save."

THE LURE OF TECHNOLOGY
AND TECHNOLOGICAL SOLUTIONS
TO HUMAN PROBLEMS

The legend of Dr. Faustus reveals a moral ambivalence toward the power to control nature that is deep within the traditions of Western culture. Extraordinary mastery has been associated with malevolent, antihuman, black magic. But it has been associated with white magic as well. Goethe revealed his own ambivalence toward the magic of technology—it could be black magic, but it could be benevolent, humane, white magic, if its uses were controlled by a humanistic and humanitarian morality.

Until recently the traditional ambivalence toward technology has become increasingly absent from the modern Western world. An ever more intricate and powerful technology, continually replenished and renewed by scientific research and maintained by powerful engineering professions, became for many the very measure of human progress, as it did for Veblen (1914) and Ayres (1944).[1] The decline in moral ambivalence toward the power of technology has been accompanied by a decline in the traditional humanistic checks on its undirected growth.

Nevertheless, the consequences of expanding technology were often far from benevolent. Technology often meant that community life was destroyed and then replaced by a functional and inorganic rationalization of personal life, a rationalization that served best the developing bureaucratic form of social organization. These consequences were often explained away by the advocates of technology as part of the necessary price of human progress. To the advocates of the technological society, a technological solution is always available, even for the deeper concerns of human existence. The alienation of persons from themselves, from each other, and from the social economy on which they depend will all be solved by the intensification of technique. Technology became the new faith, promising the believer an end to war, poverty, and political disharmony. Only human beings stood in the way—a new problem for technology to solve.

An illustration of what I mean by a technological solution to a human problem may help to make my point clear. Let us accept without argument that some emotional difficulties of persons are induced by the technicalization and dehumanization of our society and economy. Chemotherapies, shock therapies, and cerebral lobotomies are examples of "technological solutions" to such difficulties. Their "technological" nature is revealed as they are contrasted with psychotherapeutic approaches to similar difficulties. In the latter, the person in distress is invited to enter and is supported in entering into a dialogic relationship with another person or with other persons, as in reeducative groups or therapeutic communities. The voluntary character of the relationship is sedulously maintained. It is assumed that the person in distress has regenerative strengths, though these strengths are now concealed or denied. It is further assumed that such strengths are elicited by other persons committed to listen to, respond to, understand, and care for the person in distress, even as that person is invited to listen to, respond to, understand, and care for them. In the process, ideally at least, the person assumes responsibility for managing his or her own choices and relationships with others.

In the "technological solution," the person in distress becomes an object, an occupant of the patient role vis-à-vis the role of the expert therapist. The relationship is defined in nonmutual, nonreciprocal terms. The therapist withholds his or her feelings, values, and empathy—his or her subjectivity—from the process of treatment. The therapist supplies only his or her know-how and expertise. The subjectivity of the patient is not seen or valued as a strength, a prime resource in the "communal" process of reeducation and renewal. The relationship is depersonalized and dehumanized in the interest of objectivity and predictability of results.

I have, of course, idealized the psychotherapeutic or reeducative approach for purposes of contrast with a "technological solution" to a patient's problem by an expert psychiatrist. In a technologically oriented society, the psychotherapist is continually tempted to externalize, objectify, and standardize his or her "techniques," to "treat patients," to withhold his or her person from participation in a process of dialogic regeneration. No lobotomist probably can ever divest himself or herself entirely of the human feelings evoked in transactions with "patients," however hard he or she may try. The contrast is, nevertheless, valid.

Voices have, of course, been raised over the years urging that education should be grounded in a moral authority that transcends and guides technological development. But many of these voices, whether religious or secular, have spoken in behalf of a traditional authority from a pre-industrial past. It was thus easy for a society committed to progress and to defining progress in terms of scientific and technological advance to dismiss these voices as echoes from a dead past.

Disenchantment and Despair

It was not argument and criticism but rather the evidence of cataclysmic historic events that cast deep doubts upon the beneficence of the technological god. After the day in August 1945, when a U.S. bomber dropped a nuclear bomb upon Hiroshima, many sensed that humankind had moved, in Karl Jaspers' (1961) term, into a new Axial period of human history. Ingenuity and creativity had given us the power to pollute our planet and destroy all life.

The release of atomic energy was only the most dramatic event signaling to the modern world that we are living in a new period of human history, in which moral responsibilities are vastly extended and continuation of the old moral irresponsibilities in controlling the vast technological powers at our command is fatal. Yet the power of technology is such that even the likelihood of total human destruction is not sufficient to bring it under control, and in a vast number of ways we continue to destroy the "nature" upon which our life depends. We are mining and exploiting the resources of nature without replenishing them, meeting each new problem with an abstract technology sufficient to meet the present crisis only, while generating new problems. For example, we create better highways to relieve problems of traffic glut. As a consequence, the hordes of cars moving into the city pollute the air to the point where health is threatened and, if the pollution continues, life is destroyed. We are destroying, in a thousand insidious ways, the life support systems, the ecological balances, on which continuation of our existence depends.

One common reaction to awareness of the power of total destruction is despair. But despair does not serve to maintain life. The problem is for us to reeducate ourselves as we subordinate technique to moral ends. It is not difficult to locate the general area of human problems to which our new education must address itself. Disparate and contradictory moral visions guide the current uses of the plethora of powers with which our science and technology have endowed us. We live and choose within a maze of moral contradictions. A well-intentioned effort to rid farmers' crops of insect pests may unintendedly rob forests of birds, and lakes and streams of fish. Our power to build and to destroy is evident in deserts made into fertile fields and in fertile fields transformed by bombs into eroded and defoliated deserts, with both sorts of projects financed by the same nation-state. Our command of effective means in the biological sphere is evident in human lives restored, sustained, and extended by people through applied biochemical and nuclear knowledges, and in human lives indiscriminately snuffed out and horribly mutated by variant applications of the very same biochemical and nuclear knowledges. Our power to modify behavior finds expression in devoted and sensitive nurture and support of scientists and artists, and of creative minds engaged in building new knowledge and new images of human potentiality; and in the brainwashing of masses of people into robot servitude to some fuehrer's or party's whim or will.

Such contradictions are not meant to suggest that the solution to the problems of the modern world is the abandonment of technology. They suggest rather that technology is not an unambiguous blessing. It is sometimes argued that because technology got us into the mess we are in, the way out is to return to some pretechnological state of nature—perhaps sometime before the wheel. The intention is not willfully to condemn vast numbers of men and women to starvation, disease, or lives of grinding toil unrelieved by comforts or leisure, but that would be the effect. Technology is not inherently evil or inherently good. What is bad is the uncritical adulation that people have recently granted it, along with the moral authority granted its expert practitioners to manage the lives and education of people. What is needed is not a rejection of the powers of technology, but a moral community that can bring these powers under competent, humane control. In brief, we must make a commitment to seeking and creating "the Good" for our Axial period of human history and to bringing our recreated conceptions of "the Good" into play in human choosing, deciding, and planning at all levels of human organization.

People who have lost hope in something they have depended on may try to return to some mythical, primitive state of nature. Others, like American neo-conservatives, may try to rededicate themselves to a conception of the good found in traditional religious or nationalist dogma and seek to impose it on life in a technological world. Their misguided efforts are certain to fail.

Our despair and our anguish are the result of the magnitude of our responsibility and of the inefficacy of our traditional ideas and values to build a moral community that can adequately control and direct our technology. During the time when they sought to find adequate authoritative bases for life and education in technological expertise and in technological solutions to human problems, people were buoyed up by a faith in inevitable progress. They did not despair but they also did not feel themselves to be responsible. They felt a confidence in a presiding providence that would automatically bring the conflicting plans and actions of individuals and groups into the service of a common good. Confidence in some preestablished ordering principle thought to guarantee that conflicting decisions will result in a coherent moral order has taken many forms in the history of human affairs, and has been given many names—the will of God, Fate, the Nature of Stoics and Taoists, the Unseen hand of Adam Smith and the free-market mechanism of the classical economists, the idea of progress in Western liberalism, the historical inevitability of socialism in Marxist thought. We can recognize the common function that all these versions have played in shaping people's view of their future, without denying the differences that adherence to one version or another has made in the organization and development of human energies and resources. The effect of this confidence has been to narrow the range of human responsibility and to turn people's attention to the evaluation of means, to the neglect of an analysis of human ends. The recent decline of confidence has often resulted in despair, but it might also result in a widening of our responsibility for designing and inventing our own future. If we are to take responsibility for planning our own future, there must be an appeal to a principle that attends to the conservation and augmentation of human values. This principle cannot be imposed upon us from an external source, such as the authority of the expert; rather it must be constructed through the communal exercise of human intelligence and volition. Neither technology nor a forlorn return to some earlier set of traditions is sufficient for this task.

There are many paths toward the rehumanization of humankind that will need to be traveled, but one important path leads to a commitment *by those in charge of education* to building a human, moral community. Such a task requires the acknowledgment and criticism of normative assumptions that function authoritatively both in traditional culture and in our technological society.

A Faustian Educational System

Despite the discontent with technology that has arisen in some circles, our formal educational system continues to be guided by those committed to the dominance of technological expertise that accompanies a "fatuous progress theory of history" (Hendel, 1958).[2] The "authority of technology" and of technological expertise has permeated the orientations and practices of our educational institutions (see Essay 5 for a fuller development of this condition in higher education). Yet it is these very institutions that must be reconstructed if the task of moral reeducation is to be initiated, and this reconstruction requires a reassessment of the concept of authority. The authority of the technological expert has become a perverted expression of the more appropriate relation that can exist between an authority and a client. In order to clarify the effects of the technological expert, it is useful to express the more ideal relationship that *can* and *should* exist between an authority and a client. The form of the expert–authority relation can be rather simply described: A person unable to meet some need or achieve some purpose through his or her own unaided powers puts himself or herself under the guidance and direction of someone who claims to know how the need or purpose can be expeditiously met. This grant of authority is not an unlimited one. Its boundaries are set by the limited field of alleged competence of the bearer and the need and purpose of the subject. The triadic relationship among bearer, subject, and field is thus ideally collaborative in some degree, in that it requires a mutual fitting of need to resource. The subject must legitimize the authority of the bearer in controlling and directing the subject's conduct. After all, it is the subject's need and purpose that ideally are being served through the authority relation.

The collaboration, however, becomes minimal if the subject willingly grants to the expert the right to determine the former's need and purpose, or if the expert assumes the right to tell the subject what the latter's need really is, as well as how to behave in meeting it. Because of the general adulation of the technological expert, many people in industrial societies have been willing to grant the expert such extended powers.

So far, I have spoken as though the subject of expert authority is an individual person. This, of course, is not always the case. Groups and organizations of various sizes depend on experts and expert information and advice in forming plans and policies and in finding their way out of or through recurrent crises. The staffs of industrial organizations, governmental agencies, universities, and school systems are made up largely of specialized experts. And even more specialized experts than the staffs can provide are brought in for advice and recommendations in times of emergency and confusion.

The use of expert authority is, of course, nothing new in the history of human affairs. What is new is the kind of expertise that practical men and women consider useful and dependable, along with the increasing specialization and fragmentation that characterize the composition of contemporary expertise, particularly in its scientific and technological forms.

The commitment to the maintenance of an intricate bureaucracy has come to be accentuated in the educational systems of America. This is particularly true of universities and colleges, as Essay 5 will make clear. Faculty members are chosen for their demonstrated expertise in one or another field of specialized knowledge. The same credentials are considered meritorious for teaching or for research appointments. Because the basic credential is successful completion of a graduate school program, and because graduate schools typically require a demonstration of research competence in some highly specialized field of knowledge as a condition of successful completion of advanced degree requirements, the university, even more than government or industry, has become, in George Kelly's (1963) phrase, "a world steadily reduced to conceptual particles" (p. 531).

The lack of cultivation of any common intellectual or moral basis to support communication between faculty members in a university led Robert Hutchins (1936), when he was president of the University of Chicago a generation ago, to remark, exaggeratedly but truly, that the only thing that united the parts of the university was a central heating system. And Clark Kerr (1964), when he was president of what he chose to describe as a multiversity rather than a university, noted that all that united faculty members and administrators in common debate were endless discussions of what to do about the parking problems of the university. Heating and parking technologies may thus have a "communifying" function to perform, when all else fails.

George Kelly (1963) pointed out that the novelty in the utilization of contemporary expertise is "that the form of official expertise seems finally to have caught up with the needs of a complicated bureaucracy and been assimilated to it" (p. 535). While Kelly had in mind the fit between the form of expertise and the needs of governmental and industrial bureaucracies, his observation is nowhere better validated than by the social organization of the contemporary university. Faculty members are organized into schools, departments, and subdepartments by similarity of field of specialization, rather than by common concern with an issue or problem. Their teaching and research programs are, by and large, laid out along departmental lines. Transactions with members of other departments are not required by the norms of the social organization of the university. In fact, they are discouraged. Rewards are given to faculty members for staying within departmental boundaries. For example, publications in highly specialized journals are ordinarily considered more meritorious than publications in general journals with a concern for issues of broad human import.

The social organization is functionally rationalized and bureaucratic. It is designed to perpetuate a system of departmental segregation between people who are committed to accumulation of ever more specialized conceptual particles, or ever more specialized expertise. The social organization brings into play another kind of authority, the authority of the rules of the game, which serves as a substitute for the human needs that the more legitimate authority is ideally designed to meet.

The bureaucratic social system is a mechanical system, in the sense that it operates by rules that try to eliminate surprise from the outcomes of its functioning and that try to guarantee a "high quality output" from its operations. It values predictability and quality control. Graduating students are in this view products of the system, no more and no less than specialized research papers. Each is expected to conform to institutional rules, whether or not a real human need is addressed.

Kenneth Boulding (1967) has argued that human systems are somehow inherently and "naturally" organic and evolutionary, rather than mechanical, systems.

One thing we can say about Man's future with a great deal of confidence is that it will be more or less surprising. This phenomenon of surprise is not something which arises merely out of man's ignorance, though ignorance can contribute to what might be called unnecessary surprises. There is, however, something fundamental in the nature of our evolutionary system which makes exact foreknowledge about it impossible, and as social systems are in a large measure evolutionary in character, they participate in the property of containing ineradicable surprises. (p. 199)

If Boulding is right about the nature of human systems, and I believe that he is, it is not difficult to understand why universities, having become so mechanical and bureaucratic, must depend on extrinsic motivations and rewards to maintain a minimum degree of morale and institutional identification among their various subgroups. Given the mechanical adherence to the rules of the game, it is not surprising that these systems have tended to be so uncreatively defensive and vulnerable in their responses to protests against their dehumanization, moral irresponsibility, and irrelevance.

Of course, the university system is not thoroughly mechanical in its organization or operation. Some of the most creative breakthroughs in knowledge understandably have come in the interstices between traditional university departments—biochemistry, nuclear studies (are they physics or chemistry?), social psychology, and so on. And universities have experimented with alternative organizations that cut across departmental lines, such as centers, institutes, and area studies; often these alternative organizations select their personnel on the basis of the needs generated by the issues under examination. But traditionally, these organizations are breaks in the system that have often been regarded as temporary, *ad hoc*, maverick suborganizations. They have had to struggle against continual pressures exerted upon them to become indistinguishable from departments. These pressures arise from the influence of the norms of the larger system operating in crucial day-to-day areas of practice, such as promotion, budgeting, and accounting procedures.

The content—the conceptual particles—offered to students through the intricate system of bureaucratized relationships is varied. The content is by no means all technological, in the narrow sense of information translated, readied, and developed for particular application and use. In fact, most professors in arts and science pride themselves on selecting and presenting nonutilitarian content in their own courses. Nevertheless, professors are selected for their technical competence. They are professors of know-how, albeit a know-how for finding and testing conceptual particles in their own specialized field. Most operate under the "scientific" norm of "not taking sides" on issues of wide human concern, on the assumption that "universal" knowledge is morally neutral, applicable to both good ends and bad. Generally overlooked, however, are the choices they have made in selecting and organizing the content, and the emphasis that these choices generally give to one cultural tradition at the expense of another. Often neglected too are the moral implications of the information selected, and the likely use that will be made of it, given the power and direction of private industry and government.

An even more powerful norm operating in selecting and presenting content is a kind of territorial imperative. This might be stated as "Thou shalt not in thy teaching get into another faculty member's field of specialization." Of course, the moral implications of conceptual particles ordinarily do not become evident until it is understood how they fit together, but it is precisely this understanding that is taboo. The atmosphere of the learning situation is ordinarily competitive and individualistic. Rewards, in terms of credentials such as grades, honors, and recommendations, are determined by a comparative ranking of individual students, according to individual achievement. Students' cooperation and helping each other with their work is considered a violation of the norm and is called cheating. Relations between teachers and students are impersonalized, often to the point of depersonalization.

When the various aspects are taken together, however potentially liberalizing the content involved, the result is a technicalization of education. Its basis is noncommunal. Its human "products" issue from its programmed processes as specialists, motivated to get ahead in their own fields, with little awareness of the relationships of their specialities to the moral and political issues that now divide the "human community." "Generalists" and "moralists" do not function happily or entirely safely in such an environment.

There have been strong resistances in the university to the extension of its facilities and resources into programs of continuing education and reeducation for persons, groups, organizations, and communities outside the university. Part of this resistance is no doubt due to economic considerations—the university never has enough funds to support all the campus programs that its ingenious faculty members imagine as desirable to do. But even where continuing education programs might add to inadequate funding, the resistance persists. The resistance is least in "vocational" fields like agriculture, engineering, business, health, and welfare. It is greatest where general moral, political, and civic enlightenment and empowering of outside persons and groups is the aim of the continuing education project or program. Probably, the main resistance rests on grounds similar to those that led Abraham Flexner (1930), arch exponent of the technicalized university I have been describing, to urge a stance of social irresponsibility upon the university so far as the melioration of social life and the resolution of society's moral and political dilemmas are concerned. Flexner feared that university people who assumed responsibility for social improvement would be corrupted into soothsayers, alchemists, magicians, astrologers, and prescientific recommenders to society on the basis of faith, lore, and superstition rather than on the basis of valid knowledge. The corruption he feared was corruption of the role he passionately recommended to and for university-based men and women, that of the pursuit and propagation of disinterested, scientific, and, for him, *valid* knowledge. That his recommendation was based on a positivist faith in the objectivity of knowledge should be apparent. Such a faith is still widely shared in university circles. It is a faith that consigns the university to a priestly rather than a prophetic role in its relations with the established society that environs it.

The technicalization of schools below the college and university level has proceeded concomitantly with the technicalization there. This is due partly to the fact that the credentialing of teachers and administrators in public schools more and more involves successful completion of college and university programs of instruction. It is also due to the increased influence of university professors in shaping school curricula and in establishing efficient pathways of preparation for students to become successful recruits for higher education.

The attempt to substitute educational technology for human teaching has probably made greater inroads in the schools than in colleges and universities themselves. University experts have played increasingly larger roles in developing curriculum materials for the lower grade levels. Much of this material is still printed, but more and more of it is issued with accompanying tapes, films, and computer programs. Whatever the medium, the big selling point is often the extent to which these instructional devices are teacher proof. They are advertised as enabling the student to proceed with his or her own learning at his or her own individual pace, and they are designed to relegate teachers to the role of technicians implementing a *prescribed* learning program.

The "best" materials are thought by many to be self-instructional, providing immediate feedback to students as to whether a certain response is right or wrong. Students can proceed to learn through interaction with their materials without any necessity for messy, subjective, and unpredictable dialogue with either their teachers or their fellow students. Such materials are urged as a technological solution to problems of large numbers of students and a paucity of well prepared teachers. They are urged also as an efficient way of individual-

izing instruction, usually without awareness of the irony involved—
that "individualization" in this usage seems to be equivalent to further "depersonalization" of the instructional process.

Thus, the search for technological solutions to the human problems of teaching and learning goes on among educators who have not
heard the news that we are living in an Axial period, a tragic period,
of human history. And the exploitation of multiple media of "communication"—visual, auditory, electronic—is part of the search.

COMMUNITY AS THE BASIS
OF EDUCATIONAL AUTHORITY

The ultimate bearer of educational authority is a community in which
people are seeking fuller and more valid membership. Actual bearers
and subjects of this authority must together build a proximate set of
mutually helpful relationships in which the aim is the development
of value orientations, perceptions, skills, and knowledges that will
enable the subjects to function more fully, adequately, and autono-
mously as participants in a still wider community life.

Authority relations are educationally valid insofar as they operate to cultivate mutual processes of association and dialogue that, by
design, reach beyond these relationships into the life of the wider
community. All such education, whether occurring in schools or elsewhere, is at once a mothering and a weaning, a rooting into ongoing
authority relations and a pulling up of roots.

The educator develops authority in relation to a community process in which he or she works as a co-participant. The authority of a
teacher is exercised as he or she seeks to give form, focus, and direction to the participative medium. Yet the justification of the teacher's
efforts to shape processes of learningful participation cannot be found
primarily in the intrinsic satisfactions of the school. The teacher is
granted authority only by virtue of efforts to mediate between the
present community involvements of those being educated and their
expanding and deepening affiliations in the common life of a wider
community, and their fundamental interest in growing up into free
and responsible men and women.[3]

It is the traditional bases of community that the advance of our
technological civilization has destroyed. The rebuilding of open,
future- rather than past-oriented communities of inquiry to sustain
the continued growth of people has not been a high priority. In education, the focus has been on the development of special skills and

knowledges, because people with highly specialist mentalities have ordinarily been put in charge of curricular planning. Even when the need for *general* education has been recognized, it has usually been handled by requirements that students study with *specialists* outside the students' own major field of specialization for some percentage of their course work. Or it has been conceived as a need for a smattering of *general knowledge* of humankind, nature, and society drawn in diluted form from various specialities. Rarely has the need been interpreted as a need for people to live and be in a community of developing persons—of various ages, backgrounds, cultures, life-styles, and moral and religious outlooks—as each together with others inquires into the meaning of being a human person, a man or woman, today and tomorrow, in our increasingly interdependent but increasingly segregated and alienated world. Learning in such a setting comes primarily from the experience of building a community and from trying to understand what happens to self and to other selves in the process. The learning uses specialist knowledges and skills, of course, but uses them to face and meet the choices and dilemmas of community building and living. Such education, if widely practiced, might very well undermine the Faustian educational system and the unexamined authority of expertise and of bureaucratic rules of the game, as well as the larger social and political system from which the educational system draws its models and support.

Community, in a normative sense of that term—as an association of people, mutually and reciprocally involved with each other, caring for each other, aware of the human effects of their actions upon those within and outside the association, committed to being responsible for these effects—is dangerously missing both in our institutions of formal education and in the society that environs those institutions. The resistance of the bureaucrat and the expert notwithstanding, a validly authoritative education must become committed to building and utilizing community both in places set apart for learning the arts of living, loving, knowing, choosing, working, and playing, and also in other parts of society not focally responsible for the "education" of people. The range of reeducative community must, in idea at least, extend to the inclusion of all humankind in its scope.

IS IT POSSIBLE TO BUILD VALID AUTHORITY RELATIONS IN TODAY'S SCHOOLS AND COLLEGES?

The fact that we now possess the power to destroy our lives and the lives of all other human beings on earth constitutes the essential moral plight of contemporary humankind. The responsibility for bringing this power into the service of common human purposes and values is a human responsibility. Tradition alone cannot direct people toward the good of human survival. The idea of progress, conceived of as the development of an ever more refined and powerful technology, continually replenished by scientific research, has betrayed us. If there is to be a viable future for humankind, those now alive must invent and create it.

The task of reeducation for modern humankind involves major reconstruction of traditional normative orientations and the creation of new value orientations more apt to the purposes of human survival. There can be no technological solution to this task. Only the sustained and dialogic deliberations of human persons, cutting across various extant lines of human segregation and cleavage, and addressed to the resolution of conflicting views of what human beings should come to do and be, can accomplish rehumanization and moral regeneration.

Our present system of schooling and education is inadequate for this task of reeducation because it operates under the authority of technical expertise, reinforced by the authority of a functionally rationalized organization of work and learning. It has largely forsaken the arduous tasks of general and civic education and reeducation. Its priorities and its social organization must be radically altered if it is to accept the authority of community as its basis of operation. I do not know whether our institutions of formal education will successfully achieve this reorientation, but we should make the effort.

The outlines of the authority relations now required in education become clearer through a probing of three major difficulties confronted by educators as they try to locate and build a community adequate to our contemporary moral plight.

Uncertainty About the Future

We do not know the shape of the future society in which we as educators, along with those we are helping to educate, are moving. We can be sure that it will be different from the society and culture that shaped our own development, and from the society and culture in which we, along with our colleagues and students, are now enmeshed. The traditions of the past and the "realities" of the present offer us suggestions. However, they cannot provide any certain grounding for our authority as educators.

The unpredictability and ambiguity that color all attempts to anticipate the future are frightening and anxiety-producing. We should acknowledge and accept our fear and anxiety. Such acknowledgment and acceptance are a first step toward the wise exercise of educational authority, whether as bearers or as subjects.

But uncertainty and ambiguity are conditions of hope as well as of fear and anxiety. An open future is one in which our aspirations for a better society can make a difference in shaping a culture that is still to be formed, partly through our own decisions and efforts. Human beings must now invent their future, and it is in the context of this project that educational authorities can help others to acquire the disciplines needed to create a more desirable way of life, one that can take into account both the validity of different cultures and life-styles as well as the overarching needs of human survival.

Of course, our knowledge of some matters is more trustworthy than our knowledge of others. It is wrong, however, to build our contemporary curriculum around what we now know best. For we can have no prior assurance that what we now know best is what we will most need to know in order to meet the responsibilities of our new historical situation. We must make value judgments about what it is most important for us to learn. And our best knowledge alone cannot automatically determine these judgments for us. Whatever the eventual judgments may be, however, they will affect all of us, and hence the process by which they are made is as important as the nature of the judgments themselves. The process must be communal, involving cooperative thought and dialogue about human issues for which there are no experts. Thus the judgments and the issues must be determined by those engaged in the inquiry, teachers along with students, and the selection of the knowledge most needed must wait upon this determination. It is a determination that must be revised continually by those engaged in learning and teaching, not alone in the light of new knowledge and new technology, but more fundamentally in the light of new human aspirations, new actions, and new evaluations of actions taken. The basis of educational authority will change as the outlines of the community into which men and women, boys and girls, are learning their way are altered in the minds of educators and of those with whom they work. We must honestly acknowledge the fallibility of our authority even as we work to decrease that fallibility.

Conflicts over What Is Desirable

The second difficulty in defining the basis of educational authority arises from the existence of deep and pervasive conflicts among nations and between groups within nations as to what is the desirable shape of future society and culture. This issue is closely linked to the various images of the kinds of personalities that will be required to build and maintain a self-renewing society and culture. Determinations of educational purposes, curricula, organization, and management are bound to be affected by these moral and political conflicts, even though those committed to a technologized society may attempt to discount the importance of such issues.

The current conflicts between clashing utopias and ideologies in and around educational programs and institutions in America—indeed throughout the world—are a sign that denial and suppression of conflict are no longer a viable or desirable strategy for educators. The function of a nontechnical authority is to focus processes of responsible deliberation and inquiry upon the very issues involved in the conflicts. For within these conflicts may be found the alternatives that will guide people in creating a desirable future for themselves. However, the method of learning from conflict presupposes that the status and prestige of parties to the conflict are equalized, and it presupposes too that some people are available to encourage sustained communication among the partisans. It also presupposes that conflicting feelings and partisan attitudes are respected, that such differences are recognized as part of the materials to be utilized and reconstructed within the processes of conjoint learning, and that part of the outcome of the dialogue is a commonly accepted commitment by all parties to deal with each other in mutually respectful ways, as members of a human community. Wielders of educational authority must learn to support others who differ, as they learn together to build community out of conflict. In other words, educators must seek to use conflicts of value and interest openly and responsibly and in a way that is educative both for themselves and for others.

Once the context of a communal educational authority is established, the role of the expert can be reevaluated in terms of its subservience to the purposes to which the communal commitment is directed. When such a reevaluation takes place, it will not be the rules of the game or the pressures generated by a self-serving bureaucracy that will determine the requisite skills and knowledge, but rather the needs generated by the communal process itself.

If communal authority relations are to be built and rebuilt in our disoriented and tension-ridden institutions of education, teachers and administrators must learn to accept conflict as part of the reality of contemporary life. Once such acceptance occurs, the conflict itself can be used to provide a focus and a motivation for the learning process. This requires an orientation to education as dialogically regenerative and reconstructive, not monologically transmissive. Teachers and administrators can learn much of this orientation from each other if they invest themselves in projects of mutual self-reeducation addressed to the meaning of education in our historical period. But part of their reeducation will require them to learn from their students as well.

Whether such learning communities can be designed into the life of the educational institution as a legitimate and accepted part of its mission, and not just as grudging and *ad hoc* accommodation to "trouble-making" students, blacks, women, and utopian professors, is, of course, an open question. The future offers no promises that are independent of the will and efforts of human beings.

Relationships Between Old and Young

The processes will require too that in at least some educational programs younger people validly take the lead. As pointed out in Essay 3, Margaret Mead (1970) has noted that the upsurge of youthful rebellion and protest against established ways of life and education is worldwide in scope. Its occurrence in capitalist, socialist, and communist countries, and in both technologically developed and developing societies, discourages explanations in terms of the injustices and inequities of particular forms of economic and political organization alone. The increase in tension between generations suggests to her that a turning around of human culture and of human enculturation is now underway on a worldwide scale. She believes we are on the threshold of a world culture still largely to be built—a world culture in which traditional forms of human enculturation have become outmoded.

We have already moved, in fact if not in idea and ideal, from a post-figurational culture, in which people sought and found ways of handling their present and future by lessons learned in and from the past, to a pre-figurational one. At the least, we need to develop patterns of education in which old and young learn to collaborate in inventing and reinventing a future that none of us can predict in any detail, but that will retain continuities with traditional cultures. The pattern of authority must become a collaboration of equals. A rigid hierarchy of old over young or of young over old will not work. We elders must accept the fact that, at times, those younger than us are closer than we are to the authentic pulsebeat of the future as it reveals itself in the present. And this applies to the most prestigious and doughty wielder of technical expertise. At such times, we must learn to put ourselves under the educational authority of the young without losing our self-esteem.

The temptation of teachers and administrators may be to reject the very conception of authority as I have tried to develop it. Many will continue to seek adequate bases of authority in modernized and refined or perhaps in refurbished traditional rules and codes, or in the invention and use of ever more powerful and specialized expertise. There is nothing wrong with refined rules or specialized expertise. We need and will continue to need both. But unless both can be placed in the service of the claims of a more fundamental moral, communal authority, still largely to be created, education will fall victim to a process increasingly alienated from the central dilemmas of human beings in a strange and novel world.

Whether or not such tasks will actually be accomplished is now impossible to say, but, if progress is possible, it will arise not as a blessing of history, but out of the will and effort of human beings.

Our civilization is a Faustian one. The salvation of Faustus, his restoration to membership in the human community, came through the utilization of his unusual technical power for humanely constructive purposes—the draining of the swamps. The angels chanted, as they carried the restored soul of Faustus to his eternal reward, "Whose restless striving never ceases, him we have power to save." And so too, perhaps, may come the salvation of humankind in contemporary times.

5 · The Idea of a
University in 2000 C.E.

[Newman's] "Idea of a University" was a village with its priests. The "Idea of a Modern University" [Flexner's dream] was a town—a one-industry town—with its intellectual oligarchy. The "Idea of the Multiversity" is a city of infinite variety. Some get lost in the city; some rise to the top within it; most fashion their lives within one of its many sub-cultures. There is less sense of community than in the village. . . . There is less sense of purpose than within the town. . . . As against village and town, the "city" is more like the totality of civilization as it has evolved.
. . . and movement to and fro from the surrounding society has been greatly accelerated.   Clark Kerr
The Uses of the University

IN THE PREFACE TO THIS BOOK, a distinction was made between "prophecy" and "foretelling." It is as a "prophet," not as a "foreteller," that I describe and criticize today's universities in America and project an idea of a university for the future. A prophet is always possessed of convictions that impel him or her to undertake the risks of prophecy. Responsible prophets try to make their convictions clear as they prophesy. A quotation from Alfred North Whitehead (1954) expresses one of my basic convictions concerning an essential function of any university worthy of that name.

> The universities are schools of education, and schools of research. But the primary reason for their existence is not to be found either in the mere knowledge conveyed to the students or in the mere opportunities for research afforded to the members of the faculty.
>
> Both these functions could be performed at a cheaper rate, apart from these very expensive institutions. . . .
>
> The justification for a university is that it preserves the connection between knowledge and the zest for life, by uniting the young and the old in the imaginative consideration of learning. The university imparts information, but it imparts it imaginatively. At least, this is the function which it should perform for society. This atmosphere of excitement, arising from imaginative consideration, transforms knowledge. A fact is no longer a bare fact: it is invested with all its possibilities. It is no longer a burden on the memory: it is energizing as the poet of our dreams, and as the architect of our purposes. (p. 93)

We may embrace Mr. Whitehead's justification of the university as an expensive, zestful, and responsible community shaped for "the imaginative consideration of learning"—a learning disciplined to fact and logic but stretching imaginatively into the construction of objects of aspiration and commitment—dreams and purposes, both personal and social. I do embrace it. But we need not and should not accept uncritically the "representative anecdote" out of which Whitehead's idea arose. For this is the residential teaching university, after the traditional British model—a place where the young met the old in various campus relationships. To accept it uncritically would be to prejudice, by default, the place of professional functions and extension functions, along with research and general teaching functions, within the university. I believe that all of these activities properly belong to that institution today. The unfinished intellectual and reconstructive task is to achieve a meaningful interrelationship among these functions.

Can't Mr. Whitehead's "imaginative consideration of learning" be extended meaningfully to the creation and construction of new learnings out of the disciplined, imaginative, and dialogic interplay between older learnings and new experiences? And doesn't this define what research and scholarship, shorn of mystique and technical apparatus, are as human enterprises? That the "imaginative consideration of learning" in research and scholarship is often limited to participation by members of some specialist community makes their processes no less or no more "imaginative" than the ideally more inclusive references of learning processes in general or liberal education. These specialist activities furnish the "facts" that men and women employ in liberal education in energizing and testing the poetry of their dreams and the architecture of their purposes. Productive research and scholarship, therefore, belong in the university. Questions concerning their proper interrelations with its teaching mission set some of that institution's severest contemporary problems. But "solving" these problems by eliminating an element essential to their adequate solution is a "solution" in name only.

I feel we must stretch Mr. Whitehead's criterion to include the extension activities and the professional school programs of the university. Here, as with specialized research and scholarship, the stretching of the criterion is not designed to bless all activities now carried on in extension or professional school programs as essential to the life of a university or contributory to its central purpose. Ideally, the aim of professional and extension programs is to infuse the university's spirit of imaginative rationality into the surrounding culture and society. The aim at the same time is to bring considerations of human need and importance into the policy deliberations and decisions of the university. For only in the arenas of practice and action is the criterion of "human need and importance" given substance, if not form, just as truly as the idea of "objective and valid knowledge" finds its operational definition most adequately in responsible research and scholarship. The university must hold together in some meaningful, working, though frequently conflicting unity the criterion of "human need and importance," the criterion of "objective and valid knowledge," and the criterion of the "imaginative consideration of learning," in deciding what it should be and do. Professional and extension programs are required to make this trifocal vision possible.

Mr. Whitehead expressed his vision of the essential function of the university before nuclear bombs were dropped on Hiroshima and Nagasaki. The survival of the human species on earth has become problematic. This human condition now requires not the abandonment of Mr. Whitehead's emphasis on the university's function in the "imaginative consideration of learning" but rather its refocusing and intensification. It is appropriate that Karl Jaspers (1962), who has argued most cogently that the future of the university is now intertwined with the future of humankind, should express this added conviction, which I wholeheartedly accept.

> Scientific research, performance of technological service, recollection of the past, formative participation in what is handed down, all this is excellent, but it is not enough. For the calm that is allowed at the university exists so that we may experience the storm of world events in our hearts and thoughts in order to understand it. The university ought to be the place where there is the clearest consciousness of the age, where that which is uttermost attains clarity, be it that in one spot at least, full consciousness of what is taking place is achieved, be it that this clarity, working out into the world, shall provide assistance. (p. 40)

I have said enough already to indicate that I accept the current incorporation of general teaching functions, of specialized research and scholarly functions (along with the training of new specialists), and of professional and extension functions, in the education of professionals; in extramural consultation, teaching, and service; and in applied research. All are potential contributors to the consciousness-raising missions that Whitehead and Jaspers see as essential to the work of a university in today's world.

But, for the most part, these diverse functions are segregated and compartmentalized in the operation of contemporary American universities. The sustained communication, in collaboration and in meaningful encounter, between the diverse human parts of the university are not cultivated, encouraged, or rewarded. Universities have become multiversities, to use the term coined by Clark Kerr in his honest, eloquent, factually accurate, but, to me, deeply discouraging book, *The Uses of the University* (1964). I deplore the fragmentation and segregation of specialized persons, groups, and roles, which tend to characterize both the conception and organization of research and teaching functions in the contemporary multiversity. I object to the lack of continuing attention to the development of a common purpose and tone that might infuse its varied, specialized functions. This lack tends at once to reduce to a dangerous minimum significant internal communication concerning questions of aim and responsibility and to dissipate the effective impact of the university as an institution upon its social and cultural environment. I am saddened by the inability of many university people to think dialectically about conflicts of viewpoint and interest, in which they are inescapably involved within the university, and so to use conflict to create deeper community and broader vision within and among themselves and their colleagues, including students. In an ideal university, students are not customers or clients, but junior colleagues. I am brought almost to despair by administrators and faculty members who identify the quest for community within university life with the suppression of differences, who oppose "cooperation" to "academic freedom," and who confuse the voice of outside fund-granting, contracting, and accrediting agencies with the voice of wisdom at best, and with the voice of historic inevitability, whether wise or not, at worst.

THE ROOTS OF FRAGMENTATION IN THE CONTEMPORARY MULTIVERSITY

For those who would change the contemporary multiversity into a university, wailing and deploring are of little effect. What is needed is a clear-headed diagnosis of factors and forces that contribute to the prevailing confusion, fragmentation, and lack of community. The factors diagnosed must be aspects of multiversity life that are capable of reconstruction by serious and devoted human efforts, not those grounded in historic inevitability, as analysts like Clark Kerr assume most of them to be.

I find the roots of fragmentation in three kinds of conditions. The first lies in an unresolved and frequently unacknowledged confusion of aim and image for the university. The second inheres in a radically inappropriate form of social organization of university life and effort. The third stems from pressures from outside agencies and organizations on universities to focus their energies and resources upon goals important to the outsiders and, in the process, to fragment university effort and divert universities from focusing and committing their energies toward the service of their own distinctive mission. I will discuss each of these kinds of fragmenting factors in turn and recommend some possible directions for reconstructive efforts.

First, what of the confusion with respect to aim and image? In the course of its evolution, American higher education has professed three distinctly different basic ideas of a university. One of these may be represented by John Henry (Cardinal) Newman's (1901) idea of a university as a place for liberal learning; a second has been clarified by Abraham Flexner (1930) in his notion of "the modern university" as an organization for the stimulation and support of rigorous, specialized, and objective research and scholarship; the third emerged from the distinctively American vision of the land-grant extension university (Nevins, 1962). These ideas have never been integrated into the thinking and valuations of university men and women concerning university policy and practice. The fact that these ideas have not been fully integrated but operate in uneasy and unstable compromise, with their proponents distributed unevenly in various parts of the university system, serves to produce and maintain the multiversity that today masquerades under the name of university.

When I mention Cardinal Newman's idea of a university as a current influence upon the thinking of administrators, faculty members, or students, I do not mean that most of these people have studied Newman's writings and been influenced directly by them. (I might wish that more university people had read and discussed his idea in relation to currently and historically contrasting and competing ideas about university education. In fact, I consider it a scandal that so few of those whose lives are intimately bound up with an institution have studied its history, its conflicting utopias and ideologies, and its shifting interconnections with its environing society and culture. From a liberal education point of view, ignorance of education has never seemed to me a virtue in those who direct it, participate in it, and live by it. Indeed, this ignorance, which is, I believe, widespread, may be the source of at least some of the multiversities' current confusions and difficulties.) I refer, rather, when I speak of Newman's idea of a university as an influence upon American higher education, to the living, though now highly attenuated, tradition of liberal learning out of which Newman's thought emerged as an articulation, clarification, and reconstruction of the idea underlying that university tradition. The tradition still flows through the minds and persons of some men and women in American universities, however it was communicated to them, and shapes their views of what is right and proper for a university to do or not to do. (And so it will be when I speak of Flexner as an influence or were I to speak particularly of Cornell, James, Patterson, or some other pioneer in the "land-grant" tradition.)

Newman's (1901) university was essentially a teaching institution. But Newman did not seek for his students a mechanical accumulation of knowledge as informational matter. His aim was a general intellectual proficiency, and he spoke of persistent habits of mind as the goal of instruction. His university-educated man (Newman lived before the women's liberation movement) apprehends the great outline of knowledge, the principles on which it rests, the scale of its parts, its lights and shades, its great points and its little, as he otherwise cannot apprehend them. Hence it is that his education is called "liberal." A habit of mind is formed which lasts through life, of which the attributes are freedom, equitableness, calmness, moderation and wisdom; or what in a former Discourse I have ventured to call a philosophical habit. This then I would assign as the special fruit of the education furnished at a university, as contrasted with other places of teaching or modes of teaching. (pp. 101–102)

The enlargement of mind that Newman sought required thoughtful activity and participation by the student—"a making the objects of our knowledge subjectively our own . . . a digestion of what we receive into the substance of our previous state of thought" (p. 109). Enlargement and illumination come not through mere additions to previous knowledge but through "a comparison of ideas one with another."

A truly great intellect . . . is one which takes a connected view of old and new, past and present, far and near, and which has an insight into the influence of all these one on another; without which there is no whole, and no centre. It possesses the knowledge, not only of things, but also of their mutual and true relations. (p. 135)

Newman's idea may be criticized from many viewpoints—a faulty psychology, a focus upon past knowledge (the past of the West, at that) as the exclusive basis of wisdom, and ignorance of the overwhelming inundation by specialized information, which our recent knowledge explosion has heaped upon us. Yet, for me at least, his question remains central. Can a university maintain integrity and effectiveness as an institution if it forsakes the quest for the interrelated meaning of various branches of knowledge and the cultivation of persons able to see these relationships and use them in their thinking and choosing, difficult as the quest and the cultivation may be? Or does a university that has forsaken this quest tend to become a loose collection of competing departments, schools, and technical institutes, largely noncommunicating because of a multiplicity of specialist jargons and interests?

The second image of the university as an institution devoted to the production of new knowledge through specialized research and scholarship and to the selection and training of new crops of specialized researchers and scholars had its origin in Germany during the nineteenth century. It was the Johns Hopkins University, founded in Baltimore in 1876, that first freshly institutionalized the German model in this country. Graduate studies, research, and scholarship were its *raison d'etre*. Undergraduate instruction was an appendage to the basic structure of the university. But Abraham Flexner may be seen as the prophet of the idea of a "modern" university in America, just as Johns Hopkins was its pioneering institution here. Daniel Coit Gilman, first president of that institution, was a culture hero for Flexner, and Flexner (1930) called the founding of Johns Hopkins the most stimulating influence that higher education in America had ever known. What Flexner found stimulating was that the modern university does not set itself apart from the main currents of social evolution. It does not contemplate historic knowledge in the round, seeking to shape out of such contemplation minds capable of sound and balanced judgment in a changing world. It places itself within the stream of changing knowledge, stimulating it, supporting it, adding to it.

> I am undertaking . . . to discuss the idea of a modern university. In the word 'modern' I am endeavoring to indicate in the most explicit fashion that a University is not outside the general social fabric of a given era. . . . It is not something apart, something historic, something that yields as little as possible to forces and influences that are more or less new. It is on the contrary . . . an expression of the age, as well as an influence operating upon both present and future. (p. 3)

The university was ideally, for Flexner, "an institution consciously devoted to the pursuit of knowledge, the solution of problems, the critical appreciation of achievement and the training of men [sic] at a really high level" (p. 42). Because no individual could master even one subject, excellence was measurable only in specialist terms. For Flexner, Newman's liberally educated person was a figment from an outmoded past.

Yet, even as Flexner wrote in 1930, he found much in American universities that he deplored and that he thought had no place there. Those deplorable activities came not from a dead past but rather out of the immersion of the university in its time and place, an immersion that, in idea, he seemed to favor.

> A genuine university is, I have urged, an organism, characterized by highness and definiteness of aim, unity of spirit and purpose.

But it is quite obvious that the institutions which we have used for purposes of illustration (Harvard, Columbia, Wisconsin among others)—the best that we possess—are not organisms: they are merely administrative aggregations, so varied, so manifold, so complex that administration itself is reduced to budgeting, student accounting, advertising, etc. Such aggregations, even though called universities, simply do not possess scientific or educational policy, embodied in some appropriate form. In connection with them it is absurd to speak of ideals. They are secondary schools, vocational schools, teacher-training schools, research centers, "uplift" agencies, businesses—these and other things simultaneously. In the reckless effort to expand, and thus to cater to various demands, the university as an organic whole has disintegrated. . . . Their centres are the treasurer's office, into which income flows, out of which expenditures issue, and the office of the registrar who keeps the roll. (p. 179)

So Flexner's university, like Newman's, would have boundaries to sustain it over and against the society in which it functioned and to support university people in developing an organic community of purpose. But his principles of exclusion and inclusion were different from Newman's. Actually two principles of selectivity operated in Flexner's thought in his determination of which activities belonged in the university and which did not. The first stemmed from his strong positivist faith in research science as the best hope for the future of humankind in a complex and divided world. He voted strongly for one of C. P. Snow's two cultures—the scientific. It is true that he paid homage to the humanistic disciplines, but these too for him had to become "research" disciplines if they were to merit a place in his "modern" university.

Flexner's ideas, whatever his broader intent, have done much to confirm the positivist, scientistic temper in the modern American multiversity, where this temper still reigns supreme in most graduate schools and in many graduate departments. The specialized research contribution of the "modern" university has been stupendously impressive and valuable. As industrial and government elites have become convinced of the power implicit in abstract scientific findings, they have moved to erect a "scientific establishment" in which men and women from the graduate schools and research institutes of universities play a major role. The grant system through which the efforts of such scientists have been purchased, supported, and rewarded has put powerful stresses and strains upon the integrity of universities as social systems. Various internal strains have increased—strains between undergraduate education, graduate training, and research; strains between the sciences and the humanities; strains between the graduate disciplines and the applied schools and extension services. And, as the university has acquiesced more or less uncritically in the benevolences of the grant system, the quest for unifying the meanings within our proliferating knowledges and within the processes of their utilization has become more and more neglected and unrewarded. Yet this quest alone can restore a greater measure of integrity to the university and, indirectly, to its environing culture.

The other principle of selection for Flexner grew out of his conviction that it was the service motivation of the university—the desire of its administration and some members of its faculties to assume responsibility for helping solve the problem of various segments of our heterogeneous society—that threatened the integrity of the university in America. Flexner believed that the university must be at once free, relevant, and *irresponsible* in its response to social and political problems in its environment.

Flexner doubted that a university could serve responsibly the agencies of a divided and fragmented society, with the various moral and practical values that these agencies stand for, and remain true to its own central values of truth-finding and truth-telling. In remaining faithful to its own central "pure research" values, it must be irresponsible toward the conflicting practical values that define the problems of the world outside the university. Ideally, institutions, persons, and groups in the world outside the university must remain *subjects* of university-managed studies and experiments. If they are to become *collaborators* with university people in solving problems, truth value must fall victim in the process of collaboration, or so Flexner seemed to believe.

Does collaboration between universities and outside agencies necessarily mean working on the terms of the outside agency? Cannot the university maintain its autonomy within processes of responsible collaboration with other agencies of its society? Can other agencies acquire augmented respect and commitment to the values of truth-finding and truth-telling, to the values of intelligence, in dealing with conflicts and problems—values for which the university uniquely stands? Indeed, can these intellectual values permeate the society of the university without its responsible collaboration, on *jointly* defined terms, with other agencies of the society in attempts to clarify, understand, and solve social problems? Can university-based social scientists get the data they need for developing valid theories of social processes from the vantage point of irresponsible observers alone? Or must they learn to talk and walk and work with nonuniversity men and women and keep their distinctive virtue? Did Flexner adequately assess the sources of fragmentation within university life in attributing these almost exclusively to the pressures of the fragmented society upon the university? Or are there divisive and fragmenting forces operating within the life of learning itself, as he conceived it, which must be faced and dealt with directly?

These questions must be faced and answered as we work out more adequate answers than Flexner was able to imagine concerning proper relationships between the university and the powers and principalities of its social environment. But adequate answers must embody Flexner's dogged conviction that the university must build and maintain its own distinctive community of values if it is sanely to make its desperately needed contributions to contemporary society.

Some, at least, of the applied educational and research activities that Flexner found inconsequential and incredibly absurd in university settings were given a legitimate place in higher education through the idea of the land-grant university. This is the third major idea that the contemporary American university holds together in uneasy and unstable compromise with the two other ideas already discussed. The idea of a university that emerged out of the Morrill Act of 1862—an act that granted land to state colleges and/or universities for establishing instruction in agriculture and mechanic arts—was both revolutionary and basically American in its conception of the higher learning. It was an idea rooted in populist democracy, whereas the ideas already considered were elitist in origin and conception, however differently they defined qualifications for members of their elites (see Nevins, 1962). Morrill himself, Cornell, James, Patterson, along with many other pioneers in the land-grant tradition, conceived of a higher learning available to all young men and eventually to all young women as well, whatever their social class or place or origin—a learning opportunity limited ideally only by their capacity for and interest in learning. It weakened the barrier against equality for women in higher education.

The idea was democratic in another sense. In admitting agriculture and mechanic arts into the circle of university studies, the land-grant idea broke the hold of classic humanistic disciplines and of the new basic research sciences that were elbowing their way into the university as primary subjects of university concern and responsibility.

The land-grant idea of a university democratized the higher

learning in still another way as the idea evolved. The democratization stemmed from the removal of the age barrier to participation in learning under university auspices. The Agricultural Extension Service is our most notable example of this democratization. It grew out of an effort to speed the adoption and wider testing of new knowledge through providing opportunities for continuing education of adults, off and on campuses, to become consumers and producers of the fruits of new knowledge-based practices. It opened up in turn a way of making known to university teachers and researchers the needs of populations previously distant from the university.

With its emphasis on service to the society outside, the land-grant university weakened the boundaries of the university and invited influences from the outside to shape university policies and programs.

THE ROAD TOWARD RECONCILIATION OF AIM AND IMAGE

If Newman's idea still offers hope and direction to some of the members of the university devoted to undergraduate education and if Flexner's idea still furnishes a major rationale for devotees of graduate education and of university research, the land-grant idea is perhaps most alive in those responsible for the professional and extension programs of the university, in many alumni and other clients of continuing university services, and in students who come to the university to improve their nonacademic vocational skills and to elevate their social status. Are there ways to use the tensions among these various parts of the multiversity to press toward some defensible and rational reconciliation of these divergent ideas that can lend greater integrity to university life? It cannot be a unity purchased at any price. It must be an integrity that accepts variety and difference in orientation, profession, and discipline as a positive value rather than a disvalue. It must be an integrity achieved through deep, honest, and continuing dialogue concerning the central mission of the university. And this dialogue must accept the fact that serious discussion of the way toward greater integrity within the university is inseparable in idea from serious discussion of the way toward greater integrity in our national and world society. The university alone, among our institutions, has the range of intellectual resources required to develop rationales for a more effectively integrated larger society and culture. But, in order to utilize these resources with optimum effectiveness in the larger task, it must look seriously toward justifiable bases for its own integrity. It is important that we see both tasks as intertwined.

To accept the multiplicity of muted and anomic voices within the university—voices that speak of different hopes and different despairs for the future of the university and of human society and culture more generally—and to seek to join these voices in significant dialogue is itself to achieve a considerable step toward integration. If the necessary thoughtful and continuing dialogue is released and supported—a dialogue concerning the ideas and ideals that best give meaning to the university—this is in itself a partial realization of the university's educational function. Men and women engaged in the dialogue will need to raise and deal freshly, imaginatively, and responsibly with questions concerning the nature of knowledge, of wisdom, and of the relations between the two; concerning the idea of the educated person; concerning the relations among the creative arts, the humanities, and the sciences and technologies in higher education; concerning the relationships between knowledge and society; concerning the social, moral, and intellectual responsibilities of men and women of knowledge; concerning the ways in which knowledge can be most wisely applied and utilized in action; concerning the relations of university study to the major human issues of our time—issues of race relations and human rights, issues of war and peace, issues of automation, employment, unemployment and leisure, ethical issues concerning bio-engineering, to name just a few. In thus joining serious dialogue concerning the idea of a university, the university will at once be furnishing a fundamental educational experience to the participants in that dialogue and be moving toward more common bases for decisions about policy and programs.

Students, faculty members, members of the administration, alumni, and public representatives should be involved in this continuing dialogue. The widest divergence of viewpoint and orientation should be included in the groups organized to support it. Status and prestige should be relaxed within the processes of intellectual exchange and moral encounter that will characterize the dialogue. The dialogue should take place on university time. If necessary, academic credit should be given to students for participation, and "merit badge" points for pay increases and promotions to participating faculty members. What I am recommending is that the effort, if undertaken at all, be taken seriously and that the external badges that publicly define the university's conventional system of rewards must attach to it if the effort is to be taken seriously, at least in the beginning. If we can believe that the future of the university, not to mention the future of humankind, is at stake in such study and discussion, we must take them very seriously.

What I am suggesting can be stated in still another way. The achievement of greater integrity requires serious study by university people of university education. This is long overdue. I do not mean primarily a study of pedagogy or anthropogogy in its restricted sense of teaching methodology, although such study has been neglected by most university people. I mean rather a serious and informed dialogue concerning the possible and desirable bases of contemporary and future university life in its deepest and widest ramifications. I do not know the best way of meeting the practical problems involved in beginning such a study—how many should be included initially, how they should organize themselves for their work, how they should seek to communicate their findings to their colleagues, the resources they will need as they proceed. But these problems can be solved if there is a will to solve them.

What is the spirit in which the study should be undertaken? It is the spirit expressed in the letter from a wise Roman Catholic priest to George Bernard Shaw concerning his play, *St. Joan.* Shaw (1951) quotes from this letter in his preface to the play.

> In your play I see the dramatic presentation of the conflict of the Regal, Sacerdotal and Prophetical powers, in which Joan was crushed. To me it is not victory of any one of them over the other that will bring peace and the Reign of the Saints in the Kingdom of God, but their fruitful interaction in a costly and noble state of tension. (pp. 780–781)

THE BUREAUCRATIC ORGANIZATION OF THE UNIVERSITY

We may accept "the fruitful interaction [of different and opposed viewpoints and powers] in a costly and noble state of tension" as the way toward greater integrity in university life and learning. But the practical questions raised when we attempt to translate the idea into action are, in some large measure, questions of social and human organization. How do we cross departmental and school lines in such a dialogue? Out of whose budget will the needed funds come? Will participants be able to exchange ideas fully across lines of differential status and prestige, vertical and horizontal? How can students get credit for participation in such an activity, if a course number is not assigned and if differential grades are not awarded?

The feasibility and, I fear, the desirability of any new departure from university practice are often judged more in terms of the effects of the departure upon the existing organization of its social system than in terms of the effects as measured against other, less parochial criteria. What is done by way of a proposal for university education and research is always determined both by the social organization of the university, its ways of classifying and grouping personnel, its rules and regulations, and its internal and external pyramids of power, and by the merits and demerits of the concepts and rationales that define and justify the proposal when taken as an object of thought and choice.

Communal wrestling with fundamental issues of university aim and purpose is hampered by the bureaucratic organization that has come to characterize the social organization of most, indeed almost all, American multiversities.[1] The attempt to bureaucratize intellectual life in contemporary university organization has no doubt stemmed from many sources. Whatever its sources, it has made the struggle for individual achievement a major motivation in stimulating, energizing, and evaluating both faculty and student efforts. The task of the university is conceived as a productive factory or, better, a conglomerate. Faculty members are treated, graded, and advanced on the basis of quantifiable evidences of productive achievement. And, since more intangible, qualitative, slow-maturing contributions are harder to measure and reward than tangible, quantitative, quickly produced contributions, the latter are frequently made the basis of tangible reward in salary, promotion, and preferment. Competition, rather than cooperation, among faculty departments and between faculty members is stimulated by the system.

Because faculty members are, legally as well as in certain crucial role relationships, employees, they are not encouraged except by special inducements to become responsibly involved in the life of the institution beyond the special jobs for which they are hired. They tend to deploy their energies in a way to increase their marketability in university jobs or in other better paid employment. Faculty members tend to avoid the burdens of deep emotional commitment to work for the institution, which by definition they do not own, and of deep investment of themselves in teaching students. These burdens of involvement become fetters to mobility in employment. Rather, faculty members tend to invest their talent and energy in negotiable wares— publications and other more or less quantifiable evidences of contributions to their fields—which can be easily transferred to other employment situations and are widely and easily negotiable throughout the academic marketplace, much as the sojourner in a hostile country often converts assets from real estate into diamonds in order to facilitate a quick getaway across the border.

The work of the university enterprise is highly departmentalized. For work purposes chemists are grouped together, botanists together, sociologists together. Thus when group loyalties do grow despite the generally prevailing atmosphere of individual competition, the faculty member's allegiance is invited to attach itself to the advancement of his or her discipline or subdiscipline rather than to wider projects of intellectual, moral, and academic concern. A positivistic orientation helps to rationalize this neglect of extra-departmental or cross-disciplinary problems by questioning their significance and by ascribing "real" meaning only to those questions that can be solved within the framework of a particular science or discipline.

All of us know about the organization of centers in universities—centers formed to study problems that do not fall readily into departmental pigeonholes. There are over 40 of these at the University of Michigan, and nearly 100 within the University of California system. The very movement of live thought demands the breaching of the conventional lines of university organization. New miscegenated disciplines—biochemistry, nuclear studies, clinical psychology, social psychology, communications, biostatistics, to mention only a few— emerge to handle problems, the study of which is thwarted by established departmental boundaries. Such efforts, whether organized for research or teaching or both, must struggle with the established system for acceptance within the university. Some fall by the wayside. And these are not always ones that would be deemed intellectually or morally inadequate when judged by more "objective" criteria. Others congeal into new departments in order to survive in the struggle for budget and status in the university, and, in the process, often lose the burst of vision and concern that gave them birth. Others seek and find support from grant sources outside the university. And allegiance tends, in these cases, to be transferred to these grant sources and their purposes rather than to find a meaningful anchorage within the university system.

I have, of course, overstated the degree to which the bureaucratic spirit has encompassed life in the university. This spirit is at so many points antithetical to the life of learning, whether in the form of research, scholarship, or imaginative and comprehensive teaching, that countervailing forces, as we have seen, must be set up against it by men and women genuinely devoted to learning. When I think of this condition, I am always reminded of two lines from one of George Santayana's sonnets (1939a):

As in the crevices of Caesar's tomb,
The sweet herbs flourish on their little earth. (p. 1248)

Centers for tackling larger and more significant problems than departmental organization can readily encompass do emerge and, in some instances, survive in creativity. Men and women do band together to develop programs of general education that make Whitehead's "imaginative consideration of learning" more nearly possible for students. Faculty members do make devoted investments of themselves in teaching and in work on problems of university construction and reconstruction. Some remnant of the old guild organization of scholars manifests itself in tenure systems for professors and in the establishment and operation of university senates and faculty unions. The sweet herbs do flourish in the crevices of Caesar's tomb.

But the following questions seem pertinent to me. Why, if bureaucratic organization, as I have defined it, does operate often to defeat the self-professed purposes of a university and to thwart the development in it of a pervasive common purpose and to render difficult devoted communal effort on its behalf, why do we keep it? Why do we not invent and experiment with new organizational forms for channeling, supporting, and rewarding the pursuits of learning more humanely, more effectively, and, yes, more productively than now they are typically channeled, supported, and rewarded? This cannot mean a return to the guild organization of the faculty or of students, which prevailed in medieval universities. But this guild system had its values, which are maintained only with great effort today—effort that diverts scholars from the exciting and pressing tasks of scholarship and teaching. Can we not invent organizational forms that support these values along with new values realizable only within the city and not within the village or town of intellect? The resources for doing this creative task are now distributed in the various faculties. If men and women of the university cannot invent a human organization that is intellectually responsible, knowledge-based, and morally sensitive to the conditions of our time—dynamic yet stable in its changing—how can we expect other parts of our society to make such inventions for themselves? And this type of organization is needed throughout our fragmented, conflict-ridden, bureaucratized national and world society. The university should demonstrate the possibility and desirability of such organization as well as develop and communicate ideas about it, as some of its divisions now do.

Students fare no better than faculty members in the bureaucratization of the intellectual life, if my criterion for faring well in the imaginative consideration of learning is applied. The story of the Harvard students who invented an imaginary student, got him registered, took his examinations, wrote his papers, and nearly got him through to graduation before the hoax was discovered, has a real point, whether it is legend or fact. The impersonalization of relationships in the service of effective production, which is part of the valid idea of bureaucracy, can easily become depersonalization in the university, as elsewhere. "Persons" become "personnel," and even when the managers of the institution are kindly in intent in forging and administering personnel policies, the kindness tends to take the form of an exchange between roles rather than an encounter between persons. The identification number and the registrar's record become the units to be "understandingly" managed, rather than the concrete individual student with his or her hopes and fears, despairs and exultations, and lusts and aspirations, or the informal group of individual students, whatever the basis of their grouping. The story of the imaginary student who almost graduated projects the anxiety of students that this depersonalization of relationships, this degradation of persons into manipulable personnel, may actually have come to pass within the operation of the contemporary multiversity.

OUTSIDE PRESSURES TOWARD DISINTEGRITY IN THE UNIVERSITY

I have so far mentioned two sets of factors internal to higher education in America that support and maintain the multiversity and impede efforts to create universities. There are two sets of external influences that also put severe strains upon the dwindling integrity of contemporary multiversities. Although I will discuss these more briefly than I have dealt with the internal factors, this brevity is not an indication of their relative unimportance.

The first of these stems from grants by governments and industrial organizations to university people to do research on problems that are important to the work of the government department or the industrial organization, but that have little or no bearing on the self-chosen work of the university either in its educational or research programs. Though it was sensed by some before that time, it was in World War II that research in the basic sciences and related "high technology" was seen by all to be a potent weapon both in industrial competition and in international warfare. Grants and contracts have become a major distorting factor in multiversity programs in the period since World War II.

There is an important line to be drawn between grants, whether research or training grants, that serve purposes initiated and planned by university people and those that are given to serve purposes initiated and planned by the Department of Defense, the National Institutes of Health, the Commonwealth of Massachusetts, the Roman Catholic Church, or Exxon Corporation. The line is not always easy to draw. But the effects of the latter kind of grant or contract are to reduce the already slender control of the university over its own destiny—to divert it from assuming responsibility for planning and serving its own distinctive mission in clarifying the intellectual and moral quandaries of an imperiled human species.

An important condition in converting multiversities into universities is to refuse grants and contracts of the second sort. Surgery is indicated. You will recall Mr. Whitehead's observation, quoted earlier, that research and specialist training could be done more cheaply and expeditiously in organizations other than universities. Research and training institutes outside universities can be organized to serve the knowledge-building and using purposes of governments and industries more cheaply and with less institutional friction. Members of universities whose motivations and interests are better served by work in such institutes can find employment there. Universities can serve their inquiry needs through grants of the former sort and by block rather than categorical grants from fund sources. The Canadian Government has used block grants to support its universities, public and private, for many years.

The second source of disintegrity is the use of universities as a credentialing agent for entry into the professions. Professions do need some means of accrediting and licensing their members. Usually, some system of examinations or peer review is set up outside universities to serve this purpose, along with governmental licensing. But many professions have virtually prescribed university programs that aspirants to professional membership must follow. The effect is, as in the case of categorical grants, to rob the university, both faculty and students, of control over their own self-chosen learning and inquiry programs and projects. The further effect has been to support and prolong the disease of credentialism, already rampant in our society. Universities tend to become cram schools rather than educational institutions. Students are constrained to depend on extrinsic motivation in directing their learning enterprises, are impelled to work for the external badges of reward—grades and honors—rather than for learning chosen by and for themselves. As a result, they fail to receive help toward self-direction in energizing the poetry of their own dreams and the architecture of their own purposes. The university should reject the credentialing function that has been thrust upon it. Again, surgery is indicated.

Students, of course, will and should study various human problems—some appropriate to social welfare, some to health, some to management and leadership, some to teaching and learning, and some to law. And field experiences will back up and invigorate their academic studies. But ideally they should learn and understand these problems and alternative solutions in the broadly human context of the troubled society and historical period in which they must live as persons and citizens, as well as professionals. Professionals should assume responsibility for credentialing generally "educated" persons seeking to join a profession themselves. An infusion of broadly educated men and women into the professions might offset the narrow technicalization that now often tends to dehumanize the work of "helping" professionals.

A UTOPIAN ALTERNATIVE TO BUREAUCRATIZATION OF THE CITY OF INTELLECT

One principal defense for bureaucratization in university life is the plea of size and numbers. There is no other way, many argue, to handle big faculties, big masses of students, and diverse, expensive, and far-flung projects, except by bureaucratization. There is some merit in this argument, but it is certainly not a final argument.

There are ways of dealing with bigness other than through compartmentalizing effort, depending fundamentally on competition and individual achievement as principal motivators of faculty and students, and the substituting of quantitative evaluation of progress for rounded and qualitative judgments, informed but not dictated by quantitative data. If our purpose of facilitating, energizing, and communicating imaginative and sound learning and understanding of the world in which we live is defeated by the present organization of university effort, then we must invent and test more apt forms of organization.

One answer might be to work out and establish sound units of decentralized teaching and learning within a university—units bringing together diverse disciplinary resources and a limited number of students, undergraduate and graduate students, too, particularly those who wish to become college and university teachers. The persons in the unit will organize themselves around the study of some set of broad human issues. Different units probably will be concerned with different issues. Students and some faculty members in a unit might live in adjacent residences. All will have access to common university facilities—library, laboratories for skill and informational development, and other laboratories and field sites for observation, study, and experimentation. The aim of the unit will be to study, explore, investigate, discuss, and clarify the issues chosen for study in relation to existing relevant knowledge and to new knowledge needed in order to understand the issues fully. Research and original scholarship will be encouraged in its bearings upon the human issue occupying unit members at any one time—whether war and peace, automation and the new leisure, euthanasia, or problems of bioengineering; there is no end to important issues.

The resources of the creative arts, the humanities, philosophy, and theology, as well as the natural and social sciences, will be required in the faculty and student membership of the unit. All members will seek not primarily to master the major fields from which relevant knowledges and insights are drawn but rather to project the meanings of these knowledges and technologies in terms of the possibilities for good and for evil that they entail for human beings in the future, as such knowledges and technologies are worked into the fabric of human living. Facts studied will, as Whitehead and Jaspers suggested, be invested with all, or at least many, of their value possibilities. The outcome sought will not be dead-level agreement. Different individual and subgroup choices and a diversity of orientations will be encouraged and sustained. But it will be required that all choices be illuminated by rational argument and dialogue, by relevant knowledge and insight from whatever sources, and by the projected values implicit in such knowledge as it is imagined in its bearings upon our human future.

This kind of activity will call for a new discipline on the part of the specialized scholars and scientists engaged in it. But it is a discipline that will help them to reconcile their specialized intellectual pursuits with their social and moral responsibilities as persons and as citizens.

Responsible seeking for the value shape of our world in its future trend rather than in its past development is in keeping with our uneasy movement as men and women into a non-tradition-directed world. We rightly say that the alternative to depending on tradition to determine the direction of our future should lie in knowledge. But knowledge that is not illuminated by awareness of the value-possibilities implicit in it, that is not brought into meaningful relationship with living traditions in their future thrusts, furnishes no confident direction for the choices we must make, individually and collectively, in a changing world. A university should illuminate and enlarge, not dictate, the choices of men and women. It should illuminate human choices in a way that honors, respects, and utilizes the knowledge available to persons through ongoing research and scholarship. To do this, living links between the life of knowledge and the nonintellectual, practical-moral-political choices confronting men and women must be forged. The forging of such links requires a refocusing of intellectual effort and a reorganization of the relationships of various kinds and ages of men and women jointly involved in a responsible effort to learn wisdom for the world of today and tomorrow.

We must make certain in our Utopian university unit that older relics of university organization do not intrude upon and destroy the community of imaginative learning that the unit will be working hard to build. Faculty members should be employed with a presumption of tenure, though procedures for termination should be commonly agreed upon and understood. Students should not be expected to either measure up to externally imposed standards of achievement or flunk out. Once admitted, the presumption will be that students will stay and participate, until they are no longer benefiting by life in the community and are ready to move out of the university or into some more specialized academic or professional course of studies. And the students should share with the staff in judgments about separation.

But where is the larger university in this picture of decentralized learning subcommunities within it? A genuine university community might grow out of such neighborhoods of learning. All persons in the university will be required to have a connection with one or another subcommunity, with the amount and character of their involvement in it depending on their responsibilities and on the ingenuity of the unit in finding a place in its life of learning for their special talents. Units will find ways of reporting their findings to other units, and I would hope the full range of symbolic media—prose, poetry, cinema, painting, drama, and dance—will be used in this reporting and that the symbolic adequacy of all members of the unit will be stretched and enlarged in the process. They will find ways of putting their findings into more permanent and retrievable storage for the use of others seeking to illuminate the same human issue. Collected on an inter-university basis, the findings from various teaching-learning units will be contributions to the "museum of the future," which Gardner Murphy (1958) has envisaged.

A museum of the future: a systematic and orderly display of the various potentialities which the future may indeed bring. . . . A study by all the methods of analysis and extrapolation might reveal to us the possible future directions of cosmic and human development . . . The task would be to . . . fill the gaps and at the same time extrapolate in directions suggested by existing trends for upon this possibility intelligent planning depends. . . . The more serious social science predictions, the Utopias, the science fiction of today would all occupy alcoves in such a museum. (p. 273)

Unit representatives will meet to discuss and decide university-wide policies in collaboration with administrators and boards of trustees. Professors and graduate students will rotate between primary involvement in a teaching-learning unit and involvement in special graduate instruction or work in a research institute or in extension assignments. Work in these various assignments will count equally in the awarding of whatever honors, recognitions, and special emoluments the university finds it wise and expedient to grant to its individual members.

Continuing all-university conferences for specialists—faculty members and students—from the same field, though rooted socially in different parts of the university, will provide an opportunity to advance specialist concerns and disciplines. These should serve the valid functions of departments in existing university structures, but hopefully without the present fragmenting effect upon the life of learning.

I would hope that students and faculty members from various national cultures will find their way into the community life of the nonbureaucratized university. The visions of value-possibilities for good and for evil growing out of new knowledge and technology and requiring the choices of men and women of all ages, personally and communally, in increasing the good and diminishing the evil, should take a world shape in the contemporary university rather than exclusively or primarily an American shape.

I am not at all sure that this vision of an alternative organization of university life is the best one conceivable. In fact, I am quite sure that it is not nearly so good as one that can be forged out of the deliberations of men and women with various resources now available in any university, deliberations informed by the continuing organizational studies of university life that I have already recommended. I have wished here to suggest that the present organization of the multiversity, plagued with problems of size and numbers, is only one alternative among many and that other forms of social organization might better support the mission of a multiversity striving to become once again a university than its present ways of organizing, motivating, rewarding, punishing, and coaching the efforts of those who live by it and in it.

Throughout this essay, I have urged that men and women in our present multiversity find ways to move toward greater community of purpose and effort, toward a university. The reasons for such movement lie within the requirements of a sane development of the life of learning itself. They lie also in the need for a university to speak more intelligibly to the confusions and conflicts of national and world cultures, in stimulating and supporting efforts to build an adequate knowledge base and valuational base for the more rational resolution of those conflicts and confusions. This movement toward greater community of purpose and effort in the university requires the release and joining of a continuing dialogue among various internal and external voices concerning the distinctive aims and responsibilities of a university in today's world. It requires also a reconsideration and revision of the social and human organization of university life. There is good reason to believe that a more adequate organization, if achieved by universities, might provide a model for the sane and humane organization of other social, economic, and political enterprises as well.

A university needs boundaries. If it is to serve people in many parts of society consistently with its central devotion to sound and imaginative learning, it must be able to say no as well as yes to external demands upon its resources, and to set conditions for the use of its services, whether the petitioner for service be a government agency, an industry, a foundation, a labor union, a profession, a church, or some other special interest group. If a university is to be able to say no in the rational maintenance and growth of its own integrity, it must develop a pervasive idea to which it is committed. A university will have attained its idea when it is able to say no to a proffered multimillion dollar grant from a respected outside agency and to state cogently the reasons for its refusal. Perhaps by the year 2000 some universities will have become able to do so.

6 · From Pedagogy to Anthropogogy

One is always somebody's child.

English proverb

I can tell you what my book is about, at its polemical core, by citing a distinction of John Dewey's that I first encountered in the amazing meditative labyrinth Kenneth Burke called Attitudes Toward History. *The distinction is between "education as a function of society" and "society as a function of education."*
. . . In the end, that is a way of dividing the world between those who like it and those who do not. If you are at home in society, you will accept it, and you will want education to perform the function of preparing the minds of the young and the not-so-young to maintain society's principles and directives. . . . If you hold such a theory of education, you are a conservative. . . . Insofar as you think the order should be reversed, that society should be a function of education, you are a radical or that strange, impossible utopian, the radical in reverse gear we call a reactionary.

Frank Lentricchia
Criticism and Social Change

AMERICANS TODAY EXHIBIT SOMEWHAT CONTRADICTORY ATTITUDES toward "education" in their discussions of public affairs. "Education," which Americans tend obsessively to use synonymously with "schooling," is blamed by some shapers of American opinion for the increasing prevalence of crime; for unfortunate moral lapses of people, young and old; for an alleged widespread lack of traditional religious and nationalistic American values; for lack of American competitiveness in world trade and in prestige among the nations of the world; and for sundry other blameworthy attributes of contemporary American thinking and conduct. Yet, many opinion shapers, even those most condemnatory of alleged scholastic sins of omission and commission, also advocate more generous public funding for the support of the presumably ineffective, even delinquent, institutions of education.

I will attempt, in this essay, to make a case for the desirability of a rather radical revision in our conceptions and practices of "education" in America, indeed in the world. This involves a shift from focus on pedagogy, the schooling of the young, to anthropogogy, the education and reeducation of persons of all ages. To make my case, I must examine and rectify a few of the dubious assumptions that undergird current contradictions in most popular discussions of "education."

QUESTIONABLE ASSUMPTIONS ABOUT EDUCATION

The obsessive tendency to identify "education" with "schooling" must be acknowledged and reversed, if we are to talk clearly and cogently about the shape of post-contemporary education. We must accept the validity of John Dewey's (1937) terse comment on the limitations of schooling. "School education is but one educational agency out of many, and at the best is a minor educational force" (p. 235).

Critics are quite justified in complaining about the poor quality of contemporary "education" in America. But their complaints must extend beyond the inadequacies of schools to a critique of other institutions that also shape the minds, value orientations, and characters of Americans—which now *educate* or seek to *reeducate* us. Refurbishing of schools will not suffice to correct the inadequacy of the education we now receive or to reduce the miseducation from which we suffer. Other institutions, along with schools, must be reconstructed with an eye to their educative, including their miseducative, effects on the people now shaped to their demands and cajolements, if our democracy is to attain the well-educated populace it requires, if indeed we are to survive along with the rest of humankind.

Education is inescapably intertwined with what sociologists call socialization, and cultural anthropologists call enculturation. The school is one socializing and enculturating agency among many. Schools can never encompass education, whether their clientele be children, young people, adults, or all of these. The once popular idea that schooling is deliberate or conscious tutelage, as contrasted with the mute and nonconscious shaping of persons by life in other associations and agencies, has become increasingly untenable in our fragmented society. Families (and, for many children, sitters and day-care centers); recreational, health, commercial, and industrial agencies; sundry "think tanks"; the mass media; vendors of pop culture and pornography; and various voluntary religious, political, and vocational associations are consciously and deliberately part of today's educational act. Various and often conflicting educative influences now play upon the minds, emotions, and characters of people— young, middle-aged, and old. These socializing agencies vary widely in the ethical defensibility of their influence efforts. They vary widely in their assumption of responsibility for their educational effects on people. They vary even more widely in the degree of their respect for the rights of persons to be dialogic partners in choosing the direction and quality of their own continuing socialization. But, for all that, they are agencies of education in our time.

"Pedagogy," of course, refers to the teaching of children and young people, to attempts to influence the tempo, direction, and quality of their growth toward adult membership in one culture group or another. In analyzing "pedagogical authority" more than forty years ago, I noted that there are two groups in every society that are always in need of educational help (Benne, 1943/1971, especially Chapter 5). One group is the chronologically immature. The other is made up of those who are alienated, more or less radically, from full participation in the life of their society. In slowly changing cultures, where the standard expectation for almost all persons was one career, one social status, and one locale throughout a lifetime, the drama of enculturation could well be focused on or limited to bringing evernew crops of barbarians in our midst—children and young people— into the fact or at least the semblance of viable societal membership. In such societies, education could, with only minimal distortion, be identified with pedagogy. Adequate models for human development lay within the past.

Even in such societies, the need for resocialization confronted persons at age-related turning points in their lives—parenthood, retirement, grandparenthood, aging, and dying. Rites of passage in stable societies were common and effective enough to make those "normal" transitions seem part of the "natural" cycle of living and dying. Radically alienated persons could be exiled or put to death or dealt with by special therapeutic and correctional processes and institutions. Such processes and institutions were only fitfully viewed as educational, or better reeducational, in intent and effect.

In our society, the relative urgency of education as coaching the development of the immature and of education as the reduction of alienation for persons and groups of persons of all ages has changed radically during the twentieth century. The needs for continuing education and reeducation of people throughout their life-span has risen to an unprecedented crescendo. The need for persons to learn new knowledge and skills for new or changed vocational roles has come to be widely recognized in a job market periodically revolutionized by an advancing technology. What is often not recognized with equal clarity and force is that the adaptation of persons to radically altered ways of living and making a living is not only the acquisition of new salable information and skills. What is required is rather a process of deeper reenculturation that involves the remaking of world views, value orientations, modes of civic participation, and perception and valuation of self. We must learn to think of education in terms of anthropogogy, assisting the education of persons of all ages, not of pedagogy alone. Recognition of these broader dimensions of required adaptation is delayed by the stubborn persistence of the belief that socialization occurs only or primarily in children and adolescents, that it comes to an end with the advent of biological adulthood. This false assumption supports the traditional view that the central mission of education is pedagogy, not anthropogogy.

It was reported in the *Washington Post* in 1987 that the number of adults engaged in educational programs in Arlington County, Virginia had for the first time exceeded the number of children and young people enrolled in elementary and secondary schools and in colleges. I dare say that this is true in many other counties and municipalities in the United States as well. This excess included only adults enrolled in programs labeled as "education." It did not include participation in church schools, in labor halls and board rooms, in the conferences and conventions of various organizations; the support groups formed around various conditions of health or disease; and the multitude of learner-initiated and -sponsored, informal projects dedicated to learning something new or refreshing an old learning, not to mention habitues of television viewing. Alan Tough (1979) has done several censuses of self-initiated adult learning projects in the United States and Canada and found that a large majority of adults were engaged in one or more of such projects in the late 1970s. This tipping of the balance of education from pedagogy to anthropogogy has occurred without the support, help, encouragement, or perhaps even awareness of most school administrators as well as the general public.

An assumption underlies the stubborn persistence in the minds of most Americans of an identification of education with the schooling of the young in preparation for successful adulthood, which A. N. Whitehead (1958) commented adversely upon more than 30 years ago.

> Our sociological theories, our political philosophy, our practical maxims of business, our political economy, and our doctrines of education are derived from an unbroken tradition of great thinkers and of practical examples from the age of Plato to the end of the last century. The whole of this tradition is warped by the vicious assumption that each generation will substantially live amid the conditions governing the lives of its fathers and will transmit those conditions to mold with equal force the lives of its children. We are living in the first period of human history for which this assumption is false. (p. 117)

PROGRESS AND PEDAGOGY IN AMERICA

To understand the persistence of Whitehead's "vicious assumption" in contemporary thinking about education as pedagogy—as preparation for a predictable future—it may be useful to recall the period of American history in which the ideological definition of universal schooling as a guarantor of progress took shape. This period was the 1890s. It was the decade in which "pedagogy" for the first time became a field of university instruction and research. School districts for the elementary schooling of children were functioning in nearly every state and territory of the United States. Proprietary academies were giving way to publicly supported high schools. Leaders in the land-grant college movement were proclaiming that not only elementary and secondary schooling were to be made open to all the young, but that collegiate instruction as well was to become available to all young Americans with the interest and will to receive it. Formal education, like steel making and railroad building, was emphatically a growth industry.

The mood of most noneducational leaders was also one of liberal optimism. Industrial growth and the relatively unfettered exploitation of resources, nonhuman and human, were evident to all and affirmed by most. Industrial growth, to the liberal optimist, was an incontrovertible sign of social progress, seen widely as continuing indefinitely and even inevitably. And the United States was widely hailed as earth's principal exemplar of progress.

The motor of change and progress was seen to lie in a distinctively American ingenuity, which found its purest expression in labor-saving, technological inventions and in initiative to capitalize upon inventions, transmuting them into new marketable products and into profits. This ingenuity—or perhaps these ingenuities—(Thorstein Veblen [1914] was later to distinguish sharply the ingenuity of the engineer from the shrewdness of the predatory capitalist) found free expression in America because of its then unmatched natural resources and cheap labor pool, continually replenished by immigration. However, this ingenuity was more often attributed to the absence of government restraints and an alleged lack of rigid and inherited class barriers among its people. More discerning analysts of American culture saw scientific research as providing an indispensable foundation for continuing breakthroughs in technological innovation. In the popular mind of America, no sharp distinction between "science" and "technology" has ever been made. Only a small minority have reveled in what Sidney Lanier once called the "poetry of science." This close linkage between science and technology has confirmed part of the optimistic ideology of America—the continuation of drastic economic and social change. This fact of pervasive change led Whitehead to label "vicious" the assumption that we can know the character and needs of future generations of people, even the next generation. But the notion of education as preparation for a known adulthood has persisted as part of the optimistic American dream. Ideological dreams die hard.

Of course, the same decade in which the American dream seemed a sober reality to many Americans, including school workers, had another side, which tended to be discounted or ignored. It was a decade in which a nationalistic United States was flexing its imperialistic muscles in the Spanish-American War. The great depression of 1893 had slowed the growth of industry and commerce alarmingly. It was the decade when Pullman workers struck and shed blood in George Pullman's paternalistic, model company town. A teacher's union was organized in Chicago in the early 1900s. Agrarian populists were waging their unsuccessful revolt against the deepening and hardening power of financial interests in agrarian sections of the country. Jim Crow laws, legitimizing a racial caste system, were being enacted throughout the South. "Indian Territory" was being opened to Caucasian exploitation. Our natural resources, renewable and unrenewable, were being squandered wastefully and lavishly. To liberal optimists these were evanescent blemishes upon a soundly progressive system, rather than harbingers of fundamental future challenges to that system. Somehow, universal schooling, combined with an ever-advancing technology, would heal the blemishes and guarantee the forward march of American-style progress.

Today, it has become impossible sanely to hold this optimistic view of a changed America or of American schooling in a changing world. Within our nation, the melting-pot policy of Americanization of immigrant peoples, in the implementation of which the common school was to have played a crucial part, is demonstrably a failure. Divisions among unmeltably heterogeneous ethnic, racial, and religious groups are everywhere apparent. These divisions, augmented by pressures from groups organized along lines of differing genders, sexual preferences, academic disciplines, ages, and vocations, have robbed the notion of a "common interest" of any viable reality in matters of public policy, including policies for education.

Science and technology have developed to a point where they can no longer be viewed sanely as inevitably beneficent guarantors of human progress. Without adequate moral and political controls and transnational collaboration in planning their uses and limitations, they have become also agencies of species extinction, whether rapidly in a bang of nuclear war or protractedly in a whimper of spreading poverty among expanding populations in an environment increasingly unfit for living. We are truly now aliens in a strange and dangerous world.

Contemporary human alienation is historically unusual. It is unusual because there is no stable, correct, and valid—no elite—tradition from which "lesser breeds" of women and men have been alienated. The task of reeducation is not to lead "lesser breeds" toward allegiance to a "divinely" or "naturally" based superior tradition. It was this false conception of the building of consensus upon which melting-pot policies and programs of Americanization foundered. The assumption behind these policies, frequently nonconscious to their proponents, was that the white Anglo-Saxon Protestant (WASP) tradition incorporated the core values of *the* American way of life to which immigrants, particularly those from southern and eastern Europe, Africa, and Asia, when not seen as unassimilable, like blacks and Native Americans, were to be brought, through reeducation, to accept as their own. The policy has, of course, failed. The WASPs have become one wistful, though still powerful, ethnic grouping among others in America, a beleaguered minority on the world scene. We are all now living as aliens in a novel world.

THE NEED FOR FUNDAMENTAL REEDUCATION

A viable culture, if it is to come into being at all, must be built and rebuilt through the conjoint decisions, the resolution of group-reenforced conflicts between foreign and indigenous, between men and women, between young and old, and among white, black, brown, yellow, and red.

If these decisions are to be conducive to human survival, those who participate in making them must learn mutually to reeducate each other in and through these very processes of policy and decision making. These processes must, therefore, be anthropogogical as well as political. They must be apt to the conditions and transactions they purport to order and control. This means they must be informed with the most relevant information available. Our "high" technology of information processing, transmission, and exchange will be indispensable, if, but only if, it is wisely used. Valid information is, of course, not enough. The processes of conflict resolution must not aim toward the nominal and Pyrrhic victory of one tradition or world view over the others. Such resolutions are not usually optimal. They are win–lose resolutions, which are not genuinely authoritative for the losers and which require the wasteful massing of coercive power by the winners for their enforcement, if indeed they are enforceable at all. The conflicts can be resolved sanely and adequately only by win–win resolutions. In these, participants synthesize or compromise previously conflicting interests and various traditional goods to an outcome with which all parties can identify with minimal compromise of self and of allegiance to distinctive and different ultimate values. The learning process that participants must learn to employ, and to learn through employing it, must be one of "creative bargaining," a methodology of "practical judgment," as Raup, Axtelle, Benne, and Smith (1962) named and outlined it, as well as a method of "futures invention," as Ziegler and Healy (1979) developed the process as an anthropogogical mode of learning.

The basic mode of learning in effective resocialization and reenculturation is participative, experiential, and dialogic. Kurt Lewin (1945) was, I believe, quite right in his observation that persons learn their value orientations as they acquire and experience membership in groups significant to them. It is through experience of participation in the group life of a culture that relevant norms of that culture are internalized, individually to be sure. It is in participation that reality-based barriers to fuller and freer personal functioning are modified or accepted.

The effects of participative and experiential learning upon persons are at once cognitive, moral, esthetic, and motoric. These various dimensions of learning may be internalized with various degrees of awareness on the part of the learners. In a pre-figurational culture like ours, if persons are to become partners in shaping and choosing the directions of their own continuing resocialization, it is important that concomitant learnings be raised to the level of consciousness. (See Essay 3 for a complementary account of the learning required in post-contemporary reeducation.)

Learning, adequate to the contemporary human plight, requires chosen, common actions and reflections upon their consequences. It is always a self–other transaction. Fully adequate learning requires a context that is at once supportive and dialogic, in which different world views and differing interests come to be accepted as indispensable aids to the continuing reeducation of self and others into new and wider allegiances. Differences are now too often seen by a person as threats to one's precarious personal identity and security, threats to be avoided or resisted irrationally. Effective anthropogogues must become skilled in facilitating the building of learning communities across the divisive lines of contemporary social cleavage.

Practitioners and professors of anthropogogy must come to view learning and relearning not primarily as cultural transmission but as a future-oriented process of personal and cultural renewal. This view calls for a different relationship between "teachers" and "learners." The relationship to be achieved is a mutually reeducative relationship—one of peer collaboration in reconstructive inquiry. Conflicts among those who differ are to be expected, and the working through of conflicts by the creation or invention of new common meanings becomes a valued product of the educational process. Learning experiences become "experiments" designed to link needs and resources imaginatively. As "experiments," learning experiences are problematic, and outcomes cannot be known in advance. In evaluating learning outcomes, processes employed in planning and conducting the

experience are lifted up into consciousness. The behaviors of all persons in the learning situation, including teachers, consultants, and
expert resource persons, are openly evaluated in terms of their effects, good, bad, or neutral, upon the learning processes and outcomes and, wherever indicated, modified in future learning experiences. Major learning outcomes are thus self-knowledge and skills in
ongoing processes of participative and experiential learning and in
ways of transferring these knowledges and skills to other situations
in which members are now involved or are likely to be involved in the
foreseeable future.

TYPES OF ANTHROPOGOGY

Two degrees of depth in anthropogogical efforts are now apparent in
our and other cultures. These will, I believe, continue and expand.
The first is an extension of schooling or of school-like opportunities to
more and more adults in our population. Such offerings take the form
of away-from-job-and-home classes, seminars, conferences, institutes, continuing support groups, and group meetings of various
sorts and sizes. These represent, formally, a minimal departure from
traditional ways of delivering educational services. At the second
level, the aim is so to modify organizations and institutions that their
ongoing modes of operation are positively educational for their members and, in many cases, for the outside clienteles that they purport
to serve as well. This represents a more drastic departure from traditional ways of delivering educational services.

Three principal kinds of projects and programs account for much
current anthropogogical activity at the first level. The first kind, already noted, is work- and career-oriented. New technology, new definitions of traditional vocational roles, and obsolescent and newly
emerging roles compel refresher education and training for career
changes for adults in various areas of work, professional and para-
professional, and for the unemployed. Some professions, particularly
in the health field, are now mandating refresher education by their
members as a condition of continued good standing in the professions.

A second kind of anthropogogical activity is personally and inter-
personally rather than vocationally oriented. Hundreds of thousands
of persons who are feeling disoriented or inadequate in various of
their significant relationships, or who are experiencing debilitating
stress, are each year seeking reeducational experiences that promise

to help them in finding a less distorted image of themselves and in developing skills for building and maintaining relationships more fulfilling for themselves and for significant others. It seems to me foolish for educators and others to dismiss all self-help offerings as "therapeutic" or "pseudo-therapeutic" and so beyond the scope of educational responsibility. The line between reeducation and therapy is no longer easy to draw in a society fraught with alienations. The line becomes increasingly difficult to draw as a preventive rather than a curative approach to mental health, indeed to health generally, becomes more widely supported by the health professions and by the public. The core of any preventive and maintenance health program is reeducation.

A third type of anthropogogy, still at the first level, grows out of moral, political, and social concerns felt by citizens and groups of citizens. These concerns impel them to social and political actions. The range of such concerns is wide and grows wider as alternatives to established patterns emerge and find advocates. Many are rooted in anxieties about the use and misuse of powers released by continuing developments in technology and science. Abortion and genetic counseling, the use or nonuse of nuclear energy, threats to remnants of our "natural" environment, gene-splicing, electronic threats to privacy and to employment, and human rights are labels for only a few of these. Other concerns are rooted in questions of inequity and injustice, even of survival, for "forgotten" or exploited groups, inside and outside our nation—women, children, the homeless, racial and ethnic groups, Native Americans, to name a few.

Processes of education and reeducation are inherent in such movements, both in the internal efforts of membership groups and organizations to orient and guide the views and energies of members and recruits, and in their external efforts to influence public opinion and the choices and actions of persons in positions of power and authority. They represent, just as truly as do programs of vocational reeducation and projects of personal and interpersonal reorientation, efforts to reshape patterns of thinking, valuation, authority, and behavior, which may help to reduce the alienation induced in all of us by our perilous present and indeterminate future.

I mentioned earlier that anthropogogical efforts are going on at two levels at present. So far I have focused on the level that most resembles schooling. People leave their places of living and work and meet to create a temporary society specifically designed to serve the purposes of learning, whether that temporary society be a conference, seminar, retreat, or institute. At the other level, reeducative effort is focused upon the places of living and work themselves; the organization or institution is the target of change. I will discuss only one such process here, a process that, in the United States, is usually named organizational development, transformation, or renewal. Investigations of the operation of the organization and its human effects begin with exploration and diagnosis of felt dissatisfactions within the organization—whether with productivity, morale, or dehumanization of roles and relationships. In the diagnosis, and in the invention of provisional prescriptions for change consistent with the diagnosis, all of those affected by the present functioning are involved either directly or representatively. The processes of human interaction, deliberation, and decision are akin to those already described under the labels of participative and experiential learning. In organizational development circles, these processes are sometimes talked about as cooperative action research.

The first outcomes of these processes are experimental changes in institutional policy and practice designed to alleviate the dissatisfactions that originally fueled the joint inquiry. The more enduring outcomes are of two kinds. The first is a commitment by the organization or institution to deal with future problems as they arise in a similar, though alterable, way, which I have called anthropogogical.

The second outcome is the establishment of structures, normative and procedural, to support the prompt and continuing use of such methods in the management and policy making of the organization or institution. The combined effect is for the organization to become responsible for the educative effects of its operations upon those affected by these operations—in effect, to become an agent of anthropogogy.

A few years ago I was invited to attend an international conference on "Organizational Development and Social Change" in Dubrovnik, Yugoslavia. Most participants were social scientists and students and teachers of management and public administration. A few of us, I am glad to say, were professors of education. I learned at this meeting that the United States is by no means in the forefront in introducing anthropogogy into the life and work settings of people. The best established and evaluated examples came from Scandinavia, the *kibbutzim* of Israel, and the self-management movement in Yugoslavia. But the beginnings in the United States are by no means negligible.[1]

They are promising enough to give me hope that more and more institutions, in addition to those now bearing the name of education, will come to assume responsibility for the continuing education of their members, through the introduction of collaboratively reeducative methods into their processes of management, planning, and policy making. My further hope is for the creation of viable modes and networks of collaboration between various "educators" for enhancing and sharing anthropogogical responsibilities, far beyond the primitive examples I have been able to describe here. In such responsible sharing lies the best hope for human survival in our troubled world.

7 · The Theory and Practice of Reeducation

Kurt Lewin's Contributions

*If the individual is closed to change as a result of valid informa-
tion from others and tests his hypotheses privately,—there will
tend to be little learning and little behavioral change. If the individual tests his hypotheses privately but is open to change,—
learning will tend to occur to the extent that it does not depend
on others knowingly providing valid information. If the individual tests his assumptions publicly, but is closed to change,—the
result will tend to be [a] mutually self-sealing situation. . . .
The most effective case for learning is . . . public testing of assumptions and openness to changed behavior as a result.*

Chris Argyris and Donald Schön
Theory in Practice

*A unified self does not mean a self free of all conflicts. It does
mean a self free of conflicts which cannot be treated in such a way
as to promote creative transformation. The unified self is not a
static or completed condition but the very opposite. It cannot be
achieved or approximated except by commitment to creativity.
Only by learning from others in depth and others learning from
oneself in depth, thus releasing the wholeness of individuality in
each, can man be unified and this unity be satisfied. But this involves continuous creative transformation with inner conflicts
continuously undergoing modification.*

Henry Nelson Wieman
Man's Ultimate Commitment

EDUCATION, WHEN IT IS MORE than the additive accumulation of information and of intellectual and motoric skills, always involves some elements of reeducation. Reeducation requires "unlearning" of previously learned ways of perceiving, believing, valuing, and behaving, in order that new, more adequate ways can be understood, judged to be better than the old, and accepted as one's own. Such personal transcendence of earlier learnings is seldom easy, especially when the previous learnings are consonant with the cultural norms of primary groups to which the learner belongs and when they have functioned in the past as part of the learner's ways of maintaining security in a precarious world.

The need for reeducation is most apparent in the cases of radically alienated persons. These may be criminals—persons who have willfully violated established norms and laws. Or they may be persons who are deeply distressed emotionally. Reeducation of such deviates ordinarily, where undertaken in our society, has been seen as the responsibility of specialized "alienists"—rehabilitationists, therapists, or priests. Workers in formal education have usually eschewed attempts to reeducate such "extreme" cases.

But many diagnoses of our culture in its contemporary travail suggest that the education of all of us, younger and older, must in the future undergo processes of reeducation. Earlier, I quoted approvingly Margaret Mead's (1970) observation that we are all now aliens in a strange world. Some of our traditional ways of perceiving, believing, valuing, and behaving are now leading us toward our own extinction and that of our species. New viable ways of perceiving, believing, valuing, and behaving must be created and maintained if we are to survive.

Usually, in the past, processes of reeducation have been described, analyzed, and prescribed by and for specialists, whether specialists in rehabilitation, therapy, or religious conversion. Kurt Lewin's conceptualization of reeducation, on the other hand, has been devised for understanding and use by educators, trainers, friends, and civic and action leaders. Educational methodologies and programs have been and are being built and developed that incorporate Lewinian concepts. But these have been only fitfully and distrustingly introduced into institutions and programs of formal education. As I see it, post-contemporary educators will need to conceptualize and use processes of reeducation in their normal practice. Lewin's views will become important in fulfilling that need.

Kurt Lewin had good reason to seek to reeducate people in "advanced" capitalist cultures. He was a German Jew who had been driven out of his homeland by the anti-Semitism that had become an article of official state policy in Hitler's Third Reich. His mother died in a Nazi gas chamber. He found strong currents of anti-Semitism, of racism, of ethnocentrism in his adopted country, the United States. He felt the contradictions between America's professed democratic commitment to the nurture of self-directing personalities and the self-hatred and self-rejection that persons within oppressed minorities avoided or overcame only with great effort and suffering. He saw democratic institutions eroded by the perpetuation of racial injustice and threatened by mounting and unresolved intergroup conflicts. He feared that the seeds of totalitarianism might grow to destroy democracy in the United States and in the world unless the forces of research, education, and action could be united in the elimination of social injustice and minority self-hatred, and in the wise resolution of intergroup conflicts. Kurt Lewin's fears reinforced the vigor of his efforts to serve his hopes and commitments.

KURT LEWIN'S HOPES AND COMMITMENTS

Kurt Lewin was an inveterately hopeful man. Yet this hope was more than a temperamental stance toward life and experience. It drew its substance from several deep value commitments. One of these was to science, not as a body of knowledge but as a way of life.

Science, for Lewin (1949)

> is the eternal attempt to go beyond what is regarded as scientifically accessible at any specific time . . . To proceed beyond the limitations of a given level of knowledge, the researcher, as a rule, has to break down methodological taboos which condemn as 'unscientific' or 'illogical' the very methods or concepts which later on prove to be basic for the next major progress. (p. 275)

Lewin, following the lead of one of his philosophy teachers, Ernst Cassirer, saw science as an adventuring into poorly understood yet important areas of experience and an inventing of ways to gain dependable knowledge of these hitherto unknown or vaguely known areas. Lewin had ventured in his Berlin days to bring the study of human will and emotion into the range of psychological experimentation. In doing this, he had struggled

> against a prevalent attitude which placed volition, emotion and sentiments in the 'poetic realm' of beautiful words, a realm to

which nothing corresponds which could be regarded as 'existing' in the sense in which the scientist uses the term. Although every psychologist had to deal with these facts realistically in his private life, they were banned from the realm of 'facts' in the scientific sense. (Lewin, 1949, p. 276)

This same commitment to the spirit of science as a human enterprise, as intrepid inquiry, in which current scientific taboos are overcome through bold theorizing and creative research designs and methods, had led Lewin, in his Iowa days, to collaborate with Ronald Lippitt and Ralph White in bringing small-group processes into the ambit of experimental inquiry, founding a new science of group dynamics. Lewin was a theorizer and researcher. But he saw theory not only as a way into significant inquiry and research but as a practical guide to reconstructive work in social practice and action as well, including education.

Lewin was thus a moralist as well as a scientist. But he was decidedly not a moralistic moralist, in the sense of one who seeks to impose the principles of an established moral tradition upon the realities of contemporary conduct in order to control it within the confines of that tradition. His was rather a morality of reality orientation toward confronting contemporary situations in their tensions and conflicts, a morality that focused processes of the conjoint human intelligences of persons within those situations upon investigating and inventing ways of analyzing, managing and improving them. The values to which he was most basically committed were thus methodological values, combining values inherent in scientific and democratic processes and methods.

DEVELOPMENT OF REEDUCATIVE WORKSHOPS AND "LABORATORIES"

Lewin's hope for cooperative action research as a way for human beings to solve their problems and manage their dilemmas represents best this dynamic fusion of democratic and scientific values. In a real sense, the Connecticut workshop at New Britain was a project in cooperative action research. Ronald Lippitt's book (1949) on this workshop makes this clear. Ironically, this book was relatively neglected from the day of its publication because it crossed the departmental lines of academia. It is at one and the same time a description and evaluation of a training and educational program; a treatment of one phase of a statewide action program in the reduction of discriminatory practices in Connecticut employment, education, and public accommodations; and a research report of a social-psychological field experiment. Actionists, educators, and scientists are typically segregated in American society. They read different literatures and talk different languages. Lewin's commitment was to breach the walls of this segregation; to bring researchers, humanists, educators, and actionists together into collaborative efforts to solve social problems; to create mutually satisfactory programs of personal and social change; and to add to the stockpile of knowledge of human dynamics and of methods of knowledge utilization in integrated programs of action, education, and research. It was some such vision, which undergirded his hope and commitment, that he brought to the New Britain workshop. It was a vision shared by the staff and a vision that came to animate the innovative educational programs that stemmed from the workshop.

The lure of learning answers to unanswered questions was a passion in Lewin, the man, the scientist, and the moralist. My fondest memories of him in the Connecticut workshop are of his deep engagement in discussing the problems that participants laid before him. He was prepared to learn along with anyone—he was unusually free of status consciousness. He listened and questioned avidly. From time to time he would raise a finger of his right hand and say "Ah ha! Could it be this way?" And he would then propose a new conceptualization of the problem, which more often than not opened up a new way of seeing it and new avenues of inquiry toward a solution. The lure of unanswered questions and of finding concepts and data that might lead toward better diagnoses and prognoses was strong in Lewin and in those who collaborated with him.

Large questions lay behind and ran through the workshop. How can community action leaders be educated through group participation to work effectively on problems of intergroup relations? How can persons better learn to use processes of participative inquiry, education, and action as tools of personal and social change in their own community settings? The specific research question of the workshop had to do with a comparison of retention and utilization (transfer) of workshop learnings in back-home settings by teams from the same community and by persons who had come as isolates from their communities. The hypothesis that much greater utilization of workshop learnings would be made by persons participating as community teams was, as predicted, confirmed by change data gathered through field interviews, a month before and two months after the workshop, with participants and with their bosses, selected peers, and selected subordinates as well.

This substantive research finding has been obscured by the discovery of a major method of training at the workshop—a discovery that led to the training group and various other methods of laboratory education. There was a somewhat serendipitous quality to this discovery. Yet Kurt Lewin's unquenchable curiosity and his concern for productive collaboration among actionists, educators, and researchers played a part in making the discovery possible and fruitful in its further development.

The Connecticut workshop was divided into three continuing learning groups, with Leland Bradford, Ronald Lippitt, and I acting as trainers (teachers). Each group was observed by a research observer, watching processes according to a schedule designed to help answer questions pertinent to the research design. The research observers were Morton Deutsch, Murray Horwitz, and Melvin Seeman. Kurt Lewin had arranged for the six trainers and observers to meet with him each evening to report, discuss, and analyze their observations and prognoses of the development of each learning group. These discussions were recorded on tape. Some participants who were living on campus asked if they might join these sessions. Being generally open people, the staff agreed. I have paraphrased Ronald Lippitt's (1949) lengthy description of the result in the next four paragraphs.

Sometime during the evening, a staff observer commented on the behavior of one of the three persons who were sitting in—a woman trainee in the morning session. She broke in to disagree with the observation and described it from her point of view. For a while an active dialogue ensued among the research observer, the trainer, and the trainee about the interpretation of the event. Kurt Lewin was an active prober, obviously enjoying this different source of data that had to be understood.

At the end of the evening, the trainees asked if they could come back for the next meeting at which their and others' behavior in the small groups would be analyzed and evaluated. The staff, feeling that it had been a valuable contribution, rather than an intrusion, enthusiastically agreed to their return. The next night at least half of the fifty or sixty participants were there as the result of the grapevine reporting of the exciting activity by the three delegates.

From then on the evening session became the most significant learning experience of the day, with its focus on actual behavioral events and with active dialogue about differences in interpretations and observations of the events by the same people who had participated in them.

The staff were as enthusiastic as the delegates for they found the process a unique way of exposing data about interpersonal behavior and interpreting these data. In addition, the staff discovered that feedback from others on their conduct had the effect of making participants more sensitive to their own motivations and behaviors. The process brought criticism into the open in a healthy and learningful way.

This discovery led to the basic method of laboratory learning about self, groups, and interpersonal relations, and, more particularly, to the training group (T Group) that was tried out first in a concerted way in Bethel, Maine the following summer. The T Group is a micro-application of Lewin's method of cooperative action research. (See Bradford, Gibb, & Benne, 1964.) In such a group, people undertake to make their own changing experiences in and as a developing group a major focus for inquiry and learning. They share openly their observations and interpretations of behavioral events in which they engage themselves both as participants and as observers. The development of the group is guided by continuing inquiry into the transactions between members and between members and trainer. Components of action, training, and research are integrated in a powerful process of reeducation. Whether one shares Carl Rogers (1968) estimate of laboratory training as "perhaps the most significant social invention of this century" (p. 268), we can probably all agree that it represents a very significant breakthrough in processes of self-reeducation of persons in understanding and managing themselves in their various social environments. Today we recognize the important part that Kurt Lewin, intrepid inquirer, scientist, and moralist, played in this breakthrough.

One central theme running through the concerns and curiosities of the mature Lewin and exemplified in the New Britain workshop is the theme of reeducation. Through what processes do men and women alter, replace, or transcend patterns of thinking, valuation, volition, and overt behavior by which they have previously managed and justified their lives, into patterns of thinking, valuation, volition, and action that are better oriented to the changing realities and actualities of contemporary existence, personal and social, and that are at once more personally fulfilling and socially appropriate? The processes are more complex than those of learning anew, as any action leader, therapist, or teacher of adults knows from experience. They involve not extrinsic additions of knowledge or behavioral repertoire to the self or person, but changes in the self, and the working through of self-supported resistances to such changes. And, because self-patterns are sustained by norms and relationships in the groups to which a person belongs or aspires to belong, effective reeducation of a person requires changes in his or her environing society and culture as well.

PRINCIPLES OF REEDUCATION

About a year before the Connecticut workshop, Lewin, along with Paul Grabbe, formulated 10 general observations on reeducation (Lewin & Grabbe, 1945). These principles of reeducation were not simple derivations from Lewin's field-theoretical perspective on human conduct. They grew out of his and Grabbe's attempt to interpret, out of that perspective, reports of a number of projects in reeducation as various as Alcoholics Anonymous, a retraining program for police officers in diminishing intergroup prejudices, and a successful attempt to change a stereotype of older workers in an industrial organization.

What I propose to do is to assess these Lewinian generalizations in the light of the knowledge and know-how concerning reeducation accumulated in 45 years of experience and experimentation with programs in the development of human resources since their original publication. My assessment will, of course, reflect the limitations of my knowledge of these cumulative experiences and of my own theoretical and value orientation.

Lewin's analysis assumed that effective reeducation must affect the person being reeducated in three ways. The person's *cognitive* structure must be altered. For Lewin this structure included the person's modes of perception, his or her ways of seeing the physical and social worlds, as well as the facts, concepts, expectations, and opinions with which a person thinks about the possibilities of action and the consequences of action in his or her phenomenal world. Reeducation must involve the person in modifying *valences* and *values* as well as cognitive structures. Valences and values include not only the learner's principles of what should and should not be done or considered, which, along with his or her cognitive views, are embodied in beliefs. They include also attractions and aversions to other groups and their standards, feelings in regard to status differences and authority, and reactions to various sources of approval and disapproval. Reeducation finally must affect a person's *motoric actions*, the repertoire of behavioral skills and the habitual ways of a person's conscious control of his or her physical and social movements.

The complexities of reeducative processes arise out of the fact that they must involve correlative changes in various aspects of the person—cognitive-perceptual structure, valuative-moral and volitional structures, and motoric patterns for coping with the person's life-world(s). Changes in these various aspects of the person are governed by different laws and relationships. Thus reeducation runs into contradictions and dilemmas. For example, a person's learning facts that run counter to previously learned stereotypic attitudes toward members of an out-group may actually lead to denial of this knowledge and increased guilt and more frantic defense of his or her stereotypes, unless these values are somehow opened up, explored, and altered. Changed stereotypes may leave the person awkward in dealing with members of the out-group, if his or her habitual motoric skills have not been brought into line with new cognitive and value orientations. This awkwardness may evoke responses in his or her dealing with members of the out-group in new ways that reconfirm the old stereotypes or lead to immobilization because of augmented inner conflicts. Reeducative experiences must be designed with the multi-faceted aspects of behavioral change in mind and in a way that will help persons become aware of and responsible for the dilemmas and contradictions that arise out of this inescapable complexity. I believe that experiments with reeducation since Lewin's formulation have confirmed his assumption that the "whole person" must somehow be involved in processes of effective reeducation.

Lewin's principles dealt with the complex interrelationships between changes in cognitive-perceptual orientation and value orientation. He did not deal with the involvement of motoric changes in their interrelationships with the other two. Experimentation with body movement and with operant behavioral conditioning in achieving behavioral change has thrived during the more than 40 years since Lewin wrote. My supplementation of his principles of reeducation arises from this fact.

1. Lewin stated his first principle as "The processes governing the acquisition of the normal and the abnormal are fundamentally alike" (p. 53). This principle breaks cognitively through the wall that has traditionally separated dealing reeducatively with persons manifesting "abnormal" behavior and with those who are seen as "normal" behaviorally. Behavioral abnormalities have been classified as pathological or as criminally or quasi-criminally deviant. Special per-

sonnel with special training, working in special, often socially isolated settings with special techniques, have been developed to deal in segregated fashion with the therapy of the pathologically abnormal and rehabilitatively with the criminally deviant. "Education" for the normal has been sharply separated, conceptually and institutionally, from "therapy" for the pathological and "rehabilitation" for the deviant.

The wall between education on the one hand and therapy and rehabilitation on the other has now been breached on many fronts—in community mental health programs, in prison reform, and in various converging movements between education and therapy. But the resistance to thinking about and dealing with reeducation of persons as they are, normal and abnormal, and in the same processes is still powerful in the thinking and practice of most people, including educators. Probably, this is related generally to the persistence of class-theoretical modes of thinking as contrasted with field-theoretical thinking in the management of human affairs, a distinction with which Lewin, the philosopher of science, was much concerned. For people whose ways of thinking are class-theoretical, classifications devised as artifacts, as abstract tools of thought, not as representations of reality—"abnormal" and "normal," for example—are given the status of realities, with class membership constituting a difference of kind or substance between the individuals in each class. Field-theoretical thinking about people and the processes of their reeducation keeps a focus on the reality of concrete persons in their actual manifold relationships and situations and does not let abstract classifications of persons prescribe the mode or manner of differential treatment. I see field-theoretical thinking as highly desirable in contemporary analyses and in the management of human affairs. This Lewinian construction of a way of thinking about thinking seems to me more conducive both to the fuller actualization of humane values and to effectiveness in our policies and practices of education and reeducation.

Controversies about what is "therapy" and what is "education" have dogged the development and extension of practices in laboratory education since its inception. Actually, the lines between the two have become fuzzy and blurred in a number of ways, and rightly so in my opinion. Educational programs may be slowly escaping the fetters of their traditional exclusive preoccupation with cognitive development and may be taking responsibility for the affective and volitional development of persons as well. As this happens, expressive behavior, which might once have been considered abnormal in educational settings, will become legitimized as consonant with the varying idiosyncratic development of different persons. In fact, we have discovered that behavioral manifestations in intensive group experiences that might once have been coded as pathological, and so to be avoided and repressed in learning situations, are actually aspects, even necessary aspects, of processes of personal growth and self-discovery. The lines between the pathological and the growthful in behavior still need to be drawn. But experiences in human relations training, along with extensions from therapeutic practice into preventive mental health education, have shown that the lines are not easy to draw. As they are drawn, I hope they will be taken as practical judgments of the kinds of reeducation that persons may require from time to time in their lives and careers, not as a restoration of nonfunctional distinctions between the "normal" and "abnormal," which Lewin's first principle of reeducation wisely repudiates.

2. The theory and practice of reeducation are only beginning to catch up with Lewin's second principle—"The reeducative process has to fulfill a task which is essentially equivalent to a change in culture" (p. 55). Counseling and therapy have traditionally sought to facilitate changes in persons, with little or no assumption of responsibility for facilitating changes in the cultural environment in which persons function outside the counseling or therapeutic setting. This tends to place the entire burden of behavioral adjustment or adaptation upon the individual. Changes in the cultural environment, which was involved in precipitating the dysfunctional behavior that brought the person to counseling or therapy, have not been focused on in the reeducative process, which is often carried on in a specially designed setting apart from the social and cultural involvements of the person's ongoing life. There is now a tendency to involve significant other persons and their common culture in the process of reexamination, reevaluation, and commitment to change, along with the person who felt the environmental stress most deeply—as in therapy for a family in place of or as an adjunct to therapy for a disturbed individual family member; or treatment of disturbed individuals in their home and work settings, not in segregated situations. In training, work with what are sometimes called embedded groups—work staffs, entire organizations, whole families—has come to supplement or to replace "cultural island" training of persons drawn away from their home setting for education. This involves changes in culture that are ideally consonant with and supportive of changes in per-

sonal knowledge, value orientation, or motoric skill achieved through training.

At the same time as organizational development and community development approaches to personal-social-cultural changing have come into being and spread, personal growth training in settings designedly abstracted from the outside roles and institutional involvements of participants has been developing in various laboratory programs and growth centers. These seem to focus on personal reeducation, with little or no assumption of responsibility for changes in the culture, outside the center, in which persons live and function most of their lives. Do the successes claimed for such programs contradict Lewin's second principle of reeducation?

I do not think that they do. A counter-culture grew up in the United States (and outside as well) in the 1960s with norms that are markedly different from those of the "established" culture. This counter-culture found social embodiment in communes, neighborhoods, and networks of various sorts and in various associations of dropouts from established institutional life. The manifestations of the counter-culture were often closer to the norms cultivated and, in various degrees, internalized by participants in personal growth laboratories and centers—living in the moment, suspicion of deferred gratification, guidance of the choices of life by feelings, and authenticity of personal expression as a prime virtue. Though I speak here in the past tense, communes of the sort described above are by no means absent in contemporary America, though they are less publicized now.

What we are seeing in "personal growth" developments in the training field is not an abrogation of the principle that effective personal reeducation involves correlative changes in culture. It is rather a difference in the subculture of our national culture for which training is being conducted. It may be more accurate to say that community and organizational development streams in human relations training are more hopeful about the possibilities of reconstructing and humanizing established organizations and institutions than are those who train for participation in a counter-culture. Trainers who see training for personal growth without any reference to correlative training for social and cultural change as a way of changing established culture are, I think, denying the important reality embodied in Lewin's second principle of reeducation.

3. "Even extensive first-hand experience does not automatically create correct concepts (knowledge)" (p. 57). Lewin leveled his third principle against reeducators who, aware that lectures, reading as-

signments, and other abstract ways of transmitting knowledge are of little avail in changing the orientations or conduct of learners, see concrete *experience* as the way to personal change. He pointed out that thousands of years of human experiences with falling bodies did not bring people to a correct theory of gravity. What was required was specially constructed man-made experiences, or experiments, designed to reach an adequate explanation of the phenomena of falling objects, in order to achieve a more nearly correct theory. Lewin was convinced that reeducative experiences must incorporate the spirit of experimental inquiry and, insofar as possible, the form of experimentation, if more nearly correct knowledge is to be the result. I believe that Lewin is correct. It is important to recognize that the principle opens to question the effectiveness of traditional classroom practices, which seek to induce students to learn about the results of other people's inquiries and do not involve them in processes of inquiry in areas where their own beliefs are recognized by themselves to be vague, conflicting, or somehow in doubt. It is important to recognize also that the principle equally throws doubt upon the effectiveness of training where trainers and participants confuse having an exciting and moving experience with the achievement of adequate and transferable learnings through accompanying cognitive changes.

In training, it takes time and effort for a group to learn a method of experimental inquiry where their own feelings, perceptions, commitments, and behaviors are part of the data to be processed in the inquiry. But this is the goal of responsible laboratory training. At the least, experiences that have not been pre-hypothesized need to be reflected upon and conceputalized *post factum*, if valid and transferable learnings are to issue from an educational process.

Actually, this principle supports Lewin's advocacy of action research as a format for integrating personal reeducation and social change into the same process. Action research when it is most valid achieves the form of field experimentation.

4. "Social action no less than physical action is steered by perception" (p. 57). The world in which we act is the world as we perceive it. Changes in knowledge or changes in beliefs and value orientation will not result in action changes unless changed perceptions of self and situation are achieved.

Developments in the training field since Lewin's day have reconfirmed this principle. Much of the development of training technology has been focused on ways of inducing people to entertain, try out, and perhaps adopt ways of perceiving themselves and their situations that are alternative to their habitual ways of perceiving.

Openness to new knowledge and new valuations usually follows rather than precedes changes in perception. Habitual perceptions are challenged by open exchange of feedback among members of a group as they share their different responses to "the same" events. If a member attaches positive value to and trusts other members of the group or the group as a whole, he or she can accept different perceptions of other members as genuine phenomenological alternatives to his or her own ways of perceiving self and world. And he or she may then try to perceive and feel the world as others in his or her group perceive and feel it. In the process, his or her own perceptual frames may be modified or at least recognized as operating as one among other constructions of social reality.

It is, I think, true that the most impressive developments since Lewin's day in training technologies have been focused upon inducing perceptual change—more powerful forms of feedback, including the use of audio- and videotape; extending awareness to previously unnoticed processes and feelings, bodily and otherwise, as in Gestalt therapy; training in listening and in observation and psychodramatic and fantasy experiences; and experiences with the arts. These illustrate ways of cleansing, opening, and refining the doors of perception, which have been developed and tested in learning laboratories over the years. Lewin may have been a lonely phenomenologist among reeducators when he enunciated this principle more than 40 years ago. Many, if not most, reeducators have, in some measure, become phenomenologists today.

5. "As a rule the possession of correct knowledge does not suffice to rectify false perceptions" (p. 57). This principle underlines the relative independence of processes of perception from processes of cognition and valuation in the organization of the person, a point already emphasized. Lewin did not recognize so fully as most trainers do today the close linkage between social perception and self-perception. Dynamically, I tend to see others in a way to support and maintain my image of myself and my significant others. Only as the need to justify myself is reduced, as in a supportive, acceptant, loving social environment, can I freely experiment with alternative perceptions of myself and in turn with alternative perceptions of people different from myself. Changes in self-perception and in social perception come about through "experimentation" in interpersonal relations at precognitive levels of experience.

6. "Incorrect stereotypes (prejudices) are functionally equivalent to wrong concepts (theories)" (p. 58). All of us who have studied prej-

udices in ourselves and others know how incorrect stereotypes can persist as ways of explaining the motivations and behavior of persons against the weight of evidence to the contrary. The story of the man who believed he was dead illustrates the point. His friends and his psychiatrist pointed out evidences to indicate that he was alive, but the belief persisted. Finally, his psychiatrist persuaded the man to admit that dead men don't bleed and gained his permission to prick his finger with a pin. When the blood came, the man, astonished, said "Doctor, I was wrong. Dead men do bleed."

What Lewin was underlining here with respect to reeducation of incorrect stereotypes was the inadequacy of run-of-the-mill experience as such to change a person's or group's theories of the life-world. Specially designed experiments that people help to design and carry out for themselves are required to instate new, more adequate concepts in the place of those they have held habitually. One condition of experimentation is for the experimenter to accept the fact of alternative conceptualizations of the "same" event. The experimenter can then arrange experiences to furnish evidence to disconfirm one or another of the alternative hypotheses in trying to determine which of the alternatives most adequately explains the evidence. In recognizing that an incorrect stereotype is functionally equivalent to a theory in his or her mental organization, the experimenter must develop and accept an ambivalence in himself or herself toward the adequacy of some familiar stereotype. Without ambivalence, the person sees no need to submit his or her stereotypes to an "experimental" testing.

Ambivalence toward one's habitual ways of explaining social events usually comes when consensual validation of social events breaks down. Other people whose views a person prizes explain "the same" event in ways different from his or her own. If one can acknowledge ambivalence toward the stereotype, he or she can become active in gathering and evaluating evidence to disconfirm or confirm the stereotype or its alternative. Change in stereotypes will ordinarily not occur until persons are involved as self-experimenters with their own and alternative ways of explaining their social worlds. Self-experimenters must ideally have an appropriate "laboratory group" in which to work, both as a support to their persistence in arduous processes of self-inquiry and to furnish the data that the testing of alternative hypotheses requires.

7. "Changes in sentiments do not necessarily follow changes in cognitive structures" (p. 58). Just as some of Lewin's earlier principles recognized the relative independence of processes of changing cognition and processes of changing perception, this principle stresses

the relative independence of processes of cognitive change and changes in value orientation, action ideology, or sentiment.

Lewin was quite aware that many reeducative attempts verbalize only the official system of conventionally professed values and do not involve learners in becoming aware of their own personal action-ideologies, often nonconscious, which *actually* shape their personal decisions and actions. Such superficial reeducation may result in merely heightening the discrepancy between the superego (the way I ought to feel) and the ego (the way I actually do feel). The individual develops a guilty conscience. Such a discrepancy leads to a state of high emotional tension but seldom to appropriate conduct. It may postpone transgressions from the official ideology, but it is likely to make transgressions more violent when they do occur.

Subsequent training experience seems to bear out one factor of great importance in facilitating a person's reconsideration and reconstruction of his or her action-ideologies, sentiments, or value systems. This is the degree and depth to which an individual becomes involved in seeing and accepting a problem with respect to the adequacy of his or her operating values. Lacking this involvement, no objective fact is likely to reach the status of fact-for-the-individual, and no value alternative is likely to reach the status of a genuine alternative-for-the-individual and, therefore, come to influence his or her social conduct.

8. "A change in action-ideology, a real acceptance of a changed set of facts and values, a change in the perceived social world—all three are but different expressions of the same process" (p. 59). It was a part of Lewin's important contribution to an understanding of reeducation to emphasize the intimate connection between the development of a value system by a person and his or her growth into membership in a group. Individuals become socialized through internalizing the normative culture of the groups to which they come to belong. A value system is a person's own putting together, in a more or less unique way, of the various internalized normative outlooks of the significant associations that have contributed to the building of his or her social self—family, religion, age group, gender group, sexual preference group, ethnic group, and/or racial grouping. Reeducation, as it affects action-ideology, value orientation, and perception of self and social world, is a process of resocialization or, as Lewin tended to prefer, a process of reenculturation.

Reeducation of persons thus requires their involvement in new groups with norms that contrast in significant ways with those of the groups to which the persons previously belonged. The norms of the reeducative group must, as Lewin pointed out again and again, be those that support and require members to engage in experimental inquiry into their own past socialization as it affects their present functioning and their development into the future. The norms of the reeducative group are thus not accidental. They are the ideal norms of the social research community—openness of communication, willingness to face problems and to become involved in their solution, willingness to furnish data to facilitate one's own and others' inquiries, and willingness to submit ambivalences and moot points to some sort of empirical test. The material dealt with in the reeducative group is, of course, personal and social material. It is inquired into not only in the interest of gaining more valid and dependable knowledge of interpersonal and social transactions in general, but in the interest of rendering contemporary personal and social action more informed, more on target, more in line with clarified and chosen values, and in the further interest of narrowing the gap between internal intention and outer consequence in processes of decision and action.

Lewin's views of reeducation helped the workshop staff at New Britain, Connecticut to project out of their experience there the T group as a prototype of the reeducative group. The T group, as it developed, tended to focus on inquiry into interpersonal relationships between members and into the idiosyncratic aspects of member selves as they revealed themselves in T-group transactions. The "typical" T group, whatever that may be, did not ordinarily explore directly the social selves of members or the effects of significant membership and reference groups upon members and upon their attempts to deal with each other in fruitful processes of inquiry and experimental action.

Max Birnbaum (1975) and I have been developing laboratory groups with a heterogeneous membership, which we call clarification groups, in which members are encouraged to inquire into their social selves (see also Babad, Birnbaum, and Benne, 1983). The effects of membership on action-ideology, value orientation, social perception, and stereotypy are explored openly and directly. We like to think that this variation in laboratory training, which supplements rather than supplants T groups and consultation with groups and group interfaces embedded within organizations and communities, is in line with Lewin's central interest in improving community and intergroup relations.

Lewin was quite aware of one dilemma that faces all reeducators. The principle of voluntarism, of free choice by persons to engage in self- and social-inquiry, is an important element in effective reeducation. Yet the urgency of unsolved human problems leads all of us at times to try to force people into programs and processes of reeducation. The maintenance of the principle of voluntarism is very difficult in field experiments in which entire social systems—school systems, industries, community agencies—become involved. Lewin put the dilemma in this way: "How can free acceptance of a new system of values be brought about, if the person who is to be educated is, in the nature of things, likely to be hostile to the new values and loyal to the old?"

This is a real dilemma. There is no neat solution to it. Training experience has indicated that two operating attitudes or stances of reeducators are very important in dealing with the dilemma. The first is an attitude of respect for resistance and a commitment to utilize the resources of the resisters in shaping plans for experimental action and its evaluation. The second is to seek ways of helping hostile rejectors of participation in change programs to recognize that their stance of total rejection usually masks a genuine ambivalence and conflict within themselves. If they can accept this ambivalence within themselves, they are accepting the existence of a problem to be inquired into and so become candidates for voluntary involvement in the processes of its exploration and possible resolution.

9. "Acceptance of the new set of values and beliefs cannot usually be brought about item by item" (p. 61). Lewin here points out the inescapable fact that a value system is a system. It must have an integrity of its own if it is to perform its function of helping persons maintain their identity and wholeheartedness in the choices that their conflicted environment thrusts upon them. Introducing particular new values that are not coherent with other values in the person's outlook on self and world may augment the inner conflict and/or compartmentalization, the melioration of which is a part of the motivation that brings persons into a process of reeducation.

I think that many reeducators, coming as they do out of indoctrination in a social science that, however dubiously, claims value neutrality, avoid directly facing up to the dimension of inquiry into value orientations, which is a necessary aspect of effective reeducation. They may encourage participants to clarify feelings, to apply and test new concepts, and to practice skills of inquiry. They may avoid direct confrontation of differences among participants and themselves with respect to beliefs and ideologies. A piecemeal approach may be quite appropriate to skill development, expression of feelings, and even conceptual clarification. It is, and here I agree with Lewin, inappropriate in the reconstruction of a value orientation. Some of us in the training profession, following Socrates, have done some work in training for value inquiry. More work needs to be done.

10. "The individual accepts the new system of values and beliefs by accepting belongingness in a group" (p. 62). This insight of Lewin's into the indispensability of groups as media of effective reeducation and as elements in human socialization has already been emphasized. This fact of life is resisted by many persons made impatient by the urgency of widely recognized needs for behavioral change in various areas of social living. Such persons frequently try to bypass the group participation that is required for behavioral changes—put the message on TV; write more popular books on psychiatry and applied social science; get influential people, perhaps the President, to endorse it; pass a law; *require* people to change their behavior. I am not against any of these as aspects of programs of social change. But, taken as adequate means for the humanization and repersonalization of relationships in our bureaucratized mass society and culture—in which loneliness, alienation, personal confusion, and perceived self-impotence are the lot of many, if not most, people—the counsel seems a counsel of despair, not of hope. The counsel of hope seems to me to involve reconstruction of our organized life of social research, of education, and of social action. And the reconstruction will come only as collaboration among researchers, educators, and actionists comes to replace the self-segregation and autistic hostility that now tend to characterize their relationships. This was Kurt Lewin's vision of a reeducative society, and it is one in which I gladly share.

Lewin's own wise discussion (Lewin & Grabbe, 1945) of the implications of his tenth principle are worth quoting at length.

> When re-education involves the relinquishment of standards which are contrary to the standards of society at large (as in the case of delinquency, minority prejudices, alcoholism), the feeling of group belongingness seems to be greatly heightened if the members feel free to express openly the very sentiments which are to be dislodged through re-education.
>
> This might be viewed as another example of the seeming contradictions inherent in the process of re-education: Expression of prejudices against minorities or the breaking of rules of parliamentary procedures [or etiquette] may in themselves be contrary to the desired goal. Yet a feeling of complete freedom and a heightened

group identification are frequently more important at a particular stage of re-education than learning not to break specific rules.

This principle of in-grouping makes understandable why complete acceptance of previously rejected facts can be achieved best through the discovery of these facts by the group members themselves. . . . Then, and frequently only then, do the facts become really *their* facts (as against other people's facts). An individual will believe facts he himself has discovered in the same way that he believes in himself or in his group. The importance of this fact-finding process for the group by the group itself has been recently emphasized with reference to re-education in several fields. . . . It can be surmised that the extent to which social research is translated into social action depends on the degree to which those who carry out this action are made a part of the fact-finding on which the action is to be based.

Re-education influences conduct only when the new system of values and beliefs dominates the individual's perception. The acceptance of the new system is linked with the acceptance of a specific group, a particular role, a definite source of authority as new points of reference. It is basic for re-education that this linkage between acceptance of new facts or values and acceptance of certain groups or roles is very intimate and that the second frequently is a prerequisite for the first. This explains the great difficulty of changing beliefs and values in a piecemeal fashion. This linkage is a main factor behind resistance to re-education, but can also be made a powerful means for successful re-education. (pp. 62–63)

THE MOTORIC DIMENSION OF REEDUCATION

I would like now to comment briefly on an omission from Lewin's principles of reeducation of which he was quite aware. You will recall that Lewin recognized three dimensions to effective reeducation—cognitive and perceptual structures, values and valences, and motoric action—the individual's distinctive ways of control over his or her physical and social movements. It was the third dimension that Lewin chose not to conceptualize. And it is the place of physical and social movement in processes of reeducation that has become most controverted in the field of training and reeducation generally in recent years.

I recognize three developments in which the motoric dimension of behavioral change has been focused upon and made the object of research and experimentation. The first arose within the Lewinian training movement itself. This was the attempt to define human relations skills and to devise opportunities for people to practice these skills for themselves with feedback near to the time of performance—both through simulation under laboratory conditions and through field practice under reality conditions. This development thrived as an adjunct to T group experience in early laboratory designs. Then as the T group, often under the ambiguous name of sensitivity training, tended to be taken as the complete process of reeducation by some trainers and by many participants, interest in skill practice as an important part of reeducation declined. Lately, new interest in structured experiences in human relations training has been manifested, and a number of guidebooks for trainers and groups have been published, outlining skill practice exercises that have been developed and tested over the years in the emerging training profession. I think this revived interest is a healthy one and should be encouraged. Let me suggest two cautions, however. First, "putting participants through" exercises before they have, in Lewinian language, been "unfrozen," before they have seen reasons to change their present concepts, perceptions, ideologies, or skills, will likely leave little lasting deposit in their behavioral repertoire, inner and outer. Or it may leave them with new bags of tricks that are not integrated with altered and better integrated values, concepts, or perceptions, and so can be utilized only mechanically rather than organically in their life and work. Second, I tend to oppose trainers' prescriptions that do not grow out of some joint diagnosis by trainers and participants of their needs for skill development. If such prescriptions are used openly and frankly as a tool for furnishing diagnostic data to trainers and participants, such use may avoid the timing error of putting the cart before the horse.

The second use of movement as an aid to reeducation has arisen within the field of applied humanistic psychology, to which, in the broad sense of anti-Freudian and anti-Skinnerian, Lewinian psychology belongs. Humanistic psychologists draw heavily on the more organismic psychologies of Wilhelm Reich and Fritz Perls, among others. Their uses of movement draw heavily upon tactile and kinesthetic perception as a corrective to more socialized and morally tinged visual and auditory perceptions and their chief tools of expression and communication—words. Experiences in nonverbal movement help to open up people to awareness of conflicts and discrepancies within themselves and between themselves and others in their social world. I agree that dissimulation or self-delusion is more difficult in tactile and kinesthetic perceptions than in verbalized reports of what people see and hear. And I have found nonverbal movements a useful tool in extending awareness to ordinarily nonconscious bodily processes, feelings, and emotional states. "Movement" can be effectively designed into overall programs and processes of reeducation. I have two cautions that I would make about the use of experiences in nonverbal movement in training. First, it may increase the dependence of participants upon the trainer, who knows a powerful and intriguing technology that the participants do not know. It may thus, unwittingly, fail to develop the autonomy of participants in assuming more intelligent control of their own continuing resocialization in the society in which they live. Second, the hesitation to verbalize the meaning of nonverbal experiences may militate against the conceptualization of the meanings of the experience, which is a necessary part of transfer of learnings beyond the laboratory or classroom. For words are the tools of valid conceptualization as well as tools of obfuscation and self-delusion, as they are sometimes used.

The third emphasis on motoric action in reeducation comes out of behavior therapy and is based on a rather strict behavioristic psychology, particularly that of B. F. Skinner. I do not doubt the evidence of behavioral changes accomplished through reconditioning processes. I have grave doubts about the effects of such reeducation upon the "inner" processes of valuing, conceputalizing, and willing, which, on their own assumptions, behaviorists do not take into account in their experimentation or in the evaluation of its results. I have more faith in reeducation that helps persons bring their inner and outer behaviors into more integral relationship through a process in which participants play a responsible part as researchers and educators of and for themselves.

My reassessment of Lewin's views of reeducation has, I hope, convinced you, as it has convinced me, of their fruitfulness in guiding future developments in applied social science and in education more generally.

8 · On Learning to Believe in Persons

The good life will be a struggle to extort freedom, individuality and personal significance from a system that on the face of it denies all of them. . . . There is no lack of evil to be conquered, and the awareness that we have the power to remedy it disturbs any complacency we may be tempted to enjoy.

Harry Broudy
"Unfinishable Business"

LEARNING TO BELIEVE IN PERSONS begins with believing in myself. Belief in persons does not stand by itself. It is interrelated with other knowledges and beliefs about human beings in society, in history, in nature, in the world. But it begins with the originating center of all my knowing and believing—myself—whatever and whoever the objects of my knowledge and belief.

I aspire to believe in myself as a human person. I often, perhaps always, fall short of my aspiration. When I fall far short, I recognize familiar processes of self-obfuscation, self-division, self-diminution occurring within me. My thinking becomes confused and divided. I listen to the evidence, pleas, and demands of some voices in me and ignore or reject the evidence, pleas, and demands of other voices. My choices become partisan as among various parts of myself. My energy flows into defense and justification of partial and partisan positions taken against the criticisms of repressed or rejected interests and evidences within myself. I project minority positions within myself hatefully upon others around me. In diabolizing these others, I diabolize part of me and in the process further weaken and divide myself. I grow rigid in defending thoughts, orientations, and courses of action that were formed in the past—which were, perhaps, liberating, unifying, and strengthening at some past time, but which now deflect me from investment in creative and integrative processes that might liberate, unify, and strengthen me in present and future thought, choice, and action.

When, recognizing processes of self-obfuscation, self-division, self-diminution within myself and naming and accepting these for what they are, I reenact my belief in myself, and the voices within me are joined again in fruitful, dialogic conflict. I become open to the invention and incorporation of new, liberating, unifying, and strengthening patternings of impulse, aspiration, and response in and to my world. I become open to the resources of others outside me in pursuing my creative quest. I learn and grow. I am reconfirmed in my belief in myself as a human person.

PERSONS IN HISTORY, SUBMERGENT AND EMERGENT

It is difficult for me, as it is for others, to maintain faith in the capacity of human persons to learn and to grow as the main resource and hope of humanity in our historical period. We are painfully aware of deep schisms in the body social. Familiar ways of dealing with such schisms, familiar rites, have lost their power to suppress, repress, or reconcile. And schisms in the body social, not surprisingly, have engendered schisms in the human soul. We live in a period of time in which historical movements and events are experienced by most persons as "meteorological" or "geological" cataclysms. In this view, no individual body, mind, or spirit can stop, divert, or direct them. Individuals who once emerged from history to choose for themselves have lost the support of beliefs and institutions that once gave credibility to their assertion of effective freedom and to their belief in their creative power to shape events through their own thoughts and actions. Human beings feel lost, alone, in the midst of historical eruptions and counter-eruptions. Their personal lives seem to count for little or nothing in the massive reequilibrations of institutions, societies, and cultures in which their personal lives are fatefully involved. Can a person sanely maintain faith in himself or herself in such a period of history? And, even if it could be demonstrated that a person can, because such faith requires that personal choice not be dissolved in the machinations of historical necessity, should one do so? I believe that I can and should maintain faith in myself, in my capacity to learn, to grow and create. And I feel justified in recommending the same faith to others as a saving faith. I have found justifications as I have come to trust the power within myself to say no to the environing powers that threaten to engulf and destroy me.

The rhetoric of power is a potent rhetoric in a time such as ours. It is largely out of a feeling of impotence to resist the commands and cajolements of collective power in the presence of cataclysmic events that persons are now alienated from faith in themselves. It is in negation of this rhetoric of power that faith in one's self is both manifested and generated. A poem, which, when I wrote it, I called "A Dream," seems to me now to depict a reality for persons if they choose to see and believe it.

A DREAM

The light—so dim it drew the horizon near—
Showed giant figures, almost human, hemming me round,
Faceless or with averted faces. I stood alone and I could hear
Their almost human voices—impressive sound,
Well-amplified, most high fidelity—commanding "Kneel!"
I did not kneel. And from me came a bleat—
Most poorly modulated, low fidelity—"I do not feel
Your right to make me kneel." Came their repeat
"Kneel!"—computer-programmed, nuclear-driven now—"We
    have the power.
We are the nations, churches, races, collectivities.

You are a piece of us—without us, nothing. In this dark hour
Of dire emergency, to stand upright is treason, sacrilege—down
    on your knees!"
Darkness had further dimmed the scene and it was cold.
Wavering, my voice came to my ears, perhaps into their almost
    human ears, whispering "No!"
From near around me, like a significant secret told
By friend to friend in private, came fellow-sounds—at first low
Then amplified by human power—a chorus free
Praising Man and singing "NO!" Above me dawned a dim but
    brightening star.
I saw faces of men—a company of little men standing tall and
    welcoming me.
Now there was light enough to fling the horizon far.

COLLECTIVITY AND COMMUNITY

Human beings depend on their institutions for facilitating and regularizing the satisfaction of many of their needs. In turn, institutions depend on the internalization and acceptance by persons of patterns of conduct, belief, and relationship, and of subordination and command, for their viability and perpetuity. In an historical view, institutions are artifacts invented and affirmed by people at some past time, recent or remote. But they must continually be reinvented and reaffirmed by those who live in and through the patterns of conduct and rationalization that their operability requires, if they are to survive in actuality.

When persons bow down to institutions—familial, economic, political, or religious—granting to them some rightful power to create and to destroy the persons who depend on them, they are engaging in idolatry, worshiping that which they themselves have created and recreated, alienating themselves from their own inherent power to create and to destroy. When persons say no to the demands of any institution for their unquestioning allegiance and obedience, they are reducing their alienation from their original power to legitimize any and all social arrangements—a power that lives only within and among themselves.

To assert the originating power of persons to destroy and to create institutions is not to deny the social nature of human beings. It is rather to assert the validity of Martin Buber's (1935) distinction between collectivity and community. Collectivity lives in the regularization of predictable I–It relationships among people. Relationships between persons are functionally rationalized into role relationships in the service of externalized objectives and goals. In a just collectivity, there is reciprocity in role relationships, and equity in the distribution of the products of joint efforts. But in a community, persons meet as persons in I–Thou relationships. Relationships in a community do not depend on the curtailment or arrest of personal existence in the interest of efficient service of external goals, as in a collectivity. The intention and result of communal relationships is the enhancement and augmentation of personal existence. There is, as Aristotle once said, no need for justice among friends. I–Thou relationships are characterized by spontaneity, creativity, surprise. Collective relationships are characterized by predictability, routinization, minimal surprise. Persons in a livable society must maintain an intricate and precarious balance between collective and communal relationships.

THE IDOLATRIZING OF ARTIFACTS

It has been a temptation of contemporary scientific students and managers of social life to conceive sociality and to coach the practice of sociality in the image of collectivity to the virtual exclusion of community. Most have yielded to the temptation. I have already mentioned human beings' tendency to idolatrize their artifacts in commenting on their worship of institutions that live only through continual personal recreation and reaffirmation of these arrangements. This has been apparent also in human beings' use of the latest and most powerful technological creations analogically to shed light on their own nature. In the heyday of machines, scientific students of humanity sought to interpret persons as machines. No doubt this mechanical metaphor shed much light on mechanical aspects of human functioning, both in body and in mind. And no doubt also, it led many to strenuous efforts to organize human effort after a mechanical model. But it also trapped human beings into forgetting that the creators of the machine were not exhaustively explained after the model of their own creations.

It is not surprising that with the human creation and development of computer technology, persons are widely interpreting their mental operations after the model of computer functioning. Nor is it surprising that human efforts are being widely coached and organized to conform to the demands and to the image of the computer. Cybernetic Man is an idol just as Mechanical Man was and is an idol to many. The difficulty lies not in the invention and use by human beings of mechanical or computer models and technologies in facilitating their projects. The difficulty lies in the tendency of the creators to deify their own creations, to ascribe to these a reality prior to the reality of themselves, and to put themselves abjectly into the service of their own artifacts. In this process persons come to feel powerless before the powers that they have released and lose faith in the creative power that lies within themselves to use their artifacts in the service of personal and communal ends or to refuse to use them at all.

The accelerated march of bureaucracy in the organization of human life in the modern world combines two of the depersonalizing tendencies already noted. It reflects the human tendency to conceive and to practice sociality in the image of collectivity to the attempted exclusion of community in the organization of human relationships. Another way of saying this is to say that contemporary human beings have attempted to cultivate and foster I–It relationships throughout the range of organized life to the exclusion of I–Thou relationships. It reflects also the modern human tendency to place faith in technologies as a way of solving human problems, even to the extent of modeling their view of themselves in the image of their most recent and most powerful technology. Persons have tended to forget that only they themselves can heal the schisms in their souls. That these tendencies of modern persons have proved abortive is evidenced by the widespread despair, quiet or clamorous, of people, affluent or poor, who live their lives enmeshed in bureaucratic structures; by widespread withdrawal of personal investment in the fate and fortune of bureaucratized institutions, whether this withdrawal takes the form of psychological or physical dropping out; by growing attempts, especially among the young, to destroy and discredit bureaucratized forms of life and relationship; and by the weakness of bureaucratic leadership to learn from these various forms of protest and withdrawal and to generate the spontaneous allegiance of persons that the renewal and perpetuity of established institutions require.

THE AFFIRMATION OF PERSON AND COMMUNITY THROUGH THE NEGATION OF IDOLS

It is in the widespread and, I hope, growing negation by persons of dehumanizing and depersonalizing demands placed on them by many of our customs and institutions that I find reason to believe that faith by persons in themselves today is not a forlorn faith. For in the negation there is also an affirmation. Actually, there is a double affirmation in every negation of dehumanized and depersonalized ways of life and of the idols that people have made of these. When I negate demands on me that contravene my humanity and my personhood, I am affirming the irreducible and ineradicable reality of the human and the personal in me and in others. But I am also, as I negate a dehumanizing and depersonalizing social order, affirming an alternative social order that is dedicated to the enhancement rather than the attenuation of the human and the personal in me and in others. In my negation, there is thus an affirmation both of person and of community.

Why is it hard for many to hear the affirmations in the voices of contemporary protests and liberation movements? The difficulty comes in part because, in the dominant vocabulary in terms of which self and society are discussed today, it is hard for protesters to name or to declare clearly or unequivocally the affirmation of themselves out of which their protests arise. In the conventional view, protest arises out of weakness and deprivation, not out of strength, and is addressed to those who are assumedly strong and undeprived. Both protesters and those against whom protest is directed tend to share this conventional view. In this view, the "haves" possess goods that the "have nots" do not possess. The protest is motivated by a desire to deprive "haves" of their valuable possessions and to endow the "have nots" with valuable possessions of the same sort. No doubt current social and political protest does in part conform to this model, both in the national and the international scene. But there are good reasons to believe that this model fails to illuminate significant aspects of current protest against established institutions, whether in Israel, China, or the United States. For protest arises from the ranks of those—students, socially conscious intellectuals and artists, voluntary adult dropouts from established institutions, the mentally ill— now in possession of the conventional goods of a society. They are saying that they do not want what the "haves" in established society now possess and tend to call good. They are rejecting conventional criteria of success. They are groping toward more life-affirming and person-affirming, more "humanized," values, and toward social forms and relationships that incorporate and support the pursuit and actualization of these values. I do not believe that it is beyond those now in charge of institutions to join the protesters in their human quest, if they can come to believe that they themselves as persons are more important than the positions they occupy or the privileges they possess.

The case is not unlike that among many of the "have nots" as well—American blacks who reject the values of the dominant society and seek to build their own society based on more life-affirming and self-affirming value orientations; Third World groups who reject the dominant values of both Soviet communism and American capitalism and who seek to image and achieve some nonimperialistic alternative in society and in culture; and "liberation" groups among women, homosexuals, and ethnic minorities.

The human struggles that many contemporary protest movements precipitate and embody are thus not fully illuminated by conventional models of political struggle, even though proponents and opponents frequently speak a political language and are often enamored of and bewitched by political modes of action as the only way out of confusion and conflict. The struggles are easier to comprehend fully if they are seen as struggles toward a way of life more human than people are now living and enjoying, toward communal arrangements that support souls in their varied quests toward a meaningful life, toward a more person-centered existence. They are struggles toward a more humanized world culture. They are religious struggles in which men and women seek ways of finding or building a home in a universe in which they have come to feel homeless. This view does not deny the political dimension of the struggle. It does tend to put that dimension in its place. Thus, widespread attempts to conceive and practice the contemporary human struggle in exclusively political terms becloud the affirmations of person and community that are implicit in contemporary protests against established institutions and ideologies.

THE FRAGMENTATION AND REPERSONALIZATION OF HUMAN BEINGS

The implicit affirmations in social protest are further obscured by factionalized support of various fragmented views of human nature and human destiny. This fragmentation of views of persons characterizes academic life, the life of social practice, and the life of contemporary action. Departmentalization in the study of human behavior and human affairs reflects the rampant specialization of language, assumptions, and activities in the conduct and organization of contemporary research. But it also supports a segregation of research efforts, with only limited communication among biologists, psychologists, sociologists, anthropologists, economists, linguists, critics of the arts, historians, political scientists, and theologians—all presumably seeking to contribute to understanding and comprehension of human nature and human destiny. Specialization and segregation characterize research efforts within each of these fields of study as well. Efforts to build communication among specialists in various segregated disciplines or to synthesize—to confront and inter-criticize—findings, concepts, and assumptions from different disciplines receive little support and are often opposed vigorously by proponents of the disciplines and by those who finance their efforts. Philosophers have widely abandoned these tasks. It is hard to say how much light specialized knowledges of human beings might shed on our dark and confused human situation, because efforts to focus such light are infrequent and unsustained.

But it is easy to see that people seeking to understand and deal with their human puzzlements and pains get either little or highly abstract and misleading intellectual help from academic sources of knowledge about humanity. This is illustrated well by students who, seeking to understand themselves and their human condition, increasingly find little help in studies organized along specialized disciplinary lines. It is dangerous to themselves and to others when they conclude that "objective" studies of human affairs, which scientific researchers often profess to do, are worthless in the pursuit of their purposes and when they are confirmed in a one-sided subjectivity in their view of what "knowledge" is apt to their purposes. It is dangerous but it is also understandable that many students and other actionists identify themselves with an uncritical and undiluted subjectivity in their choices and decisions.

Fragmentation has also come to characterize professionals in their learning and use of technologies of social practice—in and among the health professions, in social work, in administration and management, in schooling and education, in organized religion. Each operates with varying assumptions about human behavior, human potentiality, and the ends of human life. And, because professional practice has tended to shape its patterns of service to the forms and requirements of established institutions, protesters against established institutions tend to discount the validity of professional, knowledge-based expertise, and to discount also the values of objectivity and rationality, with which professional experts over-identify themselves, in seeking to coach and influence human practice and action.

The departmental and bureaucratic organization of knowledge building and of knowledge application has tended to limit interpersonal exchange both between researchers and practitioners and between them and the "ultimate" consumers and clients of research and professional practice. When they do meet, they tend to meet in formalized and stereotypic role-to-role relationships. Their differences are emphasized in such meetings. They rarely meet as selves and as persons, possessed of a common humanity but differing in needs and resources, with hope for the possible joining of needs and resources in projects of mutual and common benefit. The need for cultivating such community with scholars; between scholars and practitioners; and among scholars, practitioners, and "consumers" of knowledge and professional practice is now widely recognized in health, in education, in welfare, in religion, and in industry and business. Roles and statuses as now defined and enacted thwart the development of such community. Only persons and selves can meet in community. Specialization becomes fragmentation when specialists fail to affirm themselves as selves and persons first and as specialists second. Creative and humane mergers of specialized knowledge, of specialized technologies, and of specific human needs take place only as persons with specialized knowledge, persons with specialized technologies, and persons with specific needs meet as persons in community. And such meeting occurs only as people come to believe in and affirm themselves as human persons. Without such meetings our specializations will destroy a common humanity, as they are now tending to do.

ONLY SELVES CAN RECONCILE THE SUBJECTIVE AND THE OBJECTIVE IN HUMAN BEING AND ACTION

A more basic factionalized fragmentation of human beings has shown itself, as we have explored the effects of departmentalization of effort in the study of human beings and in the development and utilization of technologies of social practice. This has to do with the person as "subjective" and the person as "objective." Some assert the priority of subjective existence over any or all characterizations or conceptualizations of a human being as an object among other objects and see dependence by persons on these as escapes from freedom. Others assert that only "objective" knowledge of human behavior furnishes a valid basis for understanding, treating, teaching, or managing people, and relegate subjective visions of persons to an irreal world of fantasy, wish, or dream—perhaps to be totally discarded as evidence of human nature, perhaps as evidence to be explained or explained away in terms of "real," objective, publicly manipulable variables and their relationships.

The effects of this fragmentation of persons are most apparent morally in differing views of how human beings validly ground their choices and decisions about what to do with themselves and how to deal with others. In a highly subjectivist view of decision, persons make their choices alone, unjustified and without excuse, on the basis of inner spontaneous promptings and impulsions. Only in such decisions is a person freed. The objectivist view asserts that human organisms are freed only through objective knowledge of themselves and their situation. The free person makes up his or her mind to act one way or another on the basis of knowledge of the motivations and consequences of alternative actions, keeping subjective wishes and fantasies out of the "rational" calculus utilized in the decision.

It seems to me that both subjectivist and objectivist partisans have split human capacities that are conjoined in the selfhood of human beings. Whatever else selfhood includes, it involves the distinctively reflexive power of human beings. I affirm myself. I understand myself. I respond to, take responsibility for, myself. In each of these statements, "I" somehow appears as both subject and object. In self-processes I and my situation appear as objects to be understood, analyzed, and diagnosed whether historically, in terms of my present involvements, or in relation to some future perspective or project. But it is I, as subject, with various and often conflicting wishes, fantasies, impulses, aspirations, and preferences, who is objectifying myself and my situation in the hope of fuller, less deluded, more harmonious expression, investment, and fulfillment of my complex and conflicted subjective-objective person in present action and future consequence. "Selfing" is a process that conjoins subjective and objective modes of human actuality, hopefully to the mutual and beneficial service of both. It is this "selfing" process in which I believe and seek to believe more fully and responsibly.

This is not to say that all my choices and actions are at any one time involved in self-processing. I am sometimes moved by an inner impulse that impels me to actions involving no recognition of the claims and welfare of other regions of myself or of other persons within the ambit of my action. I must pay a price for such inconsiderateness. The price may not be too great to pay if the impulse that moved me was a repressed part of my person that now I am aware of and that I can include, perhaps for the first time, within the councils of myself. But the price must be paid and I would hope to develop a self, through such experiences as these, that in the future is less repressive of, and more attentive to, minority voices in and around my-self.

At other times I am moved to action by the weight of external demands and evidences that leads me to ignore or repress the demands of "subjective" voices and doubts within my person. Such action is debilitating to myself. For I am dishonoring and suppressing parts of my subjective person in such decisions, perhaps through idolatrizing some externalized projection of myself at the expense of the invention of new modes of response that might do greater justice both to external demands and to internal demands—modes of response that can become part of my learning-growing person. Such "objectively" grounded actions are, from the viewpoint of this potentiality, unfaithful slayings of myself.

Both internal and external censorships and curtailments of whole, integrated, and free responses in and to my world are possibilities and probabilities that continually threaten me. To abet internal censorship by invoking the sacred name of "subjective" freedom or to elevate external censorship in the name of "objective" reality is to perpetuate divisions within persons and to block the building of community out of the conflicts among persons.

Decisions and choices present themselves to persons as ambiguities, confusions, and conflicts. There is a strong tendency in human organisms to make a quick end to ambiguity, confusion, and conflict within the organism by externalizing the conflict, by rushing to some inner equilibrium, whether impulsive or rationally engineered, that is a willful falsification of both outer and inner reality. Belief in the self supports the human person in staying with the conflict, in joining the dialogue between inner voices and between outer voices, and in seeking and affirming the creative resolution of conflict that is most likely to issue when a conflict is taken into the persons of the contestants and worked through to a humane conclusion. For one who affirms the potency and benignity of the self, easy resolutions that would foreclose conflicts by excluding them from the self are seen as temptations to irresponsibility or, as I have expressed the idea poetically, as burdens of false peace.

THE BURDEN OF FALSE PEACE

I seek no peace which gives the lie to life—
No peace which speaks extinction to the mind
Or chills the hot projection of the will.
Oh take from me the burden of false peace.

Life is the aching pressure of the will,
The flickering, posturing pageant of the mind.

What dulls my mind and saps my will steals life.
Oh take from me the burden of false peace.

I would begin (not end) my quest for life at Bethlehem.
I would find strength to will and fail, and learn to will anew,
To know that loss and pain in love can strengthen me.
Oh take from me the burden of false peace.

ONLY PERSONS CAN RECONCILE
THE RATIONAL AND THE NONRATIONAL

The factional struggles between proponents of the "subjective" and the "objective" in human beings often polarize a related disjunction between the "irrational" and the "rational" in persons. When rationality is used to name processes of resolving issues by cool manipulation and logical processing of facts, with an exclusion of human feelings and aspirations evoked by issues from the arena of judgment as "non-facts," it is not surprising that feelingful and aspiring persons thus excluded from influence on the resolution should find in rationality an enemy. Nor is it surprising that they should seek to elevate "sub-rational" urgencies of feeling and impulse, *Blut und Boden*, or "super-rational" revelations and absolutes, whether of nation, race, or God, above rational processes as legitimate arbiters of human choice and action. The effect of the polarization is to blind both the opponents and proponents of a depersonalized and dehumanized version of rationality to their own incoherences. "Objective rationalists" are blinded to the part that their own unacknowledged feelings, aspirations, and preferences play in the judgments they make. "Subjective irrationalists," as they seek to justify to themselves and others some favored urgency or revelation as worthy of acceptance as a ground for choice and action, fail to see that they are enlisting processes of rationality in the service and propagation of their own "irrational" devotions. Both are deluding themselves.

The problem is to invent and enact a more adequate conception of rationality. The purpose of rationality in human affairs is not to suppress human impulses and their satisfaction. It is, rather, to seek to facilitate the fuller and more harmonious satisfaction of human impulses and interests where various impulses and interests present contrary and conflicting demands on finite human energies and resources. In a situation demanding harmonization, rationality creates an ideal that has pertinence and authority to persons seeking to actualize goods that are seen as irreconcilable without the mediation of such an ideal. An ideal is perforce a creative blending of things actual and things desired.

My belief in myself and in the selves of others leads me to accept Santayana's (1929) criteria for evaluating the work of rationality in human affairs.

> A rational will is not a will that has reason for its basis or that possesses any other proof that its realization would be possible or good than the oracle with a living will inspires and pronounces. The rationality possible to the will lies not in its source but in its method. An ideal cannot wait for its realization to prove its validity. To deserve loyalty it needs only to be adequate as an ideal, that is, to express completely what the soul at present demands, and to do justice to all extant interests. (pp. 254–255)

A self, when it behaves rationally in the presence of an issue, must seek reliable information concerning relevant matters of fact. And human aspirations, aversions, and preferences are important facts to be blended and reconciled with other more technical and external considerations in forming decisions and attainable ideals. Knowledge of what now is or has been never determines completely the direction or form of future action. Reason in a self that operates in self-respect is an inventive, imaginative, and reconstructive reason alive to new possibilities and desirabilities in improving human arrangements and correcting human derangements. A hopeful person learns to use failures in action to envision new desirabilities and to generate new and more attainable aspirations.

Another distinction with respect to rationality in human affairs helps to explain in part the penchant of contemporary human beings for polarizing "irrational" and "rational" in the thought and conduct of persons. This is Karl Mannheim's (1950) distinction between substantial and functional rationality in contemporary society. Mannheim used "functional rationality" to refer to the objective analysis of functions required for various collective tasks and the organization of task production through an ordered layout of interrelated functions into which "personnel" are fitted through deliberate processes of selection and training. Functional rationality in human organization was exemplified in Germany in the movement to rationalize industrial organization, and in America in the scientific management movement. With refined and augmented power, functional rationality flourishes today in the disciplines of operations research and systems analysis. The rationalization of human organization has moved out of industry into government, education, and the provision of health and welfare services, and has touched men and women in every aspect of their lives.

Mannheim used "substantial rationality" to refer to the "reason" I described earlier, operating at the personal and group levels of human organization to achieve a flexible, harmonious, and viable patterning among various and conflicting impulses and interests. But when it operates well or fully, substantial rationality operates integratively, voluntaristically, with full communication and interaction between cognitive, affective, and conative aspects of living.

Mannheim remarked that an increase in functional rationality often leads to an increase in substantial irrationality on the part of the people expected to accede to its demands on them. He did not, as I recall it, explore the opposite hypothesis. But perhaps that opposite hypothesis is what protesters against functionally rationalized organizations—student leftists, Black Power advocates, and hippies, among others—were exploring in the 1960s. Does a committed effort by a group to articulate and assert its substantial rationality lead to an increase in functional irrationality within a highly rationalized social system or organization? I think that we have evidence that it does. But the task of practical reason as it operates through selves and communities does not end there. It must move on to the normative questions: Need the requirements of functional rationality and those of substantial rationality be opposed, segregated, and polarized in the organization of human life and action? Should we invent and bring into being forms of human organization in which the claims of substantial rationality and of functional rationality are reconciled and harmonized?

Early "human relations" protests against the sweep of functional rationality within industry were often couched in terms of its neglect and frustration of the affective and conative needs of those who work but often fail to live in industry. The new "human relations" protestants must speak also of the frustration of the powers of substantial human rationality that operate in and through human persons by rampant functional rationality in the management of human life as well. In addition, the protests must be addressed not least to the organization of our life of learning, education, and research.

PERSONS IN COMMUNITY AND COMMUNITY IN PERSONS

In commenting earlier on the premature and facile pseudo-resolutions of issues that thwart growth and learning in human persons, I did not emphasize my need, the need of all persons, for the help of other persons in shedding the burdens of false peace. I must continually validate myself against others in maintaining and deepening my reality orientation. Sensory deprivation experiments with human subjects have shown how persons, deprived of encounter with and feedback from others, lose the power to discriminate between fantasy and veridical perception, lose the boundaries that, however fluidly, identify them as persons. Consensual validation is not an option, it is rather a necessity in the maintenance of a sane and viable self. Consensual validation by persons possessed of a common false consciousness confirms them in this false consciousness, whether of self-image or of ideology.

A self committed to growth in reality orientation must deliberately seek consensual validation against others who differ in value orientation, in life-style, and commitment. A growing self must seek encounter with others who can and will challenge, if necessary, the very foundations of his or her beliefs and life commitments. And such a self must reciprocate the challenge to others in mutual exchange. Each in a growthful encounter should speak truth to the other in a spirit of love and mutual respect. This, as I understand it, and try when at my best to practice it, is what Martin Buber (1970) described as a life of and in dialogue. Faith in myself places upon me the responsibility of seeking to develop an adequate validating community around me. Only through experience of such relationships can I internalize an adequate validating community within myself. As I encounter fresh conflicts between myself and others, I must renew and refresh my internal community through new encounters and dialogue with those who challenge me. Social arrangements that thwart, discourage, and punish dialogue between those who differ are poisoning the wells of personal and social renewal.

SELF IN NATURE

So far I have spoken of self and person largely in the contexts of human exchange and sociality. But faith in self requires also supporting beliefs concerning the relations between myself and nonhuman nature in which persons and societies are born, seek to flourish, and die. I have explored some of these relationships in a prose poem.

MEDITATION ON THE SELF IN WINTER TIME

And is this I? The sun around which planet roles revolve?
Despair sloughs off some non-essential trappings of the self—the

me's that batten on bright public praise, that preen before the
public smile.
The I enduring is a lonely I, yet can not spurn its debt to others—
its piety toward Man, generic and collective.
How can I find my tortuous way to Man beneath, beyond a maze
of statuses—statuses filled and yet denied by me as
inessential to myself?

There is a cruelty unfathomable in willful, will-less crowding of a
man into the shape of ruin.
The will-less cruelty—lacking light of self-awareness—is the more
unfathomable.
And yet the pain induced in victim shows a weakness there—a
lack of calm acceptance that the cosmos is in me, in my
tormentors too; that Man looks through my eyes when they
see clearly, lovingly.

A thousand you's may judge a single me, may call me devil,
thing, may name me name which canting lips can only hint
or whisper, or for my acts unnamed intone dark censure.
But Man to which essential I responds may yet elude the
judgment. So where is Man and where am I? The questions
are the same.

My floods of fantasy break into froth and foam, whirling and
churning, propelled by deep disease within myself.
Creation moves within my floods of fantasy, joining my self to
others, to Man, to world at levels which my ego can not see
by light refracted through distorting screens of conscience
and self-image.
How can I feel, follow creation through torments of prideful pain?
How can I find among all pains the pain, which, conquered,
yields a new articulation of myself, which shapes me, node
of the cosmos, into a form that shows forth truth?

And all these words are lame things, brittle defense-offense
toward human cruelty and sightlessness within myself and
others, cruelty and sightlessness which would deny myself
and other selves unquestioned human membership.
Yet heartfelt words may light a heliograph, which others on some
lonely hill beleaguered see, interpret, may fashion bonds of
new community.
Or if no heliograph gets built, if no one reads a message in the
flickering images evoked, the words may kindle new light in
myself, may quicken hope that others will be found who feel
all mankind kin;

Who do not draw harsh circles round the love they give, doling it
out to those "deserving" it, which means no gift, no
overflowing of a tribute, unmandated, undeserved;
Who look through customs, credentials, relativities to see a core
humanity, forged in despair, living by hope, which knows of
truth because it is the source of truth.

One connection with nonhuman nature with which I am intimately involved from birth to death is my body. I am not always on
good terms with my body; I sometimes resent its illnesses, its lack of
grace, its resistance to my efforts to make it into something that it
cannot be. I am most whole when I admit the voices of my body, the
voices that speak of strength and limitation, of health and death, of
lust and satiation into the councils of myself. For our animal species,
with its ancient memories of a long and continuing evolution of life
out of nonlife, of simple life forms into intricate and differentiated life
forms, of complicated energy exchanges between organism and environment, speaks to me through my body when I learn to hear its mes-
sages. To accept my body as part of myself is for me to see and feel
myself as nature becomes conscious of itself in one unique center of
feeling, thinking, evaluation, and choice. To feel myself as continuous
with nature is to see myself as responsible for continuing the process
of evolution of life through deliberate variation and selection, not
through the dumb and silent processes of inter-adjustment, which lie
behind me and others like and yet different from me. I gain strength
in negating the idolatries that would arrest and delay the continuing
processes of creative evolution of which I as a person am an indispensable part.

I believe that I am a "node of the cosmos." I have not been able to
understand those who look for evidence of the nature of nature only
outside themselves and fail to find evidence of the nature of nature
also in the self that looks beyond itself and tries to make sense of what
it sees and finds there. In myself, as I function fully and adequately, I
am nature seeking to understand itself, to direct itself consciously, to
reshape itself planfully. To recognize, as I must, if I am to become a
self at all, that otherness is as real as I does not negate myself. It
means rather to me that nature is variegated and individualized, and
that I, if I do not fail myself, am in some way unique.

When I find conflict within me and around me, I am not appalled. For I know from my own experience as a self that conflict, if I
can face it and help to work it through, can yield a wider consciousness, a creation and realization of new good in which old good is not

wholly lost. That conflict can also destroy good puts a responsibility upon me to find ways of augmenting the creative, rather than the destructive, uses of conflict. I must recognize variety, differences, and conflict within nature as I must recognize it within and around myself. I must also recognize the reality of community, which supports me both in actualizing my individuality and in the enhancement of common experience. My own power, with the help of others, to see possibilities beyond my present powers of empirical verification also endows me and others with the power to delude myself and others. Truth is not possible without the concomitant possibility of error. Without faith in myself as a node of an evolving cosmos become conscious, critical, and responsible, I lose my zest for the continuing struggle to distinguish truth from error, to communicate truth, and to try to live by it.

My realization that I will die quickens my sense of the importance of my life. I will not wholly die if I have allowed myself to become a memorable part of others even as I have welcomed others in becoming memorable parts of myself.

EPITAPH

I have found death in friends' forgetfulness
And immortality in loving memory.
Hell lives in tortured memories sharp with pain.
If hell should be the fate that I have earned,
Forget me, friends. Grant me quick death and cool oblivion.
But if love glows among the ash of time
Where we kept watch together on time's flame,
Save me from death, grant immortality.
Remember me, my friends, remember me.

And so—I aspire to believe in myself as a human being.

9 · Toward a Morality of Hope for the Future

The specific character of despair is precisely this: it is unaware of being despair.

Søren Kierkegaard
The Sickness Unto Death

When individuals sense that they are living through a period of crisis, when foundations seem to be cracking and orthodoxies breaking up, then a public space is created in which basic questions about the human condition can be raised anew.

Richard J. Bernstein
The Restructuring of Social and Political Theory

THE SPIRITUAL OUTLOOK THAT PERVADES THE MINDS of many men and women in urbanized and industrialized societies, not least in American society, is one of despair or loss of hope. It is a loss of hope for humankind and its future. The idea of inevitable progress, which had sanctioned unhampered pursuit of selfish and short-range interests by entrepreneurs, individual and corporate, and by nation-states in the hope that the dross of selfish achievement would be converted by some cosmic alchemy into the gold of human progress, is no longer convincing to most people. The class interests served by "free enterprise" and the exploitation and oppression of "backward peoples" implicit in old-style European colonialism and new-style American colonialism have been laid bare. The myth of progress through a competitive and individual achievement approach to life and living has been depotentiated. The recurrent breaks of demonic forces of war and terrorism through the veneer of a "rationalist" and self-interested ordering of life has contributed to this disillusionment. And the unintended consequences of a life-style of personal and social irresponsibility are everywhere evident—in gutted resources, in the erosion of support systems for human and other forms of life on earth, in the open, unremitting, and seemingly irreconcilable struggle between various groups of haves and have-nots.

At the personal level, lives spent in unexamined pursuit of status and material achievement have turned hollow to the spenders themselves as well as to their children. Roots in the past have been attenuated through physical and social mobility and their future perspective has been narrowed and clouded by the buffeting of unanticipated and, to many, meaningless changes in the conditions of their lives. Whatever the various dimensions and depths of the crisis that pervades contemporary experience, from a moral viewpoint, the crisis is a crisis of hope, the crisis of a desperate future. The psychological revolution that contemporary persons require, as Erich Fromm (1968) proclaimed, is a revolution of hope.

The dream of a saving future for humankind and an earth that may again become our home is thus a dream born of moral desperation and oriented toward the renewal of hope. It is important to appreciate the quality of the desperation that is parent to the dream, if we are to speculate aptly about the moral issues that confront efforts to incarnate the dream in the life and work of educators and educational institutions—whatever forms, schools or otherwise, these may take. The desperation does not stem, Icarus-like, from a perceived lack of human powers and means to serve a vision of a new society and a new culture. Evidence of human power to modify the environment and to reshape people biologically, psychologically, and politically is widely available today.

Human power to build and to destroy is evident in deserts made by human agency into fertile fields, and in fertile forests transformed into eroded and defoliated deserts, with both sorts of projects financed by the same nation-state. Human command of effective means in the biological sphere is evident in human lives restored, sustained, and extended through applied biochemical and nuclear knowledge, and in human lives snuffed out indiscriminately and horribly maimed and mutated by variant applications of the very same biochemical and nuclear knowledge. Human power to modify behavior finds expression in devoted and sensitive nurture and support of creative minds, engaged in building new knowledge and new images of human potentiality, and in the brainwashing of masses of people into robot servitude to some fuehrer's or party's whim or will.

Contemporary desperation thus stems in part from the disparate and contradictory moral visions that now quicken and guide people's uses of the vast powers at their disposal. But desperation stems as well from a view of humanity's moral plight deeper than the melodramatic view that supports a reformer's approach of bringing ends and means into balance through piecemeal changes that elevate the obviously "good" interests and put down the obviously "bad." The human situation is more complicated than that. A well intentioned effort to rid farmers' crops of insect pests may inadvertently rob forests of birds, and lakes and streams of fish. "Solutions" to problems of traffic glut in cities through building better access and egress roads and highways create polluted air, which threatens the life-support system for human life in the city and accelerates the depletion of our already dwindling supply of petrochemical energy. The inequation of intention and consequence works the other way around as well. A concerted attack by an oppressed minority group upon the property and persons of the oppressor group may build a new beneficent realization of community within the minority group and a sense of self-worth in its members, and, at times, a deepened sense of the injustice of social arrangements within members of the oppressor group. Sorting out the "good" and the "bad" effects in our uses of the powers at our command is no simple task of serving obviously "good" and disserving obviously "bad" intentions at the psychological level of human conduct.

We can no longer sanely depend on direction by tradition in our moral life. And yet our traditions are in us, shaping the way we see our human situation; the way we feel about it; the way we define the contours, the parameters, of our choices and actions; the way we evaluate the consequences of our actions as indices of progress or retrogression. Our moral deliberations must today extend to laying bare the basic normative orientations of our culture and of ourselves and submitting these to criticism as we choose and act. The reference point in our criticisms of our traditions must shift from past experience to a future still open for shaping and reconstruction through our decisions and actions, both personal and collective. Margaret Mead's (1965) advocacy of the future as the basis for establishing a shared culture grows from a perception of the crippling disjunctures in experience, which tend to divide and demoralize contemporary persons and groups. Her counsel includes a warning concerning the kind of planning that is consonant with a future in which a shared worldwide culture can develop.

> But always the surest guarantee of change and growth is the inclusion of living persons in every stage of an activity. Their lives, their experience and their continuing response—even their resistances—infuse with life any plan which, if living participants are excluded, lies on the drawing board and loses its reality. Plans for the future become old before they are lived but the future is always newborn and, like any newborn thing, is open to every kind of living experiences. (p. 154)

Mead thus suggests that a future orientation is one basis for building a morality of hope. Hope in a shared world culture will come to life only as people of various ages, nationalities, races, classes, and specialisms become participants in planning, choosing, and enacting a future desirable for all of them. If this is true, the construction and use of an adequate methodology of participative planning and policymaking is a major element in a morality of hope for the future and in educational processes that seek to advance the conception and practice of such a morality.

There are thus deep-cutting tasks of cognitive reconstruction that confront those who would wrest a justifiable morality of hope out of a climate of despair. And, as I have suggested, these tasks of reeducation have two foci—one oriented to a reconstructed methodology of political and moral judgment, individual and collective; the other oriented to laying bare the basic value orientations of Western culture and critically reconstructing them. The building of a morality of hope has extra-cognitive dimensions as well, which cannot sanely be neglected by the educator.

One function of morality within a society is to build and maintain morale within the members of that society. "Morale" is ordinarily used to describe the moral condition of a group of people and, by extension, the moral condition of a person within a group situation. High morale refers to a feeling, an attitude of *élan* in facing and coping with the conditions that the group must handle and negotiate in discharging its functions and in carrying out its task. It signifies a feeling and attitude of confidence, of hopefulness, that the group and the persons in it are in possession of adequate ways of managing its and their life situation. It connotes some clarity of direction, of necessity idealized and not now realized, into the future and a commitment to the meaning and importance of the chosen direction. It connotes, further, confidence in the viability of the means—methods, principles, leadership—for handling the difficulties, dangers, and barriers, both known and unknown, that movement and action toward desired and desirable purposes will entail. It connotes finally a feeling of potency to invest the means, external and internal, possessed by group and person in effective and meaningful choices and actions.

Low morale or demoralization connotes deficiency in any or all of the conditions that make for high morale. Demoralization may be related to a lack of attractive and compelling purposes that provide a map for the guidance of individual and collective actions into the future. Such purposes also provide for evaluating stepwise movements into the future. In effect, acceptable and accepted purposes are necessary to give operational meaning to the idea of "progress." Evaluation of particular choices and actions, by criteria consistent with the purposes, is necessary for maintaining continuing investment of personal and collective energies in taking the risks of action and overcoming difficult barriers resistant to the achievement of the purposes. Educationally speaking, meaningful and compelling purposes and derived criteria for the evaluation of actions undertaken on their behalf are both a motivational and cognitive condition of persons or groups in working to acquire the discipline required for effective, purposeful choice and action.

Without discounting the importance of common overarching goals in the remoralization of contemporary life and education, we may properly doubt whether emphasis on such goals is a sufficient prescription for generation of hope in despairing Western men and women, both young and old. To recommend commitment to utopian hopes to persons and groups doubtful of the adequacy of the available means of organizing themselves effectively in the pursuit of any common purpose and deeply troubled about their potency to offset or reverse impersonal historical trends, when undesirable, may serve to deepen the crisis of hope rather than to meliorate it. For the present, I do not wish to question the adequacy of various prescriptions for the demoralized condition of modern men and women. This would call for a more careful diagnosis of that condition. I wish now only to emphasize the relevance of considerations of morale to the envisagement and advancement of a morality of hope for the future. To make cognitively clear the requirements of a morality for our time is an important part of the task of moral reconstruction. But to help people reckon with and modify the feelings, attitudes, and self-images that thwart the meeting of such requirements in their own choices and actions is an equally important part of the task. Educationally, it is important that the two parts of the task be seen and dealt with together, however sharply they may be distinguished and separated for purposes of analysis and criticism.

The intrusion of a discussion of morale into a treatment of morality may shock the sensibilities of some students of ethics. Such a reaction may be due in part to the way in which they conceive their task. They may see their job as extending only to the theoretical clarification of moral alternatives, ideals, or language. The task of helping persons and groups in working through the emotive, attitudinal, and relationship barriers that thwart them in enacting, testing, and evaluating rationally defensible ways of living is left to educators, psychotherapists, consultants, and political leaders. Certainly, these functionaries cannot avoid problems of morale in judging how to design, carry through, and evaluate processes and programs of education, treatment, advisement, or action. These functionaries must judge the feasibility of enacting schemes and principles of moral action in the situations and within the people with whom they work. Feasibility depends in no small part upon the morale of the persons and groups in the situation. If feasibility is taken as one criterion of adequacy for a moral scheme or principle, questions of morale cannot be neglected in the settling of moral issues. Perhaps the upshot is that theoretical analysts of the moral life and applied moralists will need to collaborate in inventing, testing, and evaluating a morality of hope for the future.

THE EXAMINATION AND RECONSTRUCTION OF VALUE ORIENTATIONS

I have suggested that one of the elements in creating a way out of moral confusion and despair is to become aware of the implicit normative orientations that run deep within our culture. Even when these normative orientations remain unexposed, persons are still affected by them; they either feel impotent to meliorate the dilemmas and conflicts of our historical period or make destructive and dogmatic attempts to impose traditional "solutions" upon these problems. If persons can be made aware of these orientations, they may criticize and alter them, and commit themselves to orientations better designed to lead toward a viable future for humankind.

The effort to expose value orientations that "objectively" shape the contours of our perceptions, thoughts, decisions, and evaluations has been thwarted by two interrelated attitudes of contemporary students of personality and of society, and more indirectly by men and women of practice and action who have been influenced by these attitudes. The first stance is that of objectivity interpreted as value neutrality. The realm of "the objective" is radically disjoined from that of "the emotive"; the realm of "the collective" separated from that of "the individual." This leads to the second stance. Values tend to be relegated to the realm of the emotive and the individual. In this view, values are seen as "merely" psychological and in the process are radically relativized. Value conflicts, in such a view, cannot be adjudicated by rational criticism or modified by rational interpersuasion.

The tendency becomes very apparent in sociological studies of deviant behavior. As Richard Means (1969) has put it,

> The deviant behavior approach has to assume the validity of traditional morality, any variation from which is automatically called a problem of "deviant behavior." The study of ends, goals, and the values of society is decidedly secondary. For the deviant behaviorist, there is no objective theory of social values by which he may judge values and goals per se. Usually, insofar as values are considered at all, they are either assumed to belong to some amorphous unit called "middle class morality" (which is exceedingly vague), or they are considered to be subjective, psychological, and personal. This leads to a kind of subjectivity and relativism, which makes a sociological judgment of the objective results of value commitment in an industrial society almost impossible. That is to say, values from this point of view have little objective basis except in the emotions; therefore judgments of a society's basic values cannot be subjected to critical analysis.
>
> This makes it difficult to trace the cause of social problems to the fact that society has the wrong basic values and violates the objective demands of external reality. The discussion is locked into the mold of a radical dichotomy between fact and value. Facts are objective and scientific; values are emotional and subjective. (p. 53)

Fortunately, a way of conceiving value orientations that under-cuts the radical dichotomy between the "subjective" and the "objective," the collective and the personal, is available to moralists and educators. I will sketch the view of Kluckhohn and Strodtbeck (1961) and attempt a critique of two "objective" value orientations implicit in American culture as illustrative of the task of reconstructing value orientations, which is incumbent upon educators who would invent and communicate a morality of hope for the future.

F. H. Heinemann (1958) has defined the contemporary moral—educational—task as "the rehumanization of man."

> Whatever formula one may choose, dehumanization of man, annihilation of man, or the question whether man will survive in the face of the nihilistic destruction of all human values, the facts are indisputable. Once more the human world resembles the valley full of bones which Ezekiel saw in his vision. And again is the question put to us: "Son of Man, can these bones live?" The integration of the diffused and disintegrated parts into a whole, the rehumaniza-tion of man—that is the task with which we are confronted. (p. 180)

There are, no doubt, many paths toward rehumanization. But the enterprise of rehumanization has little meaning or focus unless there are values that are "real," in the sense that they have consequences for human beings, that they, in some sense, define what is "human" for a culture group.

We may begin with the assumption of Kluckhohn and Strodtbeck (1961) that there are a "limited number of common human problems for which all peoples at all times must find solutions" (p. 4). Kluckhohn and Strodtbeck have identified five questions that all human groups must somehow answer. These point to objects within all human environments about which people must theorize, not for the sake of theorizing, but in the practical interest of survival as a human group. These value objects may be identified as self, nature, other selves, time, and society. I hold no brief for this particular set of basic value objectives as necessarily involved in the definition of the human. I might, for example, be inclined to include death as one of these, although I realize that death might be assimilated to time or to self.

When concepts concerning self, nature, and the others become attached to sentiment or emotion, and as commitments to these concepts develop, they become institutionalized in a society as assumptions. They may be called basic values or value orientations. They define for a group the meaning of human life. They structure the modal responses of members of the group toward themselves, toward each other, and toward objects and events in the group's environment. They operate as assumptions in processes of social deliberation and action, except as they are challenged by contact and interchange with other culture groups whose value orientations with respect to self, nature, time, and so forth are different or as they receive challenges from subcultural "proletariats" within a society.

It is important to realize that value orientations, while when unchallenged define the good for those committed to them, are not, from other perspectives, evaluated as good for the persons and group committed to them or for other persons and groups affected by actions taken on their authority. The normative orientation may exclude recognition and just evaluation of objective conditions that are involved in the survival of the group. For example, the prevalent value orientation with respect to nature in our traditional culture may lead to a gutting and mining of natural resources, to a willful upsetting of ecological balances, to putting survival of ourselves and our children into jeopardy. It makes a difference in the focus and viability of criticism and reeducation directed to the conservation of nature whether we see the object of reconstruction and criticism as particular actions and projects by wicked or thoughtless persons and groups that threaten important ecological balances, or as a basic normative orientation within our culture and, therefore, within ourselves, with respect to the relations between human beings and nature. My point here is that the basic normative orientations of a culture are amenable to moral criticism and reconstruction through education and reeducation of a deep-cutting and radical sort. A precondition of moral criticism and educational reconstruction of basic cultural values is an acknowledgment of their reality and a conviction that they underlie and generate the social problems that plague us.

The basis on which the moral criticism and educational reconstruction of the value orientations of a culture, our own or any other, should rest is still problematic for many. From what vantage point or perspective does one criticize the values of one's own culture, which are indeed also part of one's own orientation as a person enculturated in that culture? Is self-criticism of one's own culture's values at best subjective maundering, a self-indulgent rearrangement of one's own feelings and prejudices, born out of individual discontent? Or, if a person chooses to criticize the basic values of another culture, is he or she perforce indulging in an unwitting exercise in cultural imperialism? These questions do pose real difficulties for the moral critic and reconstructionist. It shows an important humility to hold them in the forefront of our minds as we criticize and reconstruct.

Moral rules are, in an important sense, indigenous to a culture group. The meanings of values can be attained only through study and experience of the interconnections between culture and social organization in a particular society. There is no sane evasion, in the study and reconstruction of values, of dealing with situations in their particularity. This we must remember. And there is no better test of implicit imperialism and cultural insularity in our formulations and recommendations as moralists or educators than the thoughtful response and feedback from the people for whom we would legislate our formulations and recommendations. This wisdom is not in question here.

But the problems of finding a more generic reference point in our criticism and educational reconstruction of the values of one or another culture remain. I have found cogency and truth in Means' (1969) formulation of an "answer" to this problem.

The idea of the good is not necessarily equated with values, since a society may hold values that make it very difficult to maximize even its own standards of the good. It seems to me the utilitarians had a point, but it took history to make the utilitarian definition of the good universal. It was not the discovery of a new verbal definition, the development of a new metaphysics or psychology, that suddenly thrust the utilitarian idea of the good into the realm of universal applicability and objectivity, but rather a break in history, a new "Axial Period," to use Karl Jaspers' term, in the life of mankind—the atomic and thermonuclear age.

If the survival of life is a basic good and can be accepted and held by people throughout the world, then this good is universal. On the practical level, the terror of atomic holocaust maximizes into reality the greatest good for the greatest number, that is, survival and life, as the basic ethical rule. It is the interconnection of terror, the intricate web of world destruction, that now ties us together and lends objectivity to the consequences of our values. Thus the values of industrial civilization, of the warring powers of the East and West, are universalized in their implication and consequences and must be judged in relation to a universal good—the fact of survival itself.

The good becomes, then, an objective reality. The rule for ethical human behavior is to act in such a way as to maximize the existence and survival of mankind. Obviously time and circumstance may vary the specific ethical injunctions or rules for any particular society. But the utilitarian definition of the good, transformed into the notion of physical survival, may lie at the heart of most social ethics. In any case, the rationalization and legitimacy of an ethic may be constructed on this basis. (pp. 56–57)

I have not accepted Means' definition of the good uncritically. Nor would I argue that his recommending central priority for the criterion of human survival as the validating preference, against which all traditional value orientations and newly emerging preferences need to be tested, is a dictum for all historical periods. But the threats to human survival that our "Axial Period" of human history presents to people make it a highly plausible candidate for definitional status in characterizing the "good." The probable acceptability of it as an overarching criterion by the peoples of the world, once they become aware of the universal threat of species extinction under which all people and peoples live today, gives it an important leverage in quickening efforts toward the resolution of value conflicts and toward the building of a shared world culture. It is from this point of view that I find Means' definition acceptable.

Nor do I believe that acceptance of this definition brings in its wake all of the intellectual and moral confusions that many ethicists since G. E. Moore have feared would follow from committing the "naturalistic fallacy." One can still make and accept distinctions between factual judgments and value judgments and not confuse the two. One can still distinguish differences in the norms under which scientists and moralists pursue their differently oriented investigations, although acceptance of Means' criterion may quicken collaboration between scientists and moralists, because all, as men and women, operate under the same threats to survival.

Acceptance of Means' criterion does lend urgency to all with a commitment to the good in human life to pursue the tasks of value criticism and educative and reeducative reconstruction of value orientations. I think it a misplaced sense of urgency if it leads to an imposition of arbitrary solutions upon moral inquiry and upon experiments in moral education and reeducation. The vast tasks of moral reconstruction cannot be sanely foreclosed. After all, participation in these tasks is itself part of the process of reeducation morally required by the commitment.

I will turn now to a brief and partial critique of two of the basic value orientations of American culture, more to illustrate the task of value reconstruction, which, I have claimed, is involved in the building of a morality of hope for the future, than on any pretense that my critique is complete or definitive. I will offer a critique of two value objects—self and nature—not because I consider them more important than the others, but because I feel better prepared to deal with these two.

The Social Value of the Self

Northrop (1960) and others have emphasized the kinship of the ideology that undergirds traditional American culture and the ideas about man and society enunciated by John Locke. Nowhere is this kinship more apparent than in traditional conceptions of the human individual. The individual is seen as a passive recipient and focus of environmental influences. To make good persons we place them in good environments; the products of good environmental socialization—conditioning (call the process of molding passive individuals to the order of wise reformers or educators what you will)—will be good men or women.

The social view and valuation of the self underlies the traditional American faith in education. This typically has been and remains an education in which the correct environmental influences, predetermined by adults, who are somehow assumed to have acquired the required wisdom in terms of the kind or kinds of educational "products" wanted and needed by society, are brought to bear upon passive and intrinsically unmotivated learners to shape them to the model desired. Where resistances to educative influences so conceived are encountered by educators, they are seen not as efforts of persons to choose and create the processes and goals of their own learning, but as defects of will to be overcome through punishment or through the proffering of adult-controlled rewards and blandishments to motivate learners to learn gladly what others expect them to learn.

There have been periodic outbreaks against the passive, environmentally determined view of man's nature and nurture throughout the history of modern education in Europe and America. These outbreaks have almost invariably been generated by "romantic" emphasis upon an inherently active self, creating and becoming through its own contemplation and action. The co-opting of the ideas of Rousseau, Pestalozzi, Froebel, Dewey, and various progressives in educational reform by the triumphant environmentalism of established education may be explained in part by the continued commitments by the common people in our culture to a value orientation that elevates the passive or oversocialized self as the "right" model of the human being.

It is important to trace the degree to which the Lockean view of the passive self has permeated studies of persons in the social sciences. I can only suggest this degree here. The conception of *Homo Economicus*, motivated to action and work by the extrinsic rewards of maximizing his or her economic self-interest—a view of human motivation underlying traditional economic theory and much neoconservative economic theory as well—has been noted and criticized by various depth psychologists. The notion of "mass man," mobilized to action only by various demagogic appeals to fears, lusts, and anxieties, still popular among political scientists, reflects, though less obviously, this assumption about the essential passivity of human beings. If there is in each person no vital center that is dynamic and unique, that seeks for self-engendered, rational meanings in patterns of life and experience, then all appeals that move a person into behavior—"action" is not an apt word for mass movement—are equally valid so long as they work. Any social arrangement, from *Walden Two* to *1984*, as long as it can be sold to "mass man," is as valid as any other. As Means (1969) puts it, "A passive, nondynamic view of man's psyche fails to acknowledge the role of values in human affairs and neglects the active, creative side of human life" (p. 72).

It is perhaps most surprising that scientific psychology has, in its main line of development in America, adopted the passive view of the human being. I recall that Müller-Freinfels wrote a history of modern psychology into the 1920s as a story of psychology without a psyche. This behavioristic view of the human is perhaps most clearly evident in the work of B. F. Skinner. Means (1969) has, I think, not caricatured Skinner's work in this comment.

> According to Skinner, man does not act, he is acted upon, oversocialized; in his famous image, man is a black box. Into the box are poured stimuli (input), and out of it comes behavior (output). In between, never the twain shall meet, for nothing, absolutely nothing, can be said about what goes on in the head between input and output. One can, of course, talk about neurons, the response pathways, and the various complexities of the brain, but the inner life of man remains a blank. (p. 73)

I think it is also important to trace the assumption of passive men and women in intellectualism, which has tended to become the moralism of the university and, through it, the moralism of other professionalized institutions as well. In this view, the thinking of a person is separated radically from the living contexts, internal and external, of the human organism. Intellect is thus separated from feeling, emotion, and choice. The "idolatry of intellectualism," as Ortega (1969, p. 45) called it, separates intelligence both from its context in human life and from the other functions of the living, thinking, feeling, and valuing human being. The profession of pure and correct doctrine is elevated as the main criterion by which the excellence and worth of a person is to be judged.

Intellectualism becomes a mask behind which many of the dehumanizing tendencies of American culture are concealed. It makes a virtue of irresponsibility on the part of the person of thought by denying or demeaning the place that evaluation and decision making play in any robust and responsible intellectual process. It actually supports the growth of irrationalisms in society because of its distorted and limited view of reason and rationality. Erich Fromm (1968) has pointed to a tragic aspect of modern society in its determined separation of thinking and feeling, a separation that intellectualism reinforces and condones.

> In fact, this separation between intellect and feeling has led modern man to a near schizoid state of mind in which he has become almost incapable of experiencing anything except in thought. (p. xii)

I do not think that Means has exaggerated when he traces a specialized "intellectualism" also in the almost paranoid concern with "pure and correct doctrine" in members of the John Birch Society and in various religious fundamentalists. The content that is taken as "pure and correct" may be quite different in John Birchers, in religious fundamentalists, and in votaries of various academic disciplines in the universities; but their passionate devotion to and defense of "pure and correct" doctrine is quite similar.

In tracing the effects of a commitment to oversocialized and intellectualized selves in various aspects of American life, I have not meant to deny or discount the play of socializing influences upon persons in their growing up. What I have meant to emphasize is the typical discounting of the part that thinking-feeling-valuing-willing selves can and should play in choosing, creating, and directing the processes of their own socialization. Nor have I meant to discount the importance of intelligence in reshaping the moral life of men and women in and through their emerging future. I have rather tried to emphasize that intellectualism discounts that importance and blocks the full enlistment of the resources of intelligence in personal and collective planning of present action in the service of future goals.

Nor have I noted and emphasized the recent emergence of trends in the study of psychology, economics, government, sociology, and philosophy and in the professions of education, social work, psycho- and socio-therapy, and religious work that operate from a view of humankind not unlike that expressed by Ortega (1969) many years ago.

> Life is nothing except man's being; so that here we have the most extraordinary, extravagant, and paradoxical thing about the human condition—namely that man is the only quality that does not simply consist in being, but must choose its own being. . . . So life is a permanent crossroads, a constant perplexity. (pp. 44–45)

What I have meant to emphasize is that resistance to these trends is based in part on a persistent value orientation deep within our culture. Moralists of the future need to trace the effects of this persistent value orientation in contemporary studies of men and women and in the life of contemporary action. We can be freed from the hold of traditional assumptions about self upon our minds, our wills, our actions—assumptions that have become immoral for our time and place—only as we become aware of their power in ourselves and the lives of others about us.

I emphasized earlier that the touchstone to be applied to candidate projects for the name of *good* is their contribution to the survival of humankind in our emerging future. How does this touchstone apply to the conception and value of the self as passive, reactive, in continual need of motivation and socialization from outside itself—a self divided, with its intellect segregated from its feelings and emotions, from the wellsprings of its inherent motivations to act and to alter its environment, and from the interpersonal community that sustains it in being? Or, turned around, how does the touchstone apply to a conception and value of the self as inherently active and creative, a self proactive, going out to select, to choose, to shape through its actions its environment toward a habitat more supportive of human living?

Two considerations out of many that might be named indicate that the second conception and value of the self are more conducive to human survival in our historical period. First, we desperately need the invention of new forms and patterns of living and of making a living as a condition of human survival. We need the creation and invention of a future fit for persons and for their children. In the last analysis, invention, creation, and renewal must come from inventive, creative, and self-renewing persons, if they are to come into being at all.

The second consideration is perhaps even more fundamental. Social and cultural institutions live from generation to generation only as persons recreate them in their imaginations, their habits, and their moral commitments, only as persons continue to impute value to them. The widespread actual or psychological "dropping out" of persons from the institutions of our culture is a signal that many people are tending to withdraw the investment of their imaginations and moral commitments from any and all institutional life. The very survival of social life and culture requires the reconstruction of our traditional social value orientation toward persons and selves.

The Social Value of Nature

I shall be even more brief in my discussion of the underlying conception and value of nature in the traditional culture of America than in my treatment of the social value of the self. And this is for two reasons. The romantic dissent against traditional views of the passive and oversocialized self is better worked out and its moral ramifications in the practices of our culture and our education are more carefully traced than is dissent against the modern human rape of nature. Much more work needs to be done in this area. And secondly, because I have introduced these two discussions of value for the purpose of illustrating needed work on the part of hopeful social scientists, moralists, and educators, the critical apparatus for the needed work does not have to be elaborated once again.

The thought and practice of modern Europeans assume a more or less radical disjuncture between human culture and the natural world in which human cultures develop and, viewed historically, decline and die, or, less often, are regenerated. Whitehead (1970) used the dramatic expression "bifurcation of nature" to describe this aspect of modern European thought (pp. 30–31). Whitehead's philosophy may be seen as an attempt to reduce this bifurcation of human culture from nature by working out a metaphysics of organism explanatory of physical, biological, and human events and processes alike. John Dewey's philosophy may be read as an attempt to emphasize the continuity of the natural and the human through the use of the ideas of evolution and transactional experience.

The bifurcation of nature stems in part from the traditional Christian theological perspective, which stresses the supernatural character of the human person's essential being and views "nature" as only a temporary home for humankind and as essentially "inferior" to persons even as they are inferior to God. This is evident not only in the

Christian view of subhuman nature external to men and women but in the view of the body, of nature in persons, as in varying degrees at war with the soul of each in its pilgrimage toward eternity. It is interesting to recall that the exultation in nature by St. Francis, his feeling of kinship with mammals and birds and his preaching to them as brothers, were at first regarded as heretical by the church. The New England transcendentalists, including Thoreau and Emerson, who felt and saw spirit immanent in nature, were heavily attacked as threats to true morality and faith by those committed to traditional Christian faith and morals.

The widespread view, that the Newtonian conception of the physical world as mechanical, atomistic, and purposeless offered a true picture of the reality of nature, drove a further wedge between nature and humanity as purposeful, qualitatively experiencing, and valuing. The notion that human studies, if they are to be really scientific, must operate with physical models and by methods proved successful in physics persists widely in academic circles today. Studies of persons as aspiring, valuing, culture-building, and culture-renewing are often relegated to the "softer," and presumably less "hard-headed" and "real," domain of the humanities and humanistic studies.

The world views of Christianity and Newtonian physics thus conceived of men and women as aliens or as sojourners within nature. But it was probably the explosion of Western Europe into exploration and colonization of untamed lands still in a "natural" state that added a new and persistent quality to the conception and value of nature. Nature became something to be conquered, subjugated, and exploited by human beings to serve their material and commercial interests. This was a spirit that supported morale in a pioneering society like America through the frightening ordeals of bringing a wilderness into the service of Europeanized life.

But several attendant valuations of nature as object in relation to human society followed. One of these is what Galbraith (1967) has called the cornucopia view of nature. There will always be a supply of materials and energies to be wrested from nature—wood and soil and metals and stored carbon and hydrocarbon energy. People need not look to the future in their exploitation of the raw materials of nature; they need not conserve or replace the reservoir of nature; there will always be more where what we are using up now came from. Nor need people respect the intricate ecological balances between land and climate and plants and animals through which natural forms survive and replenish themselves. Contemporary persons in America are only beginning to sense deeply the falsity and folly of this valuation of nature.

Closely correlated with this view is an exaltation of technology and techniques. Tools and methods for shaping ever more refined and powerful tools are humanity's principal "weapons" in the burgeoning arsenal for the fuller conquest of nature. To value technology as an aid in serving various humane purposes, in making nature more fully a home for persons, and in extending and augmenting human capacities to experience life more healthily and more meaningfully is one thing. To value technology as weaponry in the taming and exploitation of nature and to measure human progress primarily or exclusively by the sophistication, power, and complexity of a society's technological weaponry is quite another. I have known more than a few Americans who drive a car as they exercise their dog with a leash through the window and who get their own exercise with the help of elaborate rowing and cycling machines in the well equipped exercise room at home. Urbanized men and women live in an artificial world. They are separated from direct experience of the "nature" on which the artificial objects and energies of their urban environment ultimately depend.

But men and women are a part of nature. They are biological organisms, basically dependent on air and water and the services of plants in trapping solar energy. Their war against nature has threatened the very support systems on which biological survival depends. Pollution of the environment by life-destroying radiation from the release of atomic energy is only the most dramatic way in which the traditional evaluation of nature threatens the demise of the human species.

We must reeducate ourselves to a new conception and valuation of nature or perish. We must learn to see and value nature as an indispensable partner in the enterprises of living, not as an enemy to be subjugated. We must learn to accept ourselves as parts of nature. This means that we must learn to accept and value our own bodies, with their feelings and desires, and to accept the wisdom of the body, as Walter Cannon once described it, as an important ingredient of human wisdom. We must learn to fit our rhythms of living to the rhythms of nature within and around us. We must learn to contemplate nature and to gain respect both for our limits and for our powers as human beings in shaping nature as our home in our own generation as well as for future generations of men and women. Natural science must come to be seen as one of the humanities, as Bronowski (1953) and others have been urging. Technology must become the servant of humanitarian processes, not the very measure of civilizational progress to which progressive men and women must conform. This reeducative task is, most basically, a task of value reconstruction, and it is required in the service of human survival.

THE RECONSTRUCTION OF RATIONALITY
IN PLANNING AND IN MORAL JUDGMENTS

I noted earlier that building a morality of hope for the future sets two major tasks of cognitive reconstruction and reeducation for contemporary men and women. The first task, laying bare the value assumptions of our traditional cultures and critically reconstructing them in keeping with the survival of humankind as the overarching definition of the good, I have dealt with illustratively.

The second task is to reconceive the methodology of choosing and evaluating courses of action, personal and collective, in dealing with the shifting dilemmas and conditions of life. Whatever technical difficulties and challenges planning for the future presents, its most basic difficulties and challenges are moral and human. The context of moral judgment for contemporary persons is the context of practical judgment within the inclusive processes, personal and collective, of planning and inventing a future for humankind, if indeed there is to be such a future. Technical and moral-political decisions must be made together; they cannot be separated if social planning is to be rehumanized as social relations and arrangements are rehumanized. But persons must understand the basic distinction between technical and moral-political decisions if this goal is to be achieved.

Whatever else planning may mean, it signifies an anticipation of some future state of affairs and the confirmation of a vision of that future in the present in order to motivate, guide, and direct present action. A planner's present situation always includes a time perspective forward—a future different from the present, yet populated symbolically with more or less clearly delineated alternatives, agents and counteragents, objects to be molded, objects to be embraced, means to empower avoidance or embracing, and some envisioned context of interrelated factors and forces, human and nonhuman, benign, hostile, or neutral. Men and women as planners must climb out of their involvement in present transactions to look beyond the horizon of present transactions.

It is the fact of change in the internal and external conditions of human life that makes planning important, even necessary, to time-bound persons. And it is the very same fact of changing that makes planning difficult for time-bound people. If the future were to be like the present, there would be no need to give thought to and take pains in preparing for it. Yet, because the future will be different from the present, human beings do not know how far to trust their present anticipations of it in preparing to meet and cope with it. All human planning is planning for change and requires judgments about the proper balance between investment of energy and resources in the pursuit or avoidance of consequences we can now anticipate, and the massing of free and uncommitted energy and resources for coping with unanticipated consequences.

I have spoken so far of the predicament of human planning in general terms. Yet planning always occurs within some time-bound historical situation. It is useful to note the characteristics of our own historical situation, which now give new point and poignancy to people's efforts to find confident direction in planning for their future.

A radical increase in the rate of change in the conditions of human life has thrown the problem of direction finding in planning into new perspective. Concentration of energy and resources in basic and applied research has resulted in a continuous revolution in the means and conditions of work, play, education, and family and social living. People have found established institutions from the past less and less dependable as guides to the effective and humane management of new knowledges and technologies in the conduct of life. People in a slowly changing culture could validly assume that the ecological contours of their future lives would be substantially similar to those of their past. Changes to be planned for could be seen as confinable and manageable within the patterns of a viable tradition. Modern men and women have been betrayed by dependence on tradition for direction. They face both the exhilaration and the terror of an unknown future more directly than their ancestors did.

Finding direction for the future by projecting the forms and values of a traditional culture upon that future has been further undermined by the omnipresent fact of intercultural contact, confrontation, and uneasy mixing within nations and between nations. The development of vast networks of interdependence, the spread of mass media, reduced security in spatial and political boundaries due to space-destroying means of transportation and other related factors, have brought about confrontations between traditionally segregated nations, classes, races, and subcultures. If there is to be a common future, it must be constructed and reconstructed by people in a way to lead beyond the present maze of disparate and conflicting traditions.

A third feature of contemporary human struggles to find viable directions into the future is a widespread decline of confidence in a presiding providence that will automatically and without human attention bring the conflicting plans and actions of individual persons and groups of persons into the service of commonly valuable purposes. Confidence in some preestablished ordering principle within history has taken many forms in the history of human affairs.

The effect of this confidence has been to narrow the range of human responsibility for finding and giving direction to the course of human history. Decline of confidence means a widening of human responsibility for designing and inventing the future. If there is to be an ordering principle in human planning today, a principle attentive to the conservation and augmentation of valid human values, men and women must find or, even better, construct and apply the principle through their own collective volition.

There is a quite understandable temptation for persons who become aware of their responsibility for planning and inventing their own future to become convinced that the task is too great for rationality and intelligence. Appeal is then made for a dependence on what Arthur Murphy (1943) has called the sub-rational urgencies of blood, soil, or race or the super-rational absolutes of revelations and mystical intuitions as providing confident direction for people through and beyond the complexities, confusions, and conflicts that beset them. I agree with Murphy that such an appeal is a derogation by persons of their own humanity. It involves an appeal to a doctrine of despair rather than assertion of a doctrine of hope.

Reason and intelligence are always embodied operationally in a methodology for dealing thoughtfully and deliberately with the situations, dilemmas, and conflicts that confront people as they choose and decide upon the actions they will take. Part of the reconstructive task for those who would develop a morality of hope is to develop a rational methodology to guide people in making the judgments they must make as they plan and invent a future for themselves and for the human beings who will succeed them. Before suggesting the outlines of this reconstructive task, I will seek to clarify the idea of reason as it operates in the direction of human conduct. Part of the temptation of contemporary persons to renounce reason and to embrace some nonrational or irrational impulse or capacity or some extrahuman idol as a more adequate arbiter of human conduct stems from constricted and erroneous conceptions of reason that are current today. These constricted and erroneous conceptions stem in part from the prevalent intellectualism in Western society, already discussed, an intellectualism that thwarts persons from understanding and utilizing fully their rational and creative capacities.

Were a person a being with only one impulse to action—or, if moved by many impulses, were the person equipped naturally with some built-in governor ordering the time and extent of the satisfaction of each one—there would be no human need for reason. If a person were moved by only one impulse, there would be only one good and that person would have no need for thought about the good and the better. But the human person is a being with many and sometimes conflicting impulses. Each presents its claims to the name of *good*, as indeed it properly may, because the natural basis of any or all good lies in the satisfaction of some human impulse. In the presence of numerous and competing claims to the name of *good*, the good does not automatically define itself. Definition requires the creation and formulation of a relevant ideal of good, which, as it is accepted as a guide to conduct, provides for the harmonious satisfaction of various impulses and for the patterned satisfaction of various needs, in this sense, for the optimum actualization of the good in human experience.

Reason, in this view, is not one human impulse among other impulses. It possesses no natural energy or motivation, save through transferred energy paid to it by the impulses, as it were, as overhead for its harmonious fulfillment.[1]

Rational processes, projecting ideals out of a setting of presently conflicting interests into an uncertain future, can carry no absolute assurance that the realization of the ideals will fulfill their speculative promise or bring their hoped-for benefit when acted upon. But the habit and practice of rationality can make learning and self-correction out of failure and disappointment as no other arbiter of human action can do.

So far my references to the work of reason in practical contexts have pertained to decision making by an individual. I have written of the guidance of conduct by ideals rationally formulated, tested, and adjudicated in relation to variant and conflicting interests, impulses, and loyalties within the person. Can and should practical reason be involved in the formulation, projection, testing, and adjudication of social ideals as well—ideals that may achieve pertinence and authority in the harmonization and reconciliation of variant and conflicting group interests and commitments? An affirmative answer to this question has been the hope and faith of philosophers and of doers of practice and action, too, who have sought less arbitrary, more knowledge-based, and more deliberative bases for the management and resolution of social and political conflicts and for the grounding of human planning and action.

The use of practical reason in social planning and action calls for criteria different from, and in some ways more complex than, criteria for its use in personal choice and decision. What are these criteria?[2]

1. The primary basis for reason in any field where it operates, and not least in the context of social planning and action, is reliable information about relevant factual matters. An intellectualist approach might limit relevant factual matters to "objective" knowledge about the environment that surrounds the process of planning. But "subjective" human aspirations, loyalties, aversions, and preferences of those affected by the planning are, rationally speaking, important facts too. Information about things hoped for and feared must be blended and reconciled with more technical and expert and external considerations in forming rational social plans and attainable social ideals. This gathering, fusing, and blending of information about the human and the technical aspects of controverted situations is only now being done well at all in fields like urban, organizational, and community development and redevelopment. The problems to be worked out are partly methodological, but they are also political. They are grounded in obscurantist efforts by some persons and groups to circumscribe the collection and dissemination of relevant information obtained by reliable methods of inquiry. These efforts are usually directed most assiduously to suppressing the collection and publication of data about hostile feelings toward the operation and human consequences of the established goals and organization of the human activity under reconstructive scrutiny. Forces that limit support and development of resources for opening up emotionalized areas of tension and dissatisfaction for rational examination and possible reconciliation are important parts of contemporary irrationalism.

2. Relevant information, however complete and "scientific," never makes wise judgments by itself. Knowledge of what now is, or of how things as they are came to be out of their past, never determines completely the direction or shape of future aspiration and action. Practical reason in social affairs must be an inventive, creative, imaginative, and reconstructive reason, alive to new possibilities and desirabilities in improving human arrangements and correcting hu-

man derangements. It requires the will and the ability to transform the now desired into the desirable, and strategies and methodologies for changing human systems to narrow the gap between the actual and the desirable. Rational men and women must learn to use failures and surprises in planned actions to stimulate the envisioning of new desirabilities and to generate new and more attainable aspirations.

3. Reason applied in social planning and action is practical reason. This means moral reason addressed to "the attainment of ends accepted as good, by means judged proper for their realization." In consequence, to eliminate moral considerations of better and worse, with respect to the ends and means of actions, from the sphere of social inquiry and social planning is to exclude from rational consideration the very factors of value orientation in the situation that most require critical reconstruction. Men and women must come to expect culture shock, a confrontation with assumptions that have become part of their identities as selves through past enculturation, as they participate in processes of practical deliberation with persons who bring different assumptions and enculturations to the processes. And they must come to expect support as they forge new assumptions and new identities that are more reality-oriented and more conducive to human survival in the world in which they hope to continue to judge and act. Most persons will achieve the required reconstruction of their traditional value orientations in processes of thoughtful decisions about what they should do in particular action situations in which issues press for resolution, not in the philosopher's seminar. Perhaps a desirable outcome is that processes of practical planning and decision should become more "practical," in the sense that they admit the moral ordeals of contemporary men and women into the seminars to provide criteria of importance for judging where philosophers should invest their energies and efforts.

At any rate, to limit the analysis of social action to descriptive analysis—in the name of "realism" and/or "the avoidance of subjective conflicts"—is to exclude reason from social action by default or design. Such limitation becomes one of our most common self-fulfilling prophecies. We commit social action to irrationality by the very terms in which we prejudge and limit the only practicable, safe, "realistic" scope of social deliberation.

4. Practical reason, in social application, must be participative and cooperative reason. The ends proposed for social action can be

attained only through the work of many men and women, who must work together and who, in times of crisis, will work well and committedly only if they believe in the worth and meaningfulness of what they are called upon to do. A plan of action that will enlist the effort and earn the loyalty of the people who must carry it out, if it is to be carried out, must be more than a recommended blueprint for action enunciated by self-selected or officially designated "planners." Men and women act rationally when they act with conviction toward the attainment of ideal ends by means honestly judged by them to be good and right. Those who limit the work of reason to fact finding, or to social engineering conceived as manipulative salesmanship, will naturally conclude that the ideals that motivate people are inherently irrational in their content—"social myths" that move the masses but are quite beyond the limits of rational substantiation or disproof. Such an arbitrarily imposed limitation is a denial of a large part of their own rational capacity, as well as a denial of rational capacity in "the masses" of people. Only genuine dialogue between laypersons and technical experts can humanize the technical experts and elicit and develop the rational capacities of laypersons.

5. To will the operation of reason in social affairs without recognizing and assuming responsibility for establishing the human and social conditions (many of which are noncognitive) of its effective exercise is to will the end of rationality without willing the means to its effective use within the refashioning of the institutions of society. One of these necessary conditions is a relative equality of power among contending parties within any area of clashing and conflicting interests. The establishment of equality in deliberation and decision is at one and the same time a political and an educative and reeducative task. Minority voices must be empowered in order to be heard in the councils of planning and of critical evaluation of existing policy and practice. Help must be given to men and women with novel and unpopular interests and views in making their voices heard. This can be accomplished only through some combination of empowering of such interests through their organization and articulation, and the reeducation of persons holding these interests toward effective participation in processes of redefining the common good.

Those who now exercise established power must be challenged and taught to listen to claims to the right to influence made by those now excluded from the councils of established power, and to reassess their right to lead and to rule, not alone or even primarily from altruistic motives but from interest in their own survival and the survival of any moral order of society in a pluralistic and radically changing world. Political processes must be reclaimed to the life of reason, and education and reeducation extended to the renovation and renewal of political processes as part of a more inclusive process of moral reconstruction of human life.

Other noncognitive conditions for the operation of practical reason in human affairs can be named: reduction of a fear of differences among persons and groups; acceptance of change rather than stability as the normal expectation of human living; expansion of each person's capacity to trust other persons; and clarification of the nature of consent and consensus as these operate within human collectivity and community.

EXPERT AUTHORITY AND PLANNING BY LAYPERSONS

One other condition with respect to contemporary rationality in human affairs has to do with the domination of social planning by specialized experts of various kinds. In dealing with the forms of contemporary authority in 1943, I remarked that modern men and women seemed to accept the growing power of expert authority in their lives without resort to the anti-authoritarian protest that has sought to confine, deny, and even destroy other authority relations in modern Western life. I could no longer write this today. There are vigorous and probably growing protests by laypersons in various settings against the right of experts to exercise authority in shaping policies and programs that affect their lives—the anti-fluoridation resistance against informed judgments of dental experts; the struggle by those in the peace movement against the influence of military experts in shaping American foreign policy; the massing of lay resistance to the judgments of experts concerning the priorities and methods of urban redevelopment among the urban homeless; and vigorous questioning by college and high school students of the right of faculties and administration to prescribe their curriculum, and so on.

When we identify the forces of reason with increased influence of expert authority in determining practical policies and programs, we are apt to label this massing and asserting of lay power against such increased influence as irrationalism. Certainly such lay protests do gather forces of irrationalism into themselves as they gain momentum and vigor.

But, as I pointed out in my earlier analysis of authority, the legitimation of a bearer of authority to exercise control over his or her or its subjects, whether the bearer be an expert or grounds a claim to authority otherwise, requires willing obedience on the part of the subjects. This means acknowledgment by them of the right of the bearer to act authoritatively; and such legitimation usually requires some collaborative negotiation between bearer and subjects in defining the scope and quality of the authority relation. There is widespread confusion concerning the nature of authority and its place in the moral life among contemporary men and women. This confusion is not least among reputed bearers of authority, whether experts— teachers, doctors, or scientists—or rulers, such as presidents, generals, or popes. Authority is widely confused with power on the one hand and with prestige on the other. Bearers of authority assume their right to be bearers, forgetting that the establishment or renewal of their right to influence others emerges only out of the willing acknowledgment, in some degree rational, of their right to exert influence by those others. Teachers have no right to authority over the learning of children without children and/or their parents rationally granting the teachers that right. It is hardly rational to label as "irrational" parent and student challenges to the right of teachers to exercise authority over students' learning processes, whatever the credentials of the teachers, while withholding the label from teachers who assume some inherent right to teach. In a time of social change, authority relations must be continually renegotiated and renewed.

Certainly professional expertise is one of the principal ways through which contemporary societies attempt to channel current and valid knowledge and know-how into processes of personal and collective planning and decision making. Insofar as valid relevant knowledge is not available in such processes, their outcomes will be less rational than they should be. But responsibility for making knowledge available in practical decision making is a responsibility jointly shared by "expert" and "layperson." Perhaps we do not have adequate ways of packaging knowledge for practical use. Perhaps some needed specialties, particularly in the arts of mediating and reconciling, are underdeveloped and lacking. Perhaps we need new linking and generalist roles to supplement the highly specialized packaging of expertise that increasingly prevails. Certainly, we need to cultivate more collaborative and mutual relationships between expert resources and lay users of such resources as a condition of greater rationality in human affairs. Such tasks are important parts of the more general task of moral reconstruction for our time.

TOWARD A METHODOLOGY OF MORAL-POLITICAL OR PRACTICAL JUDGMENT

A generation ago I worked with three colleagues over a period of years in trying to articulate the formal phases of thought and judgment addressed to situations confronting persons with moral and political (practical) perplexities, conflicts, and alternatives. We were convinced that the best human resource in responding rationally to such situations is a way of thought and intelligence addressed to those situations. We were equally convinced that the way of thought most frequently urged upon contemporary educators as an intellectual discipline for modern men and women—a generalized "scientific method" of problem solving—was deficient in important respects. While it correctly prescribed an inquiry response to perplexing and controverted situations, the mode of inquiry prescribed was designed primarily to help persons clear up cognitive confusions and perplexities rather than to help them also in intelligently shaping their affective and conative responses to situations. Our effort was to formulate a broader methodology of intelligence, which took account of the cognitive, affective, and conative aspects of choosing and deciding in a unified, though differentiated, process of judgment (Raup et al., 1962).

I do not wish to review all of this work here. But I do want to comment on selected aspects of it for several reasons. First, as already emphasized, an important element in a morality of hope for the future is a methodology of judgment that will guide human beings in making rational and adequate responses to the morally perplexing and controverted situations that confront them. This methodology must furnish guidance to the thinking of persons in practical situations where the outcome of the thinking is an answer to the questions: How should I or we act? How should I or we invest ourselves and our energies in bringing order out of the confronting chaos? The problem to which our work on practical judgment addressed itself is, I believe, still a valid approach to the moral regeneration of contemporary life, however inadequate some of its provisional recommendations have proved to be. Second, the conception and practice of *general* education in an age of cognitive and occupational specialization still has no firm or defensible basis. It will acquire such a basis only as it finds a methodology of thought and judgment that *all* men and women require in the conduct of their lives, whatever their specialized role in society. The best current candidate for such a discipline still seems to me to lie in a defensible methodology to use in choosing and deciding how people should act to make a good life for themselves. In an irreversibly interdependent world society, this question cannot be divorced from another: How can I participate with others in building a good life for humankind? Third, some developments in modern thought and education are, I believe, moving in directions consistent with these prescriptions. But other required aspects of the general task of moral and educational reconstruction are missing and neglected. It is these on which I would like to comment.

We recommended in our work that wise judgers learn to work in four moods of judging their confronting and conflicting situation as they shape actions appropriate in and to it. One of these we called the optative mood. It involves people in objectifying and projecting their wishes and desires relevant to their situation into the future. People engage in processes of interpersuasion concerning the desired state of affairs that they would bring into actuality through their action in the present. The reference of the optative mood of thinking is a future reference. Its materials are affective and aspirational as well as cognitive. Reality-orientation is relaxed. The method of dialogue between participants may involve the full range of symbolic expression, not descriptive propositional expression alone. People can paint, sing, poetize their wishes and desires for the future. Artists can be most helpful here. The dialogue is openly interpersuasive and normative, not descriptive. It is oriented to building and finding an understanding and appreciation of common and irreducibly various and different objects of desirability within and among the participants in projected action. Powers of creative imagination are honored, elicited, and practiced in the optative mood of judging the situation.

Alternative directions for action are clothed with meaning and acquire differentiated values for the participants. And participants emerge as human beings, distinctive centers of feeling, aspiration, and valuation to themselves and to others. The "speculative cruelty" that dogs all attempts in choosing to represent the future symbolically in the present, as Santayana (1929) once named it, is reduced though never eliminated. Practical utopian thinking becomes an expected part of personal and collective planning and action.

It should be remembered, of course, that projection of action alternatives and action consequences into the future is, in part, dependent on knowledge of what now is and especially of how things work, of how variables are interrelated. Laypersons without mastery of relevant current knowledge, generated in specialist communities and often published only in the established communication channels of these specialist communities, cannot be aware of the threats and promises in the human consequences of new knowledge if and when applied under various sponsorships and for various human purposes. Laypersons need the help of scientists in their processes of optative thinking. And scientists must add a "new" responsibility to their traditional publication responsibilities. They too must learn to function in the optative mood. Sir Robert A. Watson Watt (1965), the inventor of radar, has nicely summarized this "new" responsibility.

> The ethical responsibility of the scientist . . . is, I believe, crystal clear. It is this: in recognition of the privileged and endowed freedom of action he enjoys, he should, after an appraisal that may well be agonizing, declare all the social consequences he may foresee, however dimly, which are even remotely likely to follow the disclosure not only of his own contributions to science but also of those other scientists within his wide sphere of knowledge and competence. He should outline the social good that he can foresee as resulting from technological follow-up of "pure" research; he must outline the potential social evil. He will seldom be qualified to make quantitative estimates, but to the best of his ability define fields and magnitudes. Nothing less can suffice as partial payment for his privileged tenancy of the Ivory Tower. No plea that he "doesn't understand politics or economics," that, "even if behavioral science be a science (which he doubts) he is even further from understanding it," should be sustained. We must all do our poor best, with the intelligence at our disposal, toward mapping the upward and marking the downward slopes on our still long road of social evolution.

If scientists, applied scientists, and laypersons can collaborate in the optative mood, men's and women's social future may become populated with moral alternatives that can be understood, appreciated, and assessed in processes of planning action and deciding what to do.

I will mention more briefly the other moods of judging that we recommended as phases of wise planning for choice and action. A second mood is the indicative. Here our best relevant knowledge is brought to bear in reality-testing various alternatives of action, and missing knowledge is sought. Each alternative is tested for its possibility, its feasibility, its probable consequences if acted upon, and the costs, economic and in terms of the use and depletion of resources, natural and human, that the alternative would require. Wise plans and actions must be disciplined in the indicative as well as the optative mood. A third mood of judging is the imperative mood. Considerations of urgency, of the foreclosure of time upon continued deliberation, are taken into account; and moral principles pertinent to envisaged alternatives of action are applied and, where possible, reconciled. The imperative mood leads to a commitment to action and to the continuing monitoring and evaluating of action as it proceeds to feed back surprises and unanticipated consequences into the arena of thought about the redirection and replanning of action. A fourth mood of judging we named the contemplative mood.

> In this mood characters seek to express and communicate their conviction of the desirability and importance of some ideal object of contemplation. The mood is one of celebration of a common ideal, of rededication to it. . . . While the contemplative mood of "judging" is difficult to relate to the processes of forging a practical judgment, it would also be difficult to deny the social or educational economy of this mood and its expression. . . . Cultivation of the human community in the contemplative mood is indispensable to the perpetuation and service of that community through our daily choices, decisions, plans and policies. (Raup et al., 1962, p. 98)

We did not conceive the moods and phases of judgment and planning as a fixed mechanical sequence of activities or as a series of steps to be taken. Rather we emphasized their interpenetration in the characters of persons and in the processes of groups of persons seeking a wise way through moral perplexities, confusions, and conflicts. Learning wisdom in judgment, we believed, requires persons and groups to take various stances toward action alternatives as they rationally shape their choices and commitments. The claims of intersubjectivity, factuality, feeling, aspiration, and commitment are ideally reconciled in the pattern of wisdom.

We recognized that human beings must make moral choices at various levels of generality. They must make decisions about particular situations. They must forge policies concerning the handling of kinds and families of situations. They must at times reconstruct general value or normative orientations that operate deep within their cultures and within themselves and that define the human way of acting, for themselves and for persons in their culture. We recognized the need for reconstructing value orientations, which characterizes our period of historical transition. The task of such reconstruction I have already discussed and illustrated. We believed that the need for reconstruction of basic values will come home to men and women as they think deeply about the paradoxes they encounter in making current decisions and in forging viable policies. In turn, reconstructed value orientations will come to life only as men and women bring them into the ongoing processes of their everyday decision and policy making. Only through movement in thought and choice back and forth from general principle to particular case to general principle again can the enervating gaps and contradictions between professed values and actual operating values in person and culture be bridged.

EDUCATION FOR MORAL AND POLITICAL RENEWAL

Processes of general education should be focused on dilemmas of human choice and action. They should involve learners in dealing opta- tively, indicatively, imperatively, and contemplatively with situations that present dilemmas to them. Their planning should include, inso- far as practicable, dialogue with live persons affected by their deci- sions, whatever their differences in age, gender, race, occupation, or nationality. The plans that issue from their deliberations should be carried into action, insofar as possible, and tested there. Their reflec- tions on the processes of their choosing and action and the effects of actions taken open up and bring under reconstructive criticism their moral characters as expressed and operationalized in the decisions that they make.

The hoped-for educational outcomes of such a general education would be several. It should result in a growing mastery by those in- volved in it of the arts and rationales of wise choosing and judgment in confronting situations that incorporate moral and political perplex- ities and conflicts. It should result in the reconstruction of the basic value orientations within our culture that now threaten human sur- vival. It should heighten morale in people now uncertain about their potency to change themselves and their environments through their own thought and action, by providing self-directed experiences in changing both. It should not destroy individuality or differences among groups, but rather create social support for their expression and cultivation. It should permeate the societies in which it functions with more rounded conceptions of human intelligence in action and with more human resources embodying such intelligence within those societies. It should build more fruitful and mutual relationships between laypersons and specialists of various sorts. And it should break down the segregation between various academic specialisms in a fresh and growing vision of their relationships to projects of im- proving human life.

None of these outcomes will come easily, quickly, or without pain. There will be failures and disappointments. The hope is that

those who suffer failure and disappointment will learn from these outcomes. There will be powerful resistances. There will be a need for the invention of new institutionalizations of education. I do not know whether schools and universities as now established can carry the burden of such an educational process. Certainly the walls now segregating schools from their societal surround will have to be breached creatively, if they are to do so. The movement of such an education must also lead toward the breaching of international and interracial walls. The good of human survival will be realized only as the conception of a "humankind" gains meaning, substance, and commitment in the choices and decisions and actions that all men and women learn to take in their everyday lives.

One of the main enemies in attempts to conceive and to enact a morality of hope for our future is an attitude of perfectionism. No one knows the full meaning of such a morality as it will come into being. No one can know. A new culture must be learned even as the cultures that now both support and thwart us in our movement into the future were learned by human beings in the past. What post-contemporary persons must do is to become more conscious, critical, and responsible about the ongoing processes of learning and relearning, which the building of a renewed and self-renewing culture will require. The threat of human annihilation, which now hangs over all earthlings, should quicken our efforts to institute and orient processes of learning addressed to those issues in human culture where strain and conflict mark points either of breakdown or of renewal.

The threat of human annihilation should not lead us to foreclose processes of basic learning and relearning, which all of us have become morally obligated to enact and to suffer today. Rather, it should quicken our efforts to get such processes of learning underway wherever we may live and work.

Epilogue

WALK THE DARK EARTH IN WONDER

Walk the dark earth in wonder.
Walk warily, estranged, despairingly.

We swagger, prance, plod, slither and strut.
Our feet hold commerce with a dire debris
Of evils done and suffered—rickety bones
Of children orphaned, felled by war
Or famine; piteous flesh of refugees
From human conquest and at last from life;
Bones of warriors, pawns of Caesars,
Tools of some foolish dream. While here and there,
We stumble on forgotten trophies, fleshless skulls
And tumbled palace stones of kings and conquerors.
Walk warily, estranged, despairingly.

Walk the dark earth in wonder.
Walk trustfully, in love, and full of hope.

We run, leap, dance, gambol, and tread funereal cadence.
Our feet consort with relics, hidden or open to the stars,
Of goods done and enjoyed—the happy bones
Of fathers, mothers, brothers, sisters,
Dying mourned, loved, remembered;
Brave, cycling pageant—green and brown—growth and
     decay,
Life out of death and into death and into life evolving;
Relics of man-shaped forms for working, praying,
Learning, enjoying, loving—speaking
Of dreams fulfilled, terrors transcended, conflicts reconciled—
Even in relic ruins banishing despair.
Walk trustfully, in love, and full of hope.

Walk the untrodden path from last year into next year.
Move warily and trustfully, estranged and lovingly,
despairingly and full of hope.
Walk the dark earth in wonder.

KENNETH D. BENNE

209

Notes

References

Author Index

Subject Index

About the Author

ℕotes

ESSAY 2

[1]Totalitarian societies are a relatively recent exception to this separation of the state and government from other aspects of social life. They may be thought of as attempts to reunify these scattered aspects of life, usually using amplified powers of the central government as a means of reunification.

ESSAY 3

[1]I am, of course, not arguing here against any and all uses of computer assistance in desirable processes of learning. I am against the use of programmed learning, computer-assisted or not, that seeks to individualize learning through depersonalization of the learning environment.

[2]I do not mean to disparage or denigrate the research efforts of neurologists, of cyberneticists and students of artificial intelligence, or of sociobiologists like E. O. Wilson. Rather, perhaps obtusely, I find little usefulness in their work in pursuing my present purposes.

ESSAY 4

[1]Veblen believed that the morality inherent, but largely implicit, in the craft and mentality of "engineering" would not only order the uses of technology in society for good ends but bring moral order to our predatory system of capitalist enterprise as well.

[2]Hendel argues persuasively that Western people's distrust of authority is naturally linked to people's faith in inevitable progress. After all, if progress is inevitable, then authority simply becomes the cumbersome relic of a bygone age.

[3]The view of community as the basis of pedagogical or anthropogogical authority is argued more fully in Benne (1970). I have drawn heavily upon that journal article in the later pages of this essay.

213

ESSAY 5

[1] I have discussed the bureaucratic organization of contemporary life and work in Essays 1 and 4. But the excruciating clash of such organization with professed aims and ideals in American universities justifies further discussion here.

ESSAY 6

[1] The best brief survey and conceptualization of experiments in the introduction of anthropogogy (although that word is not used in it) into American work settings is in a special issue of *The Journal of Applied Behavioral Science* (Appley & Winder, 1972). See Weisbord (1987) for a profound but readable account of the evolution of "organizational development" in the United States.

ESSAY 9

[1] I am quite aware that I am discussing reason in the language of what Santayana once called literary psychology rather than in the terms of scientific psychology. This choice of language can be justified on several grounds. One is the penchant of scientific psychologists in America, until recently, for subhuman subjects, and of clinical psychologists for pathological subjects. These choices of subject matters have placed some constraints upon the usefulness of scientific and clinical terminology for discussing and illuminating issues of full-blown and healthy human conduct. If the language I am using seems anthropomorphic, I fail to see that this invalidates it for discussing human conduct and action, as it might invalidate it for discussing the movements of suns and atoms or the behavior of paramecia or rodents. However vigorously some students of humanity may pursue projects of self-reduction, human beings are still anthropomorphic.

[2] I have formulated these criteria by selection from and synthesis among those recommended by Murphy (1943, Part III, Ch. 1) and those proposed by Raup, Axtelle, Benne, and Smith (1962).

References

Appley, Dee, & Winder, Alvin (Eds.). (1972). Collaboration in Work Settings. *Journal of Applied Behavioral Science. 13*, 261–464.

Argyris, Chris, & Schön, Donald. (1974). *Theory in Practice.* San Francisco: Jossey-Bass.

Aristotle. (1946). *The Politics.* (Ernest Barker, Trans.). Oxford: Clarendon Press.

Ayres, C. E. (1944). *The History of Human Progress.* Chapel Hill: University of North Carolina Press.

Babad, Elisha; Birnbaum, Max; & Benne, Kenneth D. (1983). *The Social Self.* Hollywood, CA: Sage.

Bellamy, Edward. (1960). *Looking Backward.* New York: New American Library.

Benne, Kenneth D. (1970). Authority in Education. *Harvard Educational Review. 40*(3), 385–410.

Benne, Kenneth D. (1971). *A Conception of Authority.* New York: Russell and Russell. (Originally published in 1943. New York: Teachers College, Columbia University, Bureau of Publications.)

Benne, Kenneth D. (1967). *Education for Tragedy.* Lexington: University of Kentucky Press.

Benne, Kenneth D. (1986). The Locus of Educational Authority in Today's World. *Teachers College Record. 88*(1), 15–21.

Benne, Kenneth; Bradford, Leland; Gibb, Jack; & Lippitt, Ronald (Eds.). (1975). *The Laboratory Method of Changing and Learning.* Palo Alto, CA: Science and Behavior Books.

Benne, Kenneth D., & Birnbaum, Max. (1978). *Teaching and Learning about Science and Social Policy.* Boulder, CO: SSEC and ERIC CHESS.

Benne, Kenneth D., & Tozer, Steven (Eds.). (1987). *Society as Educator in an Age of Transition.* Chicago: National Society for the Study of Education Yearbook.

Bennis, Warren. (1973). *Beyond Bureaucracy.* New York: McGraw-Hill.

Bennis, Warren; Benne, Kenneth D.; & Chin, Robert (Eds.) (1986). *The Planning of Change.* (4th ed.). New York: Holt, Rinehart and Winston.

Bernstein, Richard J. (1976). *The Restructuring of Social and Political Theory.* New York: Harcourt Brace Jovanovich.

Birnbaum, Max. (1975). The Clarification Group. In K. Benne, L. Bradford, J.

Gibb, & R. Lippitt (Eds.), *The Laboratory Method of Changing and Learning.* Palo Alto, CA: Science and Behavior Books, Chapter 15.

Bode, Boyd. (1957). *Democracy as a Way of Life.* New York: Macmillan.

Boulding, Elise. (1987). Changing Gender Roles in Familial, Occupational and Civic Settings. In K. Benne & S. Tozer (Eds.), *Society as Educator in an Age of Transition* (pp. 112–147). Chicago: National Society for the Study of Education Yearbook.

Boulding, Kenneth. (1967). Exploring the Unexpected: The Uncertain Future of Knowledge and Technology. In E. Morphet & C. Ryan (Eds.), *Prospective Changes in Society by 1980.* New York: Citation Press.

Bradford, Leland; Gibb, Jack; & Benne, Kenneth D. (1964). *T Group Theory and Laboratory Method.* New York: John Wiley.

Bronowski, Jacob. (1953). *The Common Sense of Science.* Cambridge, MA: Harvard University Press.

Broudy, Harry S. (1974). Unfinishable Business. In Peter Bertocci (Ed.), *Mid-Twentieth American Philosophy.* New York: Humanities Press, pp. 84–103.

Broudy, Harry S. (1980). Education in a Pluralistic Society. In L. Rubin (Ed.), *Critical Issues in Educational Policy.* Boston: Allyn and Bacon.

Buber, Martin. (1935). *Between Man and Man.* Boston: Beacon Press.

Buber, Martin. (1970). *I and Thou.* (Walter Kaufman, Trans.). New York: Scribner's.

Burke, Kenneth. (1961a). *Attitudes Toward History.* Boston: Beacon Press.

Burke, Kenneth. (1961b). *A Rhetoric of Motives.* Berkeley and Los Angeles: University of California Press.

Counts, George S. (1934). *The Social Foundations of Education.* New York: Scribner's.

Dewey, John. (1916). *Democracy and Education.* New York: Macmillan.

Dewey, John. (1927). *The Public and Its Problems.* New York: Henry Holt.

Dewey, John. (1937). Education and Social Change. *The Social Frontier, III,* pp. 235–238.

Dewey, John. (1948). *Reconstruction in Philosophy.* Boston: Beacon Press.

Einstein, Albert. (1960). *Einstein on Peace.* (O. Nathan & H. Norden, Eds.). New York: Simon and Schuster.

Ellul, Jacques. (1964). *The Technological Society.* New York: Knopf.

Fisch, Max. (1950). Dewey's Place in the Classic Period of American Philosophy. In K. Benne & W. O. Stanley (Eds.), *Essays for John Dewey's Ninetieth Birthday.* Urbana, IL: Bureau of Research and Service, College of Education, University of Illinois.

Flexner, Abraham. (1930). *Universities: American, British, German.* New York: Oxford University Press.

Fromm, Erich. (1968). *The Revolution of Hope.* New York: Harper & Row.

Galbraith, J. K. (1967). *The New Industrial State.* New York: New American Library.

Giddings, Franklin. (1908). *Principles of Sociology.* New York: Macmillan.

Habermas, Jürgen. (1973). *Theory and Practice.* (John Viertrel, Trans.). Boston: Beacon Press.

Harrington, Michael. (1972). *Socialism*. New York: Bantam Books.

Heinemann, F. H. (1958). *Existentialism and the Modern Predicament*. New York: Harper & Row.

Hendel, Charles. (1958). An Exploration of the Nature of Authority. In Carl Friedrich (Ed.), *Nomos: Authority (I)*. Cambridge, MA: Harvard University Press.

Hutchins, Robert. (1936). *The Higher Learning in America*. New Haven: Yale University Press.

James, William. (1950). *Principles of Psychology*. New York: Dover Publishing.

Jaspers, Karl. (1961). *The Future of Mankind*. (E. B. Ashton, Trans.). Chicago: University of Chicago Press.

Jaspers, Karl. (1962). Truth and Science. *The Graduate Journal*. University of Texas, Spring.

Kelly, George. (1963). The Expert as Historical Actor. *Daedalus*, XC, #3, 529–548.

Kerr, Clark. (1964). *The Uses of the University*. Cambridge, MA: Harvard University Press.

Kierkegaard, Søren. (1954). *The Sickness Unto Death*. (Walter Lowrie, Trans.). New York: Doubleday.

Kilpatrick, William H. (1947). *Selfhood and Civilization*. New York: Bureau of Publications, Teachers College, Columbia University.

Kluckhohn, Florence, & Strodtbeck, Fred. (1961). *Variations in Value Orientation*. Evanston, IL: Row, Peterson.

Laski, Harold. (1931). The Limitations of the Expert. *Harpers*, CLXII, pp. 101–110.

Lee, Gordon. (1964). *Crusade Against Ignorance*. New York: Teachers College Press.

Lentricchia, Frank. (1985). *Criticism and Social Change*. Chicago: University of Chicago Press.

Lewin, Kurt. (1949). Cassirer's Philosophy of Science and Social Science. In Paul Schilpp (Ed.), *The Philosophy of Ernst Cassirer* (pp. 271–288). New York: Tudor.

Lewin, Kurt, & Grabbe, Paul. (1945). Conduct, Knowledge and Acceptance of New Values. *The Journal of Social Issues*, I, 33–64.

Lippitt, Ronald. (1949). *Training in Community Relations*. New York: Harper.

Lynd, Robert. (1935). *Knowledge for What*. Princeton: Princeton University Press.

Mannheim, Karl. (1943). *Diagnosis of Our Time*. New York: Humanities Press.

Mannheim, Karl. (1950). *Man and Society in an Age of Reconstruction*. New York: Harcourt Brace.

Marx, Karl. (1971). Theses on Feuerbach, #6. In R. Bernstein, *Praxis and Action* (p. 12). Philadelphia: University of Pennsylvania Press.

Mead, George. (1931). *Mind, Self and Society*. Chicago: University of Chicago Press.

Mead, Margaret. (1965). The Future as the Basis for Establishing a Shared Culture. *Daedalus*, XCII, 135–155.

Mead, Margaret. (1970). *Culture and Commitment*. New York: Natural History Press.

Means, Richard L. (1969). *The Ethical Imperative*. New York: Doubleday.

Muller, Herbert J. (1970). *The Children of Frankenstein*. Bloomington, IN: Indiana University Press.

Murphy, Arthur. (1943). *The Uses of Reason*. New York: Macmillan.

Murphy, Gardner. (1958). *Human Potentialities*. New York: Basic Books.

Nevins, Alan. (1962). *The State Universities and Democracy*. Urbana, IL: University of Illinois Press.

Newman, John Henry. (1901). *The Idea of a University*. London: Longmans, Green and Co.

Northrop, F. S. C. (1946). *The Meeting of East and West*. New York: Macmillan.

Northrop, F. S. C. (1960). *The Logic of Science and The Humanities*. New York: Meridian Books.

Ollman, Bertelli. (1971). *Alienation: Marx's Conception of Man in a Capitalist Society*. New York: Cambridge University Press.

Ortega Y Gasset, Jose. (1969). *Man and People*. New York: Norton.

Parsons, Talcott. (1969). The Intellectual: A Social Role Category. In Philip Rieff (Ed.), *On Intellectuals*. Garden City, NY: Doubleday, 3–24.

Pateman, Carole. (1970). *Participation and Democratic Theory*. Cambridge: Cambridge University Press.

Percy, Walker. (1975). *The Message in the Bottle*. New York: Farrar, Strauss and Giroux.

Raup, R. Bruce; Axtelle, George; Benne, Kenneth; & Smith, B. Othanel. (1962). *The Improvement of Practical Intelligence*. New York: Teachers College Press. (Revision of a 1943 volume by the same authors, *The Discipline of Practical Judgment in a Democratic Society*. Chicago: University of Chicago Press.)

Reich, Charles. (1970). *The Greening of America*. New York: Random House.

Reiche, Reimut. (1971). *Sexuality and Class Struggle*. New York: Praeger.

Rogers, Carl. (1968). USA 2000. *Journal of Applied Behavioral Science, 4*, 265–280.

Santayana, George. (1929). *The Life of Reason* (I). New York: Scribner's.

Santayana, George. (1939a). Sonnet: As in the Midst of Battle There Is Room. In Mark Van Doren (Ed.), *An Anthology of World Poetry* (pp. 1248–1249). New York: Halcyon Press.

Santayana, George. (1939b). *The Realm of Truth*. New York: Scribner's.

Schaff, Adam. (1963). *The Philosophy of Man*. New York: Delta.

Shaw, George Bernard. (1951). *Seven Plays*. New York: Dodd, Mead.

Shils, Edward. (1974). Ideology and Utopia. *Daedalus*, CI, Winter, pp. 82–94.

Slater, Philip, & Bennis, Warren. (1964). Democracy Is Inevitable. *Harvard Business Review, 42*, March, 51–59.

Stein, Maurice. (1960). *The Eclipse of Community*. Princeton: Princeton University Press.

Stroup, Thomas (Ed.). (1966). *The University in the American Future*. Lexington, KY: University of Kentucky Press.

Sullivan, Harry S. (1953). *The Interpersonal Theory of Psychiatry.* New York: W. W. Norton.

Tough, Alan. (1979). *The Adult's Learning Projects: A Fresh Approach to Theory and Practice in Adult Learning.* Toronto: Ontario Institute for Studies in Education.

Tozer, Steven. (1987). Elite Power and Democratic Ideals. In K. Benne & S. Tozer (Eds.), *Society as Educator in an Age of Transition.* Chicago: National Society for the Study of Education Yearbook, 186–225.

Veblen, Thorstein. (1914). *The Instinct of Workmanship.* New York: Macmillan.

Veblen, Thorstein. (1965). *The Theory of Business Enterprise.* New York: A. M. Kelley, Bookseller. (Original work published 1904)

Waks, L., & Roy, R. (1987). Learning from Technology. In K. Benne & S. Tozer (Eds.), *Society as Educator in an Age of Transition* (pp. 24–53). Chicago: National Society for the Study of Education Yearbook.

Watson Watt, Robert S. (1965). In Leonard Krasner, The Behavioral Scientist and Social Responsibility: No Place to Hide. *Journal of Social Issues, 21,* 9–30.

Weisbord, Marvin. (1987). *Productive Work Places.* San Francisco: Jossey-Bass.

Whitehead, Alfred N. (1954). *The Aims of Education.* New York: New American Library.

Whitehead, Alfred N. (1958). *Adventures of Ideas.* New York: Macmillan.

Whitehead, Alfred N. (1970). *The Concept of Nature.* Cambridge: Cambridge University Press.

Wieman, Henry N. (1958). *Man's Ultimate Commitment.* Carbondale, IL: Southern Illinois University Press.

Wirth, Arthur. (1987). Contemporary Work and the Quality of Life. In K. Benne & S. Tozer (Eds.), *Society as Educator in an Age of Transition* (pp. 54–87). Chicago: National Society for the Study of Education Yearbook.

Ziegler, Warren. (1979). The Concept of the Learning Stance. In W. Ziegler & G. Healy (Eds.), *The Learning Stance.* Syracuse, NY: Syracuse Research Corporation.

· Author Index

221

· Subject Index

About the Author

Kenneth D. Benne's diverse studies have led him often to breach the boundaries between specialized academic disciplines. In 1930, he earned his B.S. degree at Kansas State University with a double major in physical science and English literature. His M.A. degree from the University of Michigan was in philosophy, but he also developed there a continuing interest in comparative religions, particularly those of India, and in classic Greek literature and history. His Ph.D. studies at Teachers College, Columbia University were focused in the philosophy of education. There, his work coincided with the Great Depression, and this led him to study seriously the processes of social and political change. What has held his variety of interests together has been a faith in democracy in and through education. For Kenneth Benne, democracy requires creatively integral persons in uncoerced community, continually reborn through the cooperative resolution of human conflicts.

His career has been that of a teacher committed to initiating and facilitating effective programs of democratic education centered on the study of human issues. This career has led from teaching in a rural school and two high schools in Kansas to the professing of educational philosophy at the University of Illinois and at Teachers College. He was also Centennial Professor in the Social Sciences at the University of Kentucky in 1965. In the last 20 years before his retirement in 1973, he was the Berenson Professor of Human Relations at Boston University. In addition, he has been an inventor and consultant in a variety of adult education programs designed to improve relations between groups with conflicting interests, among others, interracial, interclass, intergenerational, and intergender groups.

Kenneth Benne is past president of the Philosophy of Education Society, the American Education Fellowship, and the Adult Education Association of the USA, and was co-founder of the Philosophy of Education Society, the NTL Institute of Behavioral Science, and the International Association of Applied Social Scientists. He has been honored with L.H.D. degrees from Lesley College and Morris Brown College, Atlanta University, and is the recipient of the Kilpatrick Award for distinguished contribution to American philosophy of education, and the Teachers College Distinguished Alumni Award.

Kenneth Benne's extensive bibliography includes *A Conception of Authority, Education for Tragedy,* and a volume of poems, *Teach Me to Sing of Winter.*